Building Power to Change the World

Building Power to Change the World

The Political Thought of the German Council Movements

JAMES MULDOON

OXFORD
UNIVERSITY PRESS

OXFORD
UNIVERSITY PRESS

Great Clarendon Street, Oxford, OX2 6DP,
United Kingdom

Oxford University Press is a department of the University of Oxford.
It furthers the University's objective of excellence in research, scholarship,
and education by publishing worldwide. Oxford is a registered trade mark of
Oxford University Press in the UK and in certain other countries

First Edition published in 2020

Impression: 1

Published in the United States of America by Oxford University Press
198 Madison Avenue, New York, NY 10016, United States of America

British Library Cataloguing in Publication Data
Data available

Library of Congress Control Number: 2020947781

ISBN 978–0–19–885662–7

DOI: 10.1093/oso/9780198856627.001.0001

Printed and bound in Great Britain by
Clays Ltd, Elcograf S.p.A.

Contents

Introduction 1

1. Between Social Democracy and Council Dictatorship: The Council Movements in Historical Perspective 16
2. Freedom as Collective Self-Determination 52
3. Building Workers' Power 73
4. Socialist Republicanism 99
5. Socialist Civic Virtues 131
6. Conclusion: After the Councils 159

Bibliography 169
Index 183

Introduction

During the chaos and political unrest of the First World War, council movements arose across Europe through soldier mutinies, mass strikes, and factory occupations. The council movements seized upon a moment of exceptional opportunity brought about by the crisis of the war to launch a project of political transformation unprecedented in its scale. Inspired by the momentum of the rising revolutionary wave of 1917–20, workers and soldiers elected delegates to councils, which acted as revolutionary committees representing the interests of the lower classes. The desire for radical change spread rapidly across boarders as council movements emerged in Russia, Germany, Austria, Hungary, Italy, and the United Kingdom. Organizing through these new models of democratic governance, council movements dramatically reshaped European politics by precipitating the fall of powerful empires and leading to the creation of new republics. Although frequently depicted as short-lived and abortive, these movements produced lasting social change in spite of their brief existence. In Germany, they contributed to ending the war, bringing down the monarchy, introducing the eight-hour workday, and instituting women's suffrage.[1]

However, these challenges to established hierarchies also generated powerful counter-movements in defence of the old order. Fears of the council movements' demands for radical social transformation drove the German government to empower the right-wing *Freikorps*, sowing the seeds for the rise of Nazism and the Second World War.[2] Attempts to establish council states were quickly crushed across Europe by counter-revolutionary forces. The political programmes raised by radical council delegates largely disappeared with the demobilization of the council movements and were soon overshadowed by other historical events and political ideologies. In Russia, the council movements were suppressed by the centralizing tendencies of the Bolshevik Party, leading to the integration of council institutions into the bureaucratic structure of a one-party state. In Germany meanwhile, council delegates voted for the establishment of a liberal parliament in which non-socialist parties won a majority of seats at the first national election. A shaky coalition was formed between liberals, the Catholic Party, and moderate

[1] Ralf Hoffrogge, *Working-Class Politics in the German Revolution: Richard Müller, the Revolutionary Shop Stewards and the Origins of the Council Movement* (Leiden: Brill Publishers, 2014), 8.

[2] Mark Jones, *Founding Weimar* (Cambridge: Cambridge University Press, 2016).

Building Power to Change the World: The Political Thought of the German Council Movements. James Muldoon, Oxford University Press (2020). © James Muldoon. DOI: 10.1093/oso/9780198856627.003.0001

socialists, creating the dangerous instability of the Weimar Republic. By 1923, the political ambitions of radical council delegates were shattered, as any hope of achieving their broader political objectives had faded from view.

Due to the openness and uncertainty of the revolutionary uprisings, this transitional period of innovation gave rise to an incredibly fertile body of political thought. German council delegates developed a radical vision of a self-determining society in which all citizens would exercise freedom through direct participation in political and economic institutions. Debates between delegates consisted of how to equalize power between citizens and combine the twin objectives of democracy and socialism in a transformative political programme. In particular, they sought ways to extend democratic principles to a broad range of social institutions such as the army, schools, cultural institutions, workplaces, and the government bureaucracy. However, there has been surprisingly little interest in the council movements in anglophone scholarship and only a handful of historical studies of their political thought.[3] On account of this scholarly neglect and their ambiguous legacy, my aim in this book is to reconstruct their political thought as a distinct contribution to the history of ideas and of ongoing relevance for contemporary politics. Drawing from the practices of the council movements and the writings of theorists such as Rosa Luxemburg, Anton Pannekoek, and Karl Kautsky, this book analyses the German council movements' programme to democratize politics, the economy, and society through building powerful worker-led organizations and cultivating workers' political agency.

Germany at a Crossroads

In November 1918, as the German war effort showed signs of exhaustion, workers and soldiers organized into democratic councils that seized power from the old royalty, industrialists, and elites of the German Empire. The formation of councils was inspired by a sailor mutiny in Kiel prompted by an order issued on 24 October 1918 by Reinhardt Scheer, Chief of Naval Staff, to launch the entire German navy in a final suicidal fight to the death against the British navy in an attempt to restore the prestige of the German Admiralty. Without consulting the civilian government, which was already in talks towards an armistice, Admiral Scheer hoped for 'an honourable battle by the fleet' which would 'sow the seed of a new German

[3] Important studies include Oskar Anweiler, *The Soviets: The Russian Workers, Peasants, and Soldiers Councils, 1905–1921* (New York: Pantheon Books, 1974); Hoffrogge, *Working-Class Politics in the German Revolution*; Yohan Dubigeon, *La démocratie des conseils: Aux origins modernes de l'autogouvernement* (Paris: Klincksiek, 2017). In German, see Hans Hautmann, *Die Geschichte der Rätebewegung in Österreich 1918–1924* (Vienna: Europaverlag, 1995); Axel Weipert, *Die Zweite Revolution. Rätebewegung in Berlin 1919/1920* (Berlin: be.bra, 2015); Volker Arnold, *Rätebewegung und Rätetheorien in der Novemberrevolution*, 2nd ed. (Hamburg: Junius Verlag, 1985).

fleet of the future'.[4] Scheer belonged to the old German Empire, a closed and hierarchical social order ruled by a wealthy military elite that resisted pressures for democratic reform. When the councils of soldiers and industrial workers arose to resist this military order, they were inspired by a radically different vision of politics, one in which power was exercised collectively through democratic organizations with accountable and recallable delegates. The slogan of the early German councils was '*Freiheit, Friede, und Brot!*' [freedom, peace, and bread] and their demands consisted of calls for democracy, pacifism, and the transformation of the hierarchical and bureaucratic apparatuses that oppressed them.[5]

The councils developed spontaneously without prior theoretical elaboration or detailed plans for their proper structure and role. Upon hearing of the formation of councils across Germany, Revolutionary Shop Steward Richard Müller recalled hastily drawing an initial plan for elections to councils in Berlin 'without checking it thoroughly, responding to the need of the hour'.[6] The swift spread of the revolution took both the authorities and the revolutionaries by surprise. The rapid development of events on the ground left competing political groups struggling to keep pace. Although the uprisings were not initiated by the established political parties, the latter quickly strove to gain influence and power over the councils by proposing their own party delegates to be elected in the councils and caucusing before council meetings. Barely a week had passed between the initial mutiny and the organization of hundreds of councils across Germany, leading to the announcement of the abdication of the Kaiser by the Chancellor on 9 November 1918.[7]

The events were met with a mixture of fear and jubilation. For the revolutionaries, the fall of the old regime sparked enthusiasm for the possibility of the beginning of a worldwide socialist revolution. Red flags were raised over the Royal Palace in Berlin as triumphant crowds of workers marched through the streets. But there were also widespread fears of impending violence, wild rumours of secret plots, and a general sense of desperation and exhaustion after years of wartime hardship.[8] During this unstable and contradictory period, desires for social change and a fundamental transformation of hierarchical social institutions were intermingled with fears of a violent revolution and a longing for peace and stability. At the same time as the Spartacus League proclaimed the revolution

[4] Otto Groos, *Der Krieg in der Nordsee* (Berlin: E. S. Mittler, 1922), 344.

[5] Alexander Bessmertny and M. Neven DuMont, eds., *Die Parteien und das Rätesystem* (Charlottenburg: Deutsche Verlagsgesellschaft für Politik und Geschichte m. b. H., 1919), 65.

[6] Hoffrogge, *Working-Class Politics in the German Revolution*, 76.

[7] Eberhalb Kolb, *Die Arbeiterräte in der deutschen Innenpolitik, 1918–1919* (Berlin: Droste, 1962), 71–82.

[8] Mark Jones notes that these fears included 'revolutionaries' belief in non-existent armed counter-revolutionaries; fears that a single organization controlled the revolution as it spread across Germany; ideas that Karl Liebknecht possessed a secret army; and more general protean fears of the total breakdown of social and political order.' Jones, *Founding Weimar*, 2.

would be 'driven forward by its inner contradictions' towards 'the realization of the ultimate goal of socialism', the new Chancellor, Friedrich Ebert, warned of the danger of 'anarchy and the most terrible misery', calling on protesters to 'leave the streets... to ensure that there is peace and order.'[9]

With conservative and reactionary groups temporarily obstructed and overwhelmed, the Executive Council of the Workers' and Soldiers' Councils declared itself the highest political authority of the Socialist Republic of Germany and ordered that the councils' power 'must be secured and expanded so that the achievements of the revolution will benefit the entire working class'.[10] For the months of November and December, 1918, there was a precarious balance of power between the old government bureaucracy and radical council delegates which was the cause of great discord.[11] While the former, assisted by the leadership of the Social Democratic Party of Germany (SPD), wished to maintain the essential aspects of the old regime, the latter envisioned 'a new worldwide society of workers, free, without fear or want, a society based on worker democracy developing into a single unit of mankind'.[12]

However, there were a number of competing forces within the council movements, ranging from the moderate SPD to a number of more radical groups such as the Independent Social Democratic Party of Germany (USPD), the Revolutionary Shop Stewards, and the Spartacus League. While the SPD leadership wished to hold the revolution back to prevent further social change, the more radical groups demanded more extensive transformations of German society. The brief months of the council movements' existence were the occasion for some of the most important debates in the history of European politics. At stake was the question of how Imperial Germany could be transformed into a free republic. Of particular concern to workers were how democratic changes could be instituted in the production process and economic institutions. Would a genuine democracy require a socialist organization of economic life and how would this function in practice? Drawing on debates that occurred within the workers' movement over the preceding two decades, socialists developed new political programmes through the application of their theories to rapidly changing circumstances.

At an institutional level, debates were dominated by the question of 'National Assembly versus Council Republic'. Moderate delegates within the councils from

[9] Institut für Marxismus-Leninismus, *Dokumente und Materialien zur Geschichte der Deutschen Arbeiterbewegung, Band 2 November 1917—Dezember 1918* (Berlin: Dietz Verlag, 1957), 418–21, 333–4.

[10] Gabriel Kuhn, ed., *All Power to the Councils! A Documentary History of the German Revolution of 1918–1919* (Oakland: PM Press, 2012), 33.

[11] Friedrich Ebert had called for all government personnel to remain in their posts, while many of the councils sought to exercise 'control' rights over the decisions of the government bureaucracy rather than completely replace them. Walter Tormin, *Zwischen Rätediktatur Und Sozialer Demokratie: Die Geschichte Der Rätebewegung in Der Deutschen Revolution 1918/19* (Düsseldorf: Droste Verlag, 1954), 89–90.

[12] Anonymous pamphlet quoted in Kuhn, ed., *All Power to the Councils!*, 13.

the SPD were in favour of holding elections to a national assembly. They called for the creation of liberal parliamentary institutions with universal suffrage and supported the maintenance of existing social and economic structures with minor social reforms. On the other hand, radical delegates in the Revolutionary Shop Stewards and Spartacus League argued that a national assembly would allow existing elites to retain power and prevent more significant and wide-reaching democratic transformations to German society. They advocated for sovereign power to remain in the council system that had arisen organically over the course of the revolution. Fearing that old elites would reassert their control, they pushed for a more profound reorganization of German society and the democratization of key social institutions such as the army, schools, cultural institutions, civil service, and workplaces. They questioned whether liberal democratic institutions could adequately challenge relations of domination between social classes or redress fundamental economic inequalities.

In addition to the 'councils or parliament' debate, radical council theorists produced an expansive vision of a participatory, self-determining society, which called for 'the workers' permanent and active participation in all economic and political areas'.[13] Revolutionary Shop Steward Ernst Däumig anticipated 'a Germany whose affairs are really determined by active people doing more than running to the ballot box every two or three years... It can only be changed by a dedicated attempt to make and keep the German people politically active.'[14] In line with this vision, they supported a form of positive liberty that I call freedom as collective self-determination, according to which freedom must be exercised rather than enjoyed as a state or condition. Workers' control did not simply entail a centralized socialist party administering the economy. Council theorists were inspired by a vision of socialism from below in which ordinary citizens would engage in deliberation and decision-making at a local level. Däumig argued that 'it is mandatory to make it a true people's movement that includes the bottom of society.'[15] They believed structures of power should be organized from the bottom up, such that rank-and-file members of the councils would play a key role in political processes. For the council movements, the very idea of what it meant for individuals to live as free and equal citizens in a free society involved a conception of active citizenship and participation in economic and political institutions.

Radical delegates also called for the extension of democratic principles from the political sphere to other domains of society where democracy-resistant institutions and forces remained embedded. Democracy was not dismissed as a bourgeois sham that needed to be replaced by a utopian alternative. Rather, a

[13] Ernst Däumig, 'The Council Idea and its Realization', in *All Power to the Councils!*, ed. Kuhn, 52.
[14] Ibid.
[15] Ernst Däumig, 'The National Assembly Means the Councils' Death', in *All Power to the Councils!*, ed. Kuhn, 41.

participatory democratic socialist society was envisaged as an extension and radicalization of democracy from the political domain to demands for more substantive social, economic, and cultural equality. In this sense, political democracy was understood as the basis for more radical egalitarian reforms. Democratizing authority structures was viewed as the pathway to a participatory society in which citizens would play an active role in self-determining institutions.

While specific proposals for democratizing authority structures differed between groups, radical council delegates argued for the election of military officers, the dissolution of the police, the creation of a peoples' militia, the replacement of state bureaucrats by elected officials, the institution of workers' management of factories, and the socialization of key industries. Their transformative programme involved overcoming the liberal separation of the private from the public sphere and intervening into closed and hierarchical institutions from which workers' voices had been excluded. Claiming new rights of democratic control, the council movements aimed to restructure social and economic institutions to guarantee workers more meaningful influence and control over authority structures.

Most importantly, this consisted of workers' control over economic production through self-managed enterprises and the creation of new institutions to exercise democratic control over the economy. Even moderate council delegates were in favour of a rapid socialization of German industry to achieve greater levels of worker autonomy in the workplace. The 'socialization' debates within the council movements concerned the appropriate methods for transferring ownership of major industrial enterprises such as coal mines into public hands and establishing workers' control over individual workplaces. Participants in the Socialization Committee, established in November 1918 in the wake of the revolution, considered ways in which new economic institutions could be established that would balance the interests of workers in individual workplaces with broader social needs.[16]

Theorists within the council movements also emphasized the subjective role that class-consciousness played in political struggle and believed that changes in the economic sphere would need to be accompanied by widespread cultural transformation and spiritual renewal. A self-determining society would require public-spirited citizens who naturally tended towards promoting the common good and acting in solidarity with their fellow citizens. Rosa Luxemburg articulated these concerns through the language of 'socialist civic virtues', which remains an important and overlooked contribution to democratic socialist

[16] See Karl Kautsky, 'Speech on "the Socialisation of Economic Life" at the Second Congress of Councils in April 1919', in *The German Left and the Weimar Republic: A Selection of Documents*, ed. Ben Fowkes (Leiden: Brill, 2014), 33.

political thought.[17] Pannekoek also emphasized the necessary changes in what he considered a people's 'spirit' [*Geist*] or mentalities in order for revolutionary action to be successful. For Pannekoek, the transformation of economic institutions 'must be accompanied by an equally fundamental spiritual revolution' through which a new ideology would gain 'ground step by step, waging a relentless battle against the traditional ideas to which the ruling classes are clinging, this struggle is the mental companion of the social class struggle'.[18]

The struggle for a self-determining society necessitated challenging entrenched hierarchical structures, which upheld strict class divisions in German society. Questions of structural power were central to the political strategies of the council movements because they believed elites would never voluntarily give up their position of dominance. They sought to shift the balance of power between classes in order to undertake social and political transformation. Although differences in perspective existed between council delegates, the general method they proposed for challenging the dominance of elites was building the independent power of the working class through strengthening worker-led institutions and cultivating the agency of ordinary workers. They operated with an expansive understanding of what constituted the 'working class', which included intellectuals, white-collar workers, and the unemployed—although this category was contested. This position of building workers' power stood in contrast to moral reformers such as Friedrich Förster who argued that those in power could be voluntarily persuaded to adopt new norms through the influence of ethical ideals without the need for coercion or open political conflict.[19] Many liberals at the time hoped that moral principles of co-operation and civility could play a pedagogical role in political life and lead to the development of a common national interest.

Council delegates, on the other hand, considered that the only way to secure lasting social change would be to develop the independent power of the working class as an essential precondition for political transformation. In contrast to liberal reformers, council theorists strategized ways in which workers' power could be enhanced while sapping the organizational and ideological power of the bourgeoisie. They held no illusions of the collapse of the bourgeois world following one single event in which the old regime would be overthrown. Rather, they thought that revolutionary transformation would be an ongoing struggle over the course of years in which the power of workers would be pitted against their class enemy. Rather than seeking out ways in which social change could be achieved without the need for developing collective power, the council movements placed

17 Rosa Luxemburg, 'What does the Spartacus League Want?'.

18 Anton Pannekoek, 'The Position and Significance of Joseph Dietzgen's Philosophical Works', in Joseph Dietzgen, *The Positive Outcome of Philosophy* (Chicago, 1906), 12–13.

19 Friedrich Förster, *Weltpolitik und Weltgewissen* (München, 1919).

considerations of the struggle for power between classes at the centre of their political strategy.

Returning to the Council Movements

The relative lack of historical scholarship on the political thought of the council movements is partly a result of their unexpected rise and rapid collapse. It is easy to view this period as an insignificant and minor episode in the history of socialist political thought. After all, by the early 1920s, the council movements had all but disappeared, with the prospects of their democratic socialist programmes buried for a generation. Yet it would be a mistake to overlook these movements as a mere historical anachronism. The problems that the council movements faced—how to challenge social hierarchies, equalize power between citizens, and implement a transformative political programme in the interests of the many—are still vexing questions for contemporary progressive political groups. The European council movements instituted the first worker-led revolutions in industrialized countries to seriously consider the necessary practical steps for socializing major industries and establishing democratic controls over the economy. They engaged in vigorous debates over the nature and scope of democratic government, including the extent to which authority structures outside the governmental sphere should be democratized. They also sought to combine Marxist analyses of political economy with theories of modern representative democracy in an attempt to conceptualize the institutional dimensions of a post-capitalist, democratic socialist society. These debates present conceptual resources that can still inform contemporary discussions.

It is a shame, then, that socialist political theorists of this era have long since fallen out of fashion in mainstream political discourse. Many of the seminal theoretical projects of the Left in the 1980s and 90s, such as Chantal Mouffe and Ernesto Laclau's *Hegemony and Socialist Strategy* and Andrew Arato and Jean Cohen's *Civil Society and Political Theory*, were *post*-Marxist in orientation and began with a repudiation of the perceived outdated perspective of the 'Old Left'. For Mouffe and Laclau, the theorists of the Second International were captive to a logic of historical necessity and adhered to an unrealistic and dangerous ideal of emancipation understood as the construction of a rational and self-determining political order.[20] Theoretical attention was turned from economic considerations to questions of 'the social' and potential alliances between new social movements.

One aim of this book is to demonstrate that the theorists of the council movements were not as rigid, dogmatic, or simplistic as has been assumed. The

[20] See the discussion of Rosa Luxemburg and Karl Kautsky in Ernesto Laclau and Chantal Mouffe, *Hegemony and Socialist Strategy: Towards a Radical Democratic Politics* (London: Verso, 1985), 8–19.

selection of theorists in this book who participated in or wrote about the council movements shows that there were a variety of political positions adopted towards the councils and different programmes for how they could be incorporated into a new society. There was no single political ideology of 'councilism' or 'council communism', which only emerged later through polemics with the Bolsheviks and criticisms of the progress of the Russian Revolution.[21] Political disagreements over the correct structure, direction, and purpose of the council movements revealed important differences in principle and strategy between theorists within the German socialist movement. The debates that occurred leading up to and during the German Revolution are an important yet overlooked chapter in libertarian socialist political thought. There are also interesting parallels with other neighbouring traditions of thought. In many respects, the generation of the council movements anticipated certain aspects of the 'participatory democracy' programme raised by the Students for a Democratic Society of the New Left. These endeavours are rooted in 'the ancient, still unfulfilled conception of man attaining determining influence over his circumstances of life.'[22] There is still much that participatory (and deliberative) democrats today can learn from the original efforts of the council movements to create a more participatory society a century ago.

Another barrier to interpretation is the distorted historical accounts offered by some of the most influential interpreters of the council movements.[23] A theory of council democracy is perhaps most well known in political theory through the famous interpretation provided by Hannah Arendt at the end of *On Revolution*.[24] However, Arendt's retrieval of the 'council system' fails to engage in a historical analysis of the main participants in the European council movements. She offers a 'mythic' idealized account of the councils depicted as the regular re-emergence of a spontaneous institution that sprang directly from the peoples' political activities and posed an alternative to parliamentary democracy. However, from the European council movements of 1917–20 to the 1956 Hungarian Revolution, Arendt disregards council delegates' socialist ideology and socio-economic concerns, arguing that councils 'have always been primarily political, with social and

[21] See James Muldoon, 'The Birth of Council Communism', in *The German Revolution and Political Theory*, eds. Gaard Kets and James Muldoon (London: Palgrave Macmillan, 2019), 339–60.

[22] Students for a Democratic Society, *The Port Huron Statement* (Chicago: Charles H. Kerr Publishing Co., 1990).

[23] John Medearis, 'Lost or Obscured? How V. I. Lenin, Joseph Schumpeter, and Hannah Arendt Misunderstood the Council Movement', *Polity* 36, no. 3 (2004), 447–76.

[24] Hannah Arendt, *On Revolution* (New York: Penguin, 2006), 247–73. See also Hannah Arendt, *The Jewish Writings* (New York: Schocken Books, 2007), 343–74, 388–401; Hannah Arendt, *The Human Condition* (Chicago: The University of Chicago Press, 1958), 215–20; Hannah Arendt, *Crises of the Republic* (New York, NY: Harcourt Brace Jovanovich, 1972), 189–91; Hannah Arendt, *Men in Dark Times* (New York: Harcourt, Brace and World, 1970), 52.

economic claims playing a very minor role'.[25] As a result, she is confounded by the councils' emergence within the workers' movement and provides an unconvincing attempt to separate instances of revolutionary councils concerned with purely political matters from workers' councils seeking to organize economic production. Arendt's depiction of the councils has led her interpreters to view the final chapter of *On Revolution* as the outline of an abstract theoretical model without due consideration of the historical manifestation of the council movements.[26] The result has been a neglect of theorists directly participating in the council movements who remain largely overlooked in Arendt's interpretation.

The political thought of the council movements has also been marginalized as an object of serious historical investigation due to Lenin's criticisms of the radical theorists within the German and Dutch sections of the Communist International as representing an 'infantile disorder' of ultra-leftism within the workers' movement.[27] While there are differences between the participants in the council movements of 1917–20 and the later development of council communism as an ideology opposed to Leninism, Lenin's negative portrayal of theorists such as Anton Pannekoek has adversely impacted upon the interpretation of the council movements.[28] Contrary to Lenin's interpretation, many of the council theorists made significant theoretical innovations within Marxism, particularly by advancing democratic republican aspects of Marx's political thought.[29] Within socialist political theory, the council movements have been most associated with a rigid form of 'councilism', which has been depicted as a dogmatic ideology based on the rejection of party discipline, parliamentary elections, and trade unions.[30] This book examines the political theories of participants in the council movements in order to reveal a more complex picture of the diversity of their theoretical programmes.

The return to the political theories of the German council movements in this book is primarily a project in the history of political thought. The council movements arose during an overlooked transitional period in European history that warrants further examination. The council movements led to the unexpected transformation of the Russian, German, and Austro-Hungarian Empires into a

[25] Arendt, *On Revolution*, 266. James Muldoon, 'The Origins of Hannah Arendt's Council System', *History of Political Thought* 37, no. 4 (2016), 761–89.

[26] Andreas Kalyvas, *Democracy and the Politics of the Extraordinary* (Cambridge: Cambridge University Press, 2009), 187–300.

[27] V. I. Lenin, '"Left-Wing" Communism: An Infantile Disorder', in *Collected Works, Vol. 31* (Moscow: Progress Publishers, 1965).

[28] On the development of council communism on the basis of the experiences of the council movements see James Muldoon, 'The Birth of Council Communism', in *The German Revolution and Political Theory*, ed. Kets and Muldoon.

[29] On Marx's democratic republicanism see Bruno Leipold, *Citizen Marx: Republicanism, Communism and Capitalism.* Princeton: Princeton University Press, (forthcoming).

[30] Gilles Dauvé, *Eclipse and Re-Emergence of the Communist Movement* (London: PM Press, 2015), 95.

number of independent republics. This represents a significant chapter in the development of modern political thought. Yet rather than interpreting this transformation as a simple movement from one set of political institutions to another, this study raises the question of forgotten political alternatives. In early November 1918, a number of different political possibilities were open for the future direction of German politics. Germany was in no sense predestined to transition from monarchical to liberal democratic institutions, which resulted from a set of historically contingent factors. An important part of this study involves uncovering the competing ideals and political programmes, which were supported during this revolutionary period, but which may not have achieved full realization in practice.

Quentin Skinner has warned that 'once a political idea achieves a position of hegemony it comes to be regarded as the only coherent way of thinking about the concept involved.' Returning to the history of the German council movements helps remind us that 'our present ways of thinking... reflect a series of choices made at different times between different possible worlds.'[31] The current dominance of liberal democracy as the only viable conception of democratic government is partly a result of this historical forgetting. Historical scholarship enables us to denaturalize hegemonic accounts of politics and expand our sense of historical possibility through encounters with foreign ways of interpreting politics. Far from being an antiquarian historical footnote, the council movements raise important questions for democratic and socialist theory today. This study seeks to reignite discussion of the possibility of the compatibility of democracy with socialism, of democratic intervention into the economy, and of achieving a more participatory democratic society.

There is also an Arendtian element to this recovery of the political thought of the council movements. I have not attempted a systematic exposition of every important theorist within the council movements. Rather, I have focused on specific ideals and programmes at the intersection of democratic and socialist thought that speak to current concerns about how democracy could be deepened and expanded. Arendt imagines the political theorist as akin to 'the pearl diver who descends to the bottom of the sea', in order to bring to the surface 'thought fragments' as something 'rich and strange' that might allow us to interpret current events in a new light.[32] This history of the councils is not aimed at resuscitating a past era, but rather seeks to uncover certain unfulfilled hopes and aspirations of political transformation that remain alive in the present.

This historical work, then, could be seen as playing a double role. First, it serves as a critical tool against existing institutions, demonstrating the contingency of the

[31] Quentin Skinner, *Liberty before Liberalism* (Cambridge: Cambridge University Press, 1996), 117.
[32] Hannah Arendt, *Men in Dark Times* (New York: Harcourt Brace and Company, 1968), 205.

current order and countering the effects of dominant political narratives.[33] Many of the political ideas and programmes of the council movements go beyond that which the present order can assimilate on its own terms. Considered in light of the future directions of democratic governments across the globe, a return to the council movements may unsettle and provoke us. Their vision of active citizens participating in a self-determining society with economic independence and participatory structures of governance prompts us to rethink the necessary underlying conditions for popular government. Comparing the council movements' ideals and political programmes to present forms of democratic government helps us reflect on our political inheritance from a new perspective.

Second, returning to political debates during a decisive period of political transformation in which a wide number of possibilities were still open expands our political imagination. This includes not only the dominant ideologies of the period, but also the partially forgotten alternatives. The radical openness of the future at times of great disruption and transition gives rise to a diverse body of new political ideas. Radical delegates within the council movements held a fundamentally different vision of political life that differs significantly from contemporary approaches to thinking about freedom and democracy. I hope to bring part of this extraordinary experiment in democratic politics to the surface to shed new light on the possibilities for democratic practices today. However, my approach does not involve a project of simple reclamation. We should be wary of methodological approaches which seek to translate past political experiences directly into present circumstances. The emergence of the councils is connected to a particular historical epoch and socio-economic environment. I address these questions in the conclusion with further discussion of the contemporary significance of the councils.

Chapter Outline

The structure of this book on the German council movements reflects a number of prominent themes in their political thought. Chapter one examines the underlying democratic and socialist impulses of the rank-and-file delegates of the German council movements, with a look back to the main historical precedent for councils in the Russian Revolution. It focuses on two periods of council activity: Russia (from the strikes in February 1917 to the crushing of the Kronstadt uprising in 1921) and Germany (from the heightened revolutionary activity of 1917 to the

[33] See Aletta Norval, 'Writing a Name in the Sky: Rancière, Cavell, and the Possibility of Egalitarian Inscription', *American Political Science Review* 106, no. 4 (2012), 810–26.

establishment of the Weimar Constitution in August 1919).[34] I show that while a diversity of political views were held by participants in the council movements, there was broad support for the deepening and extension of democratic conditions in major political, economic, and social institutions. This analysis offers a concrete historical context for the examination of political theorists later in the book.

The next four chapters address important questions in the political thought of three main theorists: Anton Pannekoek, Karl Kautsky, and Rosa Luxemburg. Each chapter is organized around a different thematic concern and pursues connected interpretive arguments related to these theorists' views on freedom, power, socialist democracy, and civic virtue. In each chapter, I tend to focus on the writings of one theorist to bring to light a partially obscured way of thinking about the political phenomenon in question. The three thinkers have been selected due to the way in which their debates reveal the political divisions of the council movements. I have aimed to offer an introduction to important theoretical questions that were debated within the council movements, but I have not aspired to create a comprehensive introduction to each of the main protagonists' political thought.[35]

A special note is needed on the inclusion of Karl Kautsky, a figure not frequently associated with the council movements. Indeed, Kautsky was critical of other council theorists and engaged in a polemic against Rosa Luxemburg and Anton Pannekoek during this period. I have chosen to include him here for two reasons. Firstly, tracing the debates between Kautsky and his interlocutors helps us uncover important questions raised within the German socialist parties over the role of council movements and the future of Germany. Secondly, his thought is not as antithetical to the council movements as is usually considered. Kautsky presents an important 'centrist' position within the USPD, which has been neglected in the history of political thought and is developed in this book.

Chapter two develops political insights into the nature of political freedom from the writings of Anton Pannekoek. It proposes that Pannekoek espoused a particular conception of freedom I call freedom as collective self-determination, which is distinct from both the dominant liberal and republican views of liberty.[36] Pannekoek was selected as the theorist who offers the clearest articulation of how

[34] For a broader periodization that includes a second period of activity of the German councils in 1919–20 see Weipert, *Die zweite Revolution*.

[35] In particular, I have paid less attention to the Revolutionary Shop Stewards whose political thought has been carefully reconstructed in Hoffrogge, *Working-Class Politics in the German Revolution*. See also Dirk H. Müller, *Die revolutionären Obleute und der November 1918: Zur Verschränkung von institutioneller Revolution und Rätebewegung* (Norderstedt: Books on Demand, 2020). For other aspects of the political thought of the council movements see Kets and Muldoon, eds., *The German Revolution and Political Theory*; and James Muldoon, ed., *Council Democracy: Towards a Democratic Socialist Politics* (London: Routledge, 2018).

[36] Philip Pettit, *On the People's Terms: A Republican Theory and Model of Democracy* (Cambridge: Cambridge University Press, 2012).

the activities of the councils were connected to questions of freedom and emancipation. The chapter claims that the framework of the recent liberty debates in political theory has obscured important dimensions of freedom from within the positive liberty tradition. Pannekoek understood political freedom as a political community's ongoing struggle against forces of domination *and* the experimentation with new practices and structures of governance. He identified the state and capitalist relations of production as two of the principal sources of domination in German society. He also saw bourgeois ideology as exercising a stultifying effect on workers' capacity to struggle for their freedom. Democratic participation, on this account, was an essential aspect of the freedom struggle because an emancipatory movement should be led by the workers themselves as the main agents of political transformation. To be free entailed actively participating in deliberation and decision-making and having a direct influence over the laws and character of a political community.

Chapter three argues that council theorists considered it important to shift the balance of power between social classes in order to achieve political transformation. It theorizes differences between those who advocated 'organization' (Kautsky) versus those who advocated 'mobilization' (Luxemburg, Pannekoek) as the most effective method of developing the independent power of the working class. It claims Kautsky advocated a strategy of developing power through building worker-led organizations such as the party, unions, and the press. His strategy involved the gradual growth of power through organization building, parliamentary activity, and developing workers' consciousness within existing organizations. Underlying this strategy of organization lay a conception of power as something that could be incrementally developed and stored through sound organizing, discipline, and patience. In contrast, Luxemburg and Pannekoek considered that power could only be developed through political struggle and direct clashes with the ruling class. They argued that previously unorganized workers could be mobilized through the escalating dynamics of political struggle and that consciousness-raising was best conducted in militant action rather than administrative party activities. These two fundamentally different analyses of how workers should develop their power cast light on different aspects of the council movements' political struggle.

Chapter four reconstructs a theory of socialist republicanism from the writings of an overlooked figure of the German Revolution, Karl Kautsky. Comparing it with the theories of Rosa Luxemburg and the SPD leadership, I argue that during the revolution Kautsky proposed an innovative socialist republican programme that called for the radical transformation of the state and society.[37] The dominance of the 'National Assembly versus Council Republic' ideological framework of the

[37] See James Muldoon, 'A Socialist Republican Theory of Freedom and Government,' *European Journal of Political Theory* (forthcoming).

revolution has obscured Kautsky's 'centrist' third option. Kautsky argued for the presence of workers' councils *alongside* a parliamentary system and understood democracy and socialism as the twin goals of a socialist revolution. He sought to combine the benefits of political democracy and civil rights for minorities with the gradual socialization of the economy. This interpretation challenges the dominant view of Kautsky as a bourgeois reformist who advocated political quietism during the revolution.

Chapter five shows that the German council movements struggled not only for the deepening of democracy and the social ownership of the means of production, but also for a broader project of human emancipation couched in terms of ideological transformation and cultural rejuvenation. A significant barrier identified at the time to the realization of democratic socialist goals was the strong ideological hold of bourgeois mentalities over workers. As a result, radical theorists such as Anton Pannekoek and Gustav Landauer emphasized the subjective role that a people's class-consciousness and 'spirit' [*Geist*] played in political struggle. An overlooked yet significant contribution to this topic was Rosa Luxemburg's theorization of 'socialist civic virtues' as a key element of class struggle and socialist democracy. Luxemburg incorporated republican language and themes into a socialist political ideology of workers' self-emancipation. She understood that worker-controlled institutions would need to be supported by widespread socialist norms that would be common knowledge and followed as a matter of habit. It would be necessary to direct workers away from the egoism, individualism, and competition that predominated in capitalist societies and towards a socialist culture of self-discipline, public-spiritedness, solidarity, and self-activity. She believed it was primarily through their own political activity and the experience of political struggle that workers could acquire the necessary habits and dispositions of self-government for living in a self-determining society. Her ideals of socialist civic virtues help provide content to the council movements' vision of the institutional and cultural order of a future socialist society. Council theorists were motivated by a participatory ideal of a self-determining society in which active citizens would be the main actors in processes of self-government and economic self-management. Reflecting on the political thought of the council movements provides an important standpoint from which to reassess our own forms of democratic government.

1

Between Social Democracy and Council Dictatorship

The Council Movements in Historical Perspective

The council movements have left an ambiguous legacy in political thought. Their historical impact has been overlooked and even some of their most important interpreters have offered distorted accounts of their structure and significance.[1] The aim of this chapter is to return to the history of the council movements in order to cast new light on their historical conditions and the motivations of key historical actors. Council movements arose spontaneously across several European countries during the immediate post-war period and had a remarkable influence on European politics. In the interwar period they redefined the contours of political struggle and represent an important chapter in the history of the workers' movement and international socialism. The two most prominent examples of council movements to emerge in Europe were those of Russia and Germany in the period 1917–1920.[2] Council movements also appeared in other countries such as Austria, Hungary, Italy, and the United Kingdom, but I will focus attention in this chapter on the German council movements. Germany was viewed by European revolutionaries as the most likely country to instigate an international socialist revolution. It was the most advanced industrial nation with a highly organized labour force of 2.5 million unionized workers and a long history of revolutionary politics. However, to the surprise of many, it was the relatively underdeveloped Russia in which council movements first emerged and were eventually incorporated into the Soviet regime.

[1] Medearis, 'Lost or Obscured? How V. I. Lenin, Joseph Schumpeter, and Hannah Arendt Misunderstood the Council Movement', 447.

[2] I concentrate on events in Berlin and Saint Petersburg, which were locus points for the development of the councils. Berlin, for example, consistently had the highest number of strikes in all of Germany and was the heart of the German labour movement. Hans Manfred Bock, *Syndikalismus und Linkskommunismus von 1918–1923* (Meisenheim am Glan: Verlag Anton Hain, 1969), 82. For an analysis of one of Germany's regional centres see Gaard Kets and James Muldoon, 'Rediscovering the Hamburg Workers' and Soldiers' Councils', in *Council Democracy: Towards a Democratic Socialist Politics*, ed. James Muldoon (London: Routledge, 2018), 51–70.

Building Power to Change the World: The Political Thought of the German Council Movements. James Muldoon, Oxford University Press (2020). © James Muldoon. DOI: 10.1093/oso/9780198856627.003.0002

The council movements have been subject to a number of competing interpretations, which have been structured by the conceptual opposition of liberal democracy and council dictatorship. The German councils have typically been portrayed as representing the chaos and disorder before the emergence of stable liberal democratic institutions. The first wave of West German historiography dismissed the period of the councils as a dangerous flirtation with Bolshevism on the path to liberal democracy.[3] In the interpretation of Karl Dietrich Erdmann, representative of this earlier West German approach, the councils embodied a radical Bolshevik ideology of council dictatorship, which was only avoided through the leadership of the German Social Democratic Party towards parliamentary democracy.[4] He posed a radical alternative between 'Western democracy' and 'Eastern dictatorship': either 'the social revolution in alliance with forces pushing towards a proletarian dictatorship, or the parliamentary republic in alliance with conservative elements such as the old officer corps'.[5] A dissenting voice within this early period was Walter Tormin, who argued that Germany had never been in any real danger of a Bolshevist takeover and the council movements strived for the democratization of German society.[6]

Similarly, in scholarship on the Russian Revolution, the story of the soviets in the early phases of the Russian Revolution tended to be overshadowed by the larger framework of the Bolshevik takeover and creation of a one-party state, such that it was difficult to discern the original intentions of participants of the council movements.[7] Meanwhile, in the Soviet Union, the councils were represented as the admirable but ultimately temporary organs of the working class that would eventually be replaced by the superior knowledge and organization of the party. A more balanced assessment of the role of the councils was hindered in the former soviet states by prejudice arising from Lenin's attack on council communist tendencies in his '"Left-Wing" Communism: An Infantile Disorder' and the purges of the left wing of the Bolshevik Party during the Stalinist era.[8]

In the 1960s, a second wave of historical research led by Eberhard Kolb, Peter von Oertzen and Reinhard Rürup paved the way for a reappraisal of the council

[3] For a study by an East German scholar see Ingo Materna, *Der Vollzugsrat der Berliner Arbeiter- und Soldatenräte 1918/19* (Berlin: Dietz-Verlag, 1978). For a good overview of the historiography of the German Revolution see Wolfgang Niess, *Die Revolution von 1918/19 in der deutschen Geschichtsschreibung* (Berlin: de Gruyter, 2013).

[4] Karl Dietrich Erdmann, 'Die Geschichte der Weimarer Republik als Problem der Wissenschaft', *Vierteljahreshefte für Zeitgeschichte* 3 (1955), 1–19.

[5] Ibid., 7.

[6] Tormin, *Zwischen Rätediktatur Und Sozialer Demokratie*. See also Erich Matthias, 'Zur Geschichte der Weimar Republik. Ein Literaturbericht', *Die neue Gesellschaft* 3 (1956), 312–20.

[7] Anweiler, *The Soviets*, 5.

[8] Vladimir I. Lenin, '"Left-Wing" Communism: An Infantile Disorder', in Vladimir I. Lenin, *Collected Works, Vol. 31* (Moscow: Progress Publishers, 1965), 17–118.

movements.[9] The publication of new historical material with the series, 'Sources of the History of the Council Movement in Germany 1918–1919' in 1968 also opened the possibility of a new historical perspective.[10] These interpretations demonstrated that the German council movements did not follow the example of the bolshevization of the soviets in Russia, but tended to be concerned with the democratization of authority structures and the socialization of the economy. During this period, there was a brief renewal of interest in the council movements which was sparked by the radical student movements and a desire to explore historical alternatives to the Weimar Republic and different possible pathways for grassroots socialism.[11] Yet after this short burst of research, there was a decline of scholarly output, with some exceptions being influential books by Heinrich August Winkler, Ulrich Kluge, and Wolfgang Mommsen.[12]

Only recently has there been an upsurge in scholarly interest in the council movements.[13] Ralf Hoffrogge published an important study on Revolutionary Shop Steward, Richard Müller, and the role of the shop stewards as the most organized radical force within the council movements.[14] Dietmar Lange analysed the use of political mass strikes in Germany in the revolutionary years of 1918–19 with an emphasis on the Berlin general strike of March 1919, which was in favour of the recognition of the workers' councils.[15] Axel Weipert recently provided more insight into not only the November Revolution of 1918, but also the 'second revolution' in 1919 and 1920 in which the councils movements mobilized a mass base and made a socialist democratic claim against the Weimar government.[16] William A. Pelz has outlined the forgotten and vital force of the common people during these mass movements, which he argues has been ignored within the historical scholarship.[17] Yohan Dubigeon has also reflected on the experiences of workers' councils as a modern form of grassroots democracy in a theoretical

[9] Kolb, *Die Arbeiterräte in der deutschen Innenpolitik 1918–1919*; Peter von Oertzen, *Betriebsräte in der Novemberrevolution* (Düsseldorf: Droste Verlag, 1963); Reinhard Rürup, *Probleme Der Revolution in Deutschland 1918/19* (Wiesbaden: Steiner, 1968).

[10] The series 'Quellen zur Geschichte der Rätebewegung in Deutschland 1918/19' began with the first volume, Eberhard Kolb, ed., *Der Zentralrat der Deutschen Sozialistischen Republik 19.12.1918 bis 8.4.1919* (Leiden, 1968).

[11] Wolfgang Niess, *Die Revolution Von 1918/19 in Der Deutschen Geschichtsschreibung. Deutungen Von Der Weimarer Republik Bis Ins 21. Jahrhundert* (Berlin, Boston: Gruyter, 2013).

[12] Heinrich August Winkler, *Von der Revolution zur Stabilisierung. Arbeiter und Arbeiterbewegung in der Weimar Republik 1918 bis 1924* (Berlin/Bonn: Verlag J. H. W. Dietz, 1984); Ulrich Kluge, *Soldatenräte und Revolution. Studien zur Militärpolitik in Deutschland 1918/19* (Göttingen: Vandenhoeck and Ruprecht, 1975); Wolfgang J. Mommsen, 'Die Deutsche Revolution 1918/19' *Geschichte und Gesellschaft* 4, no. 3 (1978), 362–91.

[13] See Klaus Weinhauer, Anthony McElligott, and Kirsten Heinsohn, eds., *Germany 1916–23: A Revolution in Context* (Bielefeld: Transcript, 2015); Fowkes. *The German Left and the Weimar Republic: A Selection of Documents*; Kuhn, ed., *All Power to the Councils!*.

[14] Hoffrogge, *Working-Class Politics in the German Revolution*.

[15] Dietmar Lange, *Massenstreik und Schießbefehl: Generalstreik und Märzkämpfe in Berlin 1919* (Berlin: edition assemblage, 2012).

[16] Axel Weipert, *Die Zweite Revolution. Rätebewegung in Berlin 1919/1920* (Berlin: be.bra, 2015).

[17] William A. Pelz, *A People's History of the German Revolution* (London: Pluto Press, 2018).

study of council democracy from 1871 to 1921.[18] These recent studies have tended to share an interest in a social history of the working classes that looks beyond the canonical figures to uncover new historical narratives.

In this chapter, I trace the rise and fall of the council movements and examine their participants' underlying democratic and socialist impulses. I argue that while a diversity of political views were held by participants in the council movements, there was broad support for the deepening and extension of democratic conditions in major political, economic, and social institutions. Workers lived in hierarchical and authoritarian societies with strict class divisions, highly disciplined workplaces, and little chance for self-direction in their lives. During the hardships of the war, discontent with existing regimes was reaching fever pitch through a steady rise of strike activities. Following initial revolutionary upheavals, both the Russian and German monarchies were toppled with relative ease as mass movements arose with desires for peace, bread, democracy, and a reorganization of social life. In the early days of both revolutions, the demand for the democratization and socialization of political and economic institutions was supported by the overwhelming majority of people, particularly the workers and sections of the liberal middle classes.[19] The council movements channelled working-class aspirations to cast off the chains of stultifying authoritarian regimes and to live in an egalitarian, self-determining society. Yet counter-revolutionary forces were quick to reorganize themselves and the emancipatory demands of the council movements were subverted, misdirected, and subdued. While the opportunity of developing a radically more democratic society was present in each case, powerful interests were able to reassert old hierarchies, which limited the emancipatory potential of the early council movements.

Situating the Councils

In standard usage, a council could be an advisory or administrative body of people that offers advice or exercises some form of power such as a committee, local authority, or board of directors. The councils I refer to in this study, however, have a specific historical origin and political significance that differentiates them from other types of councils. The European council movements developed most significantly in 1917–19 in Russia, Germany, Hungary, Austria, Italy, and the UK. Historians have pointed to similarities between these councils and a long line of direct democracy and self-determination movements 'from the urban

[18] Yohan Dubigeon, *La démocratie des conseils. Aux origines modernes de l'autogouvernement* (Paris: Klincksiek, 2017).

[19] Albert Schmelzer, *The Threefolding Movement, 1919: Rudolf Steiner's Campaign for a Self-Governing, Self-Managing, Self-Educating Society* (Forest Row: Rudolf Steiner Press, 2017), 23.

communes of the middle ages, the Swiss peasant cantons, the original collective settlements in North America, the Paris Commune of 1871 and the Russian soviets'.[20] There is a resemblance between many of these grassroots organizational forms that have emerged over the course of revolutions and uprisings. However, the councils of the early twentieth century were a very distinct institution that arose out of revolutionary situations during the big strike movements of the preceding years as a means for the recently emerged working classes to represent their interests and overturn hierarchical structures that oppressed them.[21] The structure of the councils was closely linked to the organization and cooperation of workers in large factories, which distinguished them from other pre-industrial forms of council-like institutions and democratic movements. The councils were also institutions with a distinctive class element insofar as they aimed to organize and empower the lower classes against an entrenched political and economic elite.

The main historical precedents for the councils of the immediate post–First World War period were the early workers' soviets of the 1905 Russian Revolution.[22] When the soviets first arose in May 1905 they were composed of deputies who represented primarily workers' economic interests to factory owners in disputes over conditions.[23] The Mensheviks began campaigning for 'revolutionary self-government', which was followed by the formation of the St Petersburg Soviet of Workers Deputies during the peak of the strikes in October.[24] These soviets politicized workers and gave them the opportunity to appoint recallable delegates to struggle for greater worker self-determination. Their political goal was a radically democratic parliamentary republic. The soviets conceived of themselves as revolutionary committees rather than the beginnings of a new state form.[25] At the time in 1905, Pannekoek noted that the councils 'were hardly noticed as a special phenomenon' because they were overshadowed by theoretical interest in the mass strike.[26] Though they only existed relatively briefly, these soviets left behind a revolutionary tradition amongst the workers, which emerged anew in 1917. Many of those who were young workers and soldiers in 1905 were the elders of the 1917 period.

Comparisons could also be made to the 1871 Paris Commune, which was another important precursor to the European council movements. Oskar

[20] Arthur Rosenberg, *A History of Bolshevism: From Marx to the First Five-Year Plan* (Oxford: Oxford University Press, 1934), 92.

[21] Anweiler, *The Soviets*, 4.

[22] For the most detailed account of the role of the soviets in the 1905 Russian Revolution see Anweiler, *The Soviets*, 20–96.

[23] Ibid., 40. [24] Tormin, *Zwischen Rätediktatur und sozialer Demokratie*, 14.

[25] Ibid. Although Trotsky argued that 'the substance of the Soviet was its effort to become an *organ of public authority*.' Leon Trotsky, *History of the 1905 Revolution* (Harmondsworth: Penguin Books, 1972), 176.

[26] Anton Pannekoek, *Workers' Councils*, accessible at https://www.marxists.org/archive/pannekoe/1947/workers-councils.htm. See for example Rosa Luxemburg, 'The Mass Strike, the Political Party and the Trade Unions'.

Anweiler understated the historical role of the Paris Commune in his argument that 'the Commune too had no direct influence on the formation and early activity of the soviets.'[27] More recently, Donny Gluckstein has shown that not only did the basic institutional form of the Commune mirror, to a remarkable extent, the federation of workers' councils in the 1917–20 revolutionary period, but the actions of the Parisian workers inspired generations of working class actors.[28] Marx's essay on the Paris Commune became the point of departure for Lenin's analysis of the soviets, which was influential over the Russian experience.[29] The main difference was that the Paris Commune was an attempt at municipal self-administration, while the council movements were a revolution of workers in big industries.[30] The Paris Commune was composed of a heterogeneous assortment of artisans, petit bourgeoisie, merchants, workers, and declassed individuals, which distinguished it from the twentieth-century workers' and soldiers' councils.[31]

Anweiler also distinguished between three different types of councils: workers' committees that represented workers' interests, revolutionary committees that led revolutionary movements for a limited duration, and councils that became state authorities such as the Paris Commune.[32] The issue with attempting to draw up a typology of different forms of councils is that participants in each council rarely agreed amongst themselves upon their basic structure and purpose. As these issues were contested and the precise powers and authority of the councils were rarely formally defined, I prefer to speak of *council movements*, which refers to the broader political forces that supported the formation of councils, and *council republics*, by which I mean the brief moments in which council movements succeeded in establishing council institutions as the sovereign political authority over a territory.

The council movements of the early twentieth century were composed mainly of workers, soldiers, artisans, white-collar workers, unemployed workers, and intellectuals and contained a number of competing social and political forces. There were three shared core aspirations that united most of the participants. First, they supported a democratic programme of political reforms to authoritarian regimes that would have given workers basic civic and political rights such as freedom of speech, freedom of association, and universal suffrage. Second, they aimed to institute workers' control over key industries that would allow for greater

[27] Anweiler, *The Soviets*, 11.

[28] Donny Gluckstein, 'Workers' Councils in Europe: A Century of Experience', in *Ours to Master Ours to Own: Workers' Control from the Commune to the Present*, ed. Immanuel Ness and Dario Azzellini (Chicago: Haymarket Books, 2011), 34–6. See also Donny Gluckstein, *The Paris Commune: A Revolution in Democracy* (London: Bookmarks, 2006); See also Jones, *Founding Weimar*, 4.

[29] Karl Marx, 'The Civil War in France'.

[30] Anton Pannekoek, 'Nach vierzig Jahren', *Bremer Bürger-Zeitung* (18 March 1911), 163.

[31] Martin Breaugh, *The Plebeian Experience: A Discontinuous History of Political Freedom* (New York: Columbia University Press, 2013), 173–4.

[32] Anweiler, *The Soviets*, 5.

self-determination in the workplace. Finally, they sought to challenge the central authority structures in European society and transform the underlying power relations in order to empower the lower classes and provide them with new capacities to shape public life. This radical programme was not shared by all of those who participated in the council movements, but it was a set of underlying concerns that was repeatedly expressed in council meetings and declarations.

The issue of whether the council movements desired to create council republics is a complex and ambiguous question that I will examine later in the chapter. In the few instances where political groups formed short-lived council republics such as in Bavaria, Hungary, and Bremen, they embodied three key institutional features. First, they were unified bodies that stood in place of liberal parliamentary institutions and had no separation between executive or legislative powers. Second, they were composed of directly elected delegates who were subject to immediate recall and were elected from within factories and barracks. Third, they desired to exercise political and economic functions including fulfilling basic administrative tasks and assisting in the organization of economic production.

The council movements in Germany can also be distinguished from an anarcho-syndicalist current of workers' organizations which although relatively small, constitutes an important minor tendency in the German workers' movement.[33] Ralf Hoffrogge has noted that 'although anarchism in Germany had always been a marginal fringe movement, it did attain considerable influence in the form of revolutionary syndicalism, primarily in the Ruhr region in 1918/1919.'[34] The revolutionary syndicalists also had representation in Berlin through the Free Association of German Trade Unions [*Freie Vereinigung deutscher Gewerkschaften (FVdG)*], which was the only trade union organization in Germany not to support the German state in the First World War.[35] Syndicalists were revolutionaries who prioritized the agency of workers acting directly through their trade unions over the mediation of political parties. They supported the general strike as the most decisive weapon of workers against the capitalist class. Advocates of a council system charted a middle course between anarcho-syndicalism and social democracy by arguing for the establishment of regional and national institutions that would provide coordination between different political and economic bodies. The councils were also organized primarily

[33] Hans Manfred Bock, 'Anarchosyndicalism in the German Labour Movement: a Rediscovered Minority Tradition', in *Revolutionary Syndicalism: An International Perspective*, ed. Marcel van der Linden and Wayne Thorpe (Aldershot, England: Scholar Press, 1990), 59–80. See also Hans Manfred Bock, *Syndikalismus und Linkskommunismus von 1918 bis 1923* (Meisenheim/Glan: Verlag Anton Hain, 1969); Angela Vogel, *Der deutsche Anarcho-Syndikalismus* (Berlin: Karin Kramer, 1977); Dirk H. Müller, *Gewerkschaftliche Versammlungsdemokratie und Arbeiterdeliegerte vor 1918* (Berlin: Colloquium Verlag, 1985).

[34] Hoffrogge, *Working-Class Politics in the German Revolution*, 116.

[35] Wayne Thorpe, 'Keeping the Faith: The German Syndicalists in the First World War', *Central European History* 33, no. 2 (2000), 195–216.

through existing political parties and the ideology of delegates in the councils tended to reflect their political party.

It should be clear from this brief outline that by councils I am not referring to Athenian direct democracy, a Rousseauian republic, pre-revolutionary American townships, or even the Union of Soviet Socialist Republics established by the Bolshevik Party. I will explain later in more detail why we have good reason to view the Soviet Union as a distortion of the original aspirations of the council movements. The size and the scale of the European council movements of the early twentieth century mark them out from other attempts at establishing self-managed factories and other forms of workers' control. The council movements were organized in nationwide federal structures that attempted to exercise political and economic functions in order to achieve workers' self-determination and empowerment. Councils also briefly reappeared in Hungary and Poland in 1956, which followed in the steps of the earlier councils.[36] There have since been a number of other attempts at establishing workers' councils that draw inspiration from the experiences of the European council movements, although never on the same scale or with the support of such a large workers' movement.[37]

Theoretical Precursors to the Councils

The closest direct theoretical precursors to the council system are early socialist and anarchist writers who advocated self-government, cooperative production, and mass participation in public affairs. Nineteenth-century European socialists such as Fourier, Owen, Saint-Simon, Proudhon, and Marx share with the council movements a concern for the deleterious effects of capitalism and unquestioned political authority. They also hold a common commitment to restructuring society through radical social reform. Yet while there are many commonalities in their underlying political principles, none of these precursors arrive at the organizational form of a council system as a pyramidal structure of bottom-up workers' councils that would fulfil a political and economic function. In spite of some striking resemblances, the councils have little in the way of theoretical elaboration before they dramatically appear on the stage briefly in 1905 and then more significantly in 1917.

First, I will address Hannah Arendt's somewhat misleading portrait of a forgotten tradition of the councils throughout modern politics. Arendt traces the development of the council system back to the French revolutionary societies

[36] Oskar Anweiler, 'Die Räte in der ungarischen Revolution', *Osteuropa* 8 (1958), 393–400.

[37] For a more expansive list of workers' councils in the twentieth century see Ness and Azzellini, eds., *Ours to Master Ours to Own*. See also Assef Bayat, *Work, Politics and Power: An International Perspective on Workers' Control and Self-management* (New York: Monthly Review Press, 1991).

and Thomas Jefferson's sketches of a ward system of local town hall meetings.[38] While Arendt acknowledges that there is no evidence of a direct connection between the twentieth-century councils and Jefferson's institutional design, there are also clear differences in the two systems that undermine her argument for the regular emergence of a single council form. The town hall meetings of Jefferson's grassroots democracy lacked any class-specific organizational character and were not designed to overcome the strict distinction between the political and economic spheres. Jefferson's plan for the division of the country into wards did not fulfil the main goals of the twentieth-century council movements such as organizing workplaces democratically, restructuring the capital–labour relationship, and challenging the centralized power of the bourgeois national government. Contrary to Arendt's council mythology, there is only a vague resemblance between eighteenth-century attempts at self-governance and the twentieth-century workers' councils.

From the early socialist and anarchist tradition, I will consider the three major figures of Pierre-Joseph Proudhon, Mikhail Bakunin, and Karl Marx due to their canonical status and the proximity between their political thought and the councils. Proudhon put forward a vision of a free society in which local workers' associations would be connected through a decentralized economic and political federal system.[39] He criticized private property, wage labour, and the repressive institutions of the state and believed that industries should be democratically organized by workers' associations.[40] Rejecting the model of the nation-state and traditional conceptions of government, Proudhon argued that a decentralized federal network of workers' associations constituted the 'true synthesis of freedom and order'.[41] In one of his final works, Proudhon summarized the key tenants of his political thought as follows: 'All my economic ideas, developed over the last 25 years, can be defined in three words, agro-industrial federation; all my political views . . . political federation or decentralization, all my hopes for the present and future . . . progressive federation.'[42] His thought has been directly linked to the formation of the Russian councils and exercised a significant influence on the development of left-wing political movements in Europe.[43] Proudhon's anti-authoritarianism and support for a cooperative federation of producers places him as a precursor to the leading proponents of council democracy in the early twentieth century. However, his conception of a voluntary federal system of

[38] Arendt, *On Revolution*, 249.

[39] Pierre-Joseph Proudhon, *The Principle of Federation* (Toronto: The University of Toronto Press, 1979).

[40] Pierre-Joseph Proudhon, *Oeuvres Complètes, Vol. 17* (Paris: A. Lacroix, 1868), 188–9.

[41] Quoted in George Woodcock, *Pierre-Joseph Proudhon: His Life and Work* (New York: Schocken Books, 1972), 75.

[42] Proudhon, *The Principle of Federation*, 73.

[43] Otto Seeling, *Der Rätegedanke und seine Verwirkung in Sowjetrussland* (Berlin: Pyramidenverlag, 1925), 37.

workers' associations was less centralized and hierarchical than the pyramidal form adopted by most European council systems during their brief existence. In contrast to Proudhon's political ideal, the councils tended to centralize power in an executive council and still relied on the rule of law, a military force, and systems of political representation through delegation.

As one of Proudhon's disciples, Bakunin also advocated for the formation of workers' committees as a means of organizing the proletariat and peasantry against the institutions of the state. Bakunin followed Proudhon's critique of all forms of hierarchically organized power including the state, capitalism, and the church. He also went further than his mentor in developing more clearly the methods by which revolutionary political transformation could be achieved. In line with later council theorists, Bakunin rejected participation in bourgeois elections and parliamentary institutions. He argued for the 'free federation from the bottom upward, the association of workers in industry and agriculture—first in the communities, then through federation of communities into districts, districts into nations, and nations into international brotherhood.'[44] In Bakunin's formula, these workers would join with other insurrectionary groups to form a 'federation of the barricades' as the locus of revolutionary struggle.[45] He preferred the formation of new working-class institutions that would be constituted through the election of workers' delegates with binding mandates subject to immediate recall in order to prevent delegates from becoming a new privileged class. As part of this revolutionary process, Bakunin emphasized the importance of the spontaneous organizational impulses of the workers, an inclination that would later be confirmed in the largely spontaneous formation of the workers' councils in the early twentieth century.

In spite of these affinities, there is little evidence to suggest that Bakunin's ideas were particularly influential over the political actors who developed council institutions. Although the tactics and strategies of the council delegates often corresponded to essential aspects of Bakunin's political thought, delegates were more likely to espouse Marxist rather than anarchist principles and ideology. Yet the council movements did not begin with highly developed theoretical outlines of their methods and practice. Instead, they drew their point of view from more accessible sources available in socialist newspapers and pamphlets. It is thus important not to overemphasize the coherence of theoretical differences that were not themselves clear to participants at the time.

Bakunin's confrontation with Marx, which led to the split in the First International, represented the first clash between centralizing and federalist

[44] Gregori Petrovich Maximoff, ed., *The Political Philosophy of Bakunin: Scientific Anarchism* (Glencoe, Il: The Free Press, 1953), 410.

[45] Daniel Guerin, ed., *No Gods, No Masters: An Anthology of Anarchism. Vol. 1* (Edinburgh: AK Press, 1998), 155–6.

tendencies that would later play out in the struggle over the Russian soviets. This confrontation led to Bakunin's contribution to political struggle being marginalized within the Marxist tradition, with the Bolsheviks continuing Marx's denial of any strong affinities with anarchism. While followers of Proudhon and Bakunin advocated for the development of workers' councils in the 1860s and 1870s as organs of class struggle, it was not until the early twentieth century that they received a concrete form on a national scale.[46]

Karl Marx was nevertheless the dominant influence over the ideology and political practices of participants in council movements across Europe in the 1917–20 period. Through meticulous biographical research, Sabine Roß has confirmed that the vast majority of council delegates in Germany were members of a socialist political party that was Marxist in orientation (although the ideology of soldiers participating in councils was usually more centrist).[47] Similarly, in the First All-Russian Congress of Soviets of 1917, all but a small number of delegates were socialists from the Bolshevik, Menshevik, and Socialist Revolutionist parties.[48] In spite of differences between leading figures of the workers' movement concerning the role of a workers' party in processes of social reform and revolution, the overwhelming majority of socialists adhered to the basic principles of Marx's critique of capitalism and considered that capitalism was in terminal decline. Concerning the pathway towards workers' liberation, council activists agreed with Marx that 'the emancipation of the working class must be the work of the working class itself.'[49] Council institutions were valued precisely because they appeared as the spontaneous outcome of the organizational impulses of workers. Although some council delegates participated in the councils with ulterior motives and not all socialists were Marxists, most of those who supported the continued existence of the council organizations had a broadly Marxist political ideology.

However, it cannot be said that Marx was an unambiguous advocate of council communism, since there are few references to workers' councils in his political writings and he nowhere argued directly for a council democracy in a post-capitalist society. Marx's various pronouncements on the preferred organizational form of revolutionary struggle tended to be immediate responses to events and evolved with political circumstances. During the period of 1848–50, Marx held an optimistic view of the immediate prospects of revolutionary action. In the *Communist Manifesto*, Marx set out the broad tasks of the proletariat in a revolution as follows:

[46] Paul Avrich, *The Russian Anarchists* (Princeton: Princeton University Press, 2015), 73.

[47] Sabine Roß, *Biographisches Handbuch der Reichsrätekongresse 1918/1919* (Düsseldorf, Droste Verlag, 2000).

[48] Frank Golder, ed., *Documents of Russian History, 1914–1917* (New York: The Century Co., 1927) 360–1. Although the Socialist Revolutionary party was not explicitly Marxist, many of its key participants were strongly influenced by Marxist ideas in addition to a neo-populist discourse, which emphasized the role of the peasantry as a revolutionary class against the Tsarist regime.

[49] Address and Provisional Rules of the Working Men's International Association.

> The proletariat will use its political supremacy to wrest, by degree, all capital from the bourgeoisie, to centralise all instruments of production in the hands of the State, i.e., of the proletariat organised as the ruling class; and to increase the total productive forces as rapidly as possible.[50]

Here, Marx appears to be describing a transitional period of revolutionary transformation in which the proletariat would use the instruments of a centralized state to advance its political goals. Marx discussed the important role of a communist party in this process, but there is no mention of workers' councils or how the working class would be concretely organized outside of the party.

In an address to the League in 1850, Marx speculated about a future revolutionary situation in Germany in which a feudal power will have been overthrown by a combination of bourgeois and working-class forces. It is in this address that Marx first suggested the possibility of workers forming councils that would build workers' power in order to challenge a bourgeois government:

> Alongside the new official governments they must simultaneously erect their own revolutionary workers governments, whether in the form of municipal executives and municipal councils, or of workers clubs and workers committees, so that the bourgeois democratic governments not only lose the backing of the workers, but also from the very beginning find themselves watched and threatened by institutions behind which stand the entire mass of workers.[51]

This call for revolutionary councils and committees to be established alongside official government structures anticipated the situation of 'dual power' that was created in the Russian and German revolutions following the establishment of workers' councils. Marx did not abandon his insistence on 'the necessity of an independently organized party of the proletariat' or the importance of a strong centralized state power, adding that 'workers must not only strive for one and indivisible German republic, but also, within this republic, for the most decisive centralization of power in the hands of the state authority.'[52] Elsewhere, in his critique of the Gotha Programme, Marx noted that workers would only need to use the instruments of the state for a limited period during a transitional phase before the institution of a future classless society in which the coercive force of the state would no longer be necessary to enforce class hierarchies.

The main inspiration for later council communists was not from this revolutionary era, but from one of Karl Marx's later texts on the Paris Commune.[53] Marx

[50] Karl Marx and Friedrich Engels, 'The Communist Manifesto'.

[51] Karl Marx, 'Address of the Central Authority to the Communist League'. [52] Ibid.

[53] For an analysis of this text see Bruno Leipold, "Marx's Social Republic: Radical Republicanism and the Political Institutions of Socialism," in *Radical Republicanism: Recovering the Tradition's Popular*

did not anticipate the Paris Commune and initially warned workers against establishing such a regime.[54] Yet when the Paris Commune was formed, Marx threw his enthusiastic support behind it, praising workers for establishing 'a working class government, the produce of the struggle of the producing against the appropriating class, the political form at last discovered under which to work out the economical emancipation of labour'.[55] Crucial for Marx was the Commune's capacity not simply to act as a political organ of government, but to reorganize the economic relationship between capital and labour. Marx's description of the Paris Commune is one of his most developed accounts of the potential institutional structure of a post-capitalist people's republic. Although it is unclear whether Marx envisaged that this system would eventually be supplanted, his support for the Commune gave later Marxists cause to believe that some form of federal council system could be a possible model for a socialist polity.

One distinct innovation in Marx's thought that occurred during this period was the emphasis he placed on developing alternative working-class institutions to the bourgeois state. Marx believed the lesson of the Paris Commune was that 'the working class cannot simply lay hold of the ready-made state machinery, and wield it for its own purposes.'[56] Thus, rather than seizing the administrative and coercive apparatuses of the state, Marx supported the development of alternative institutions controlled by workers that would aim to replace the government. Marx saw in the Commune an ideal of 'really democratic institutions' in which the workers would take 'into their own hands the direction of public affairs'.[57] In Marx's account, the decisive difference between bourgeois government and the Commune lies in how the communards attempted to place instruments of collective decision-making under more robust forms of democratic control by the people. This was achieved through the institution of universal suffrage and the public election of all posts in the bureaucracy, judiciary, and armed forces. These delegates would be subject to immediate recall and would all be paid a worker's wage.

It was from this new type of social organization that Marx imagined the basis for a national federation of workers' organizations. Although nothing of the sort had been developed in practice, Marx envisioned how 'the rural communities of every district were to administer their common affairs by an assembly of delegates in the central town, and these district assemblies were again to send deputies to the National Delegation in Paris.'[58] There is still a tension in this work between Marx's

Heritage, eds. Bruno Leipold, Karma Nabulsi and Stuart White (Oxford: Oxford University Press, 2020), 172–196.

[54] Karl Marx, 'The Civil War in France'. [55] Ibid. [56] Ibid. [57] Ibid.
[58] Ibid.

centralized political vision and the admission that the 'old centralised government' would have to give way to the 'self-government of the producers'.[59] Under these circumstances, Marx attempted to reconcile his older principles with the Commune's demand for local self-government and autonomy for regional towns. Allowing for certain ambiguities between the centralist and federalist tendencies within Marx's work, his sketch of a national organization prefigures the later structure of federal council institutions.

Celebrated in Marx's writing as 'the glorious harbinger of a new society', the Paris Commune proved influential over future council supporters such as Lenin, Luxemburg, and Korsch.[60] It is unclear to what extent Marx considered the Commune to be merely a transitional phase towards a new post-capitalist society or a more permanent institutional form. Engels later confirmed after Marx's death that the Commune could be regarded as 'the dictatorship of the proletariat', which adds weight to an interpretation of the councils as a more temporary form.[61] Nevertheless, the Commune entered into radical political thought through Marx's writings as an important contribution to the ongoing debate over the appropriate organizational form of revolutionary struggle. His account of the Paris Commune would later assist Lenin in understanding the role that soviets could play in the 1917 revolution after their initial appearance in 1905.[62] Marx's writings provide the single most important theoretical reference point for political actors participating in council movements. However, later council communists would also orient themselves through their experience of the Russian Revolution, the failures of social democratic parties and their response to Leninism and his theory of a vanguard party.

Russia: Towards a Council Dictatorship

After a long nadir following the repression of the 1905 Revolution, the councils (in Russian: soviets) dramatically reappeared in Russia following a wave of mass strikes in March 1917.[63] A combination of the inherent weaknesses of the old regime and the short-term crises brought on by the impact of the First World War led to the collapse of the Tsar's government and widespread expectations for political freedom. The development of the councils began with a series of strikes throughout February 1917. On 8 March, workers announced a strike at

[59] Ibid.

[60] Marx, *The Civil War in France*; Lenin, 'State and Revolution'; Rosa Luxemburg, 'The Russian Revolution'; Karl Korsch, 'Revolutionary Commune'.

[61] Engels, postscript to *The Civil War in France*.

[62] Lenin, 'State and Revolution'.

[63] Dates refer to the Gregorian calendar rather than the older Julian calendar that was used in Russia prior to 1918.

Petrograd's largest industrial plant.[64] This strike was followed the next day by large political gatherings for International Women's Day. At this rally, female workers marched from factory to factory, bringing over 50,000 more workers into the streets for the strike. By the next day industrial production in Petrograd had almost entirely been halted. When the Tsar attempted to order troops to forcefully suppress the rioters, soldiers mutinied, government authority collapsed, and the Tsar was forced to abdicate the throne.[65] Workers seized the opportunity to create workers' organizations of various kinds including trade unions, factory committees, soviets, and political parties. Soviets flourished across Russia, arising to meet the immediate needs of the workers and soldiers. The most vibrant and democratic element of this workers' movement were the factory committees and soviets that sprang up across the industrial centres of Russia.[66] In spite of different tendencies amongst the workers, Trotsky notes that 'the form of organization [the soviets] itself stood clear of all debate.'[67]

Revolutionary forces that had opposed Tsarism were split between the bourgeois and liberal coalition on the one hand, who participated in the Duma and the Provisional Government, and the workers and soldiers on the other, who all established soviets.[68] In Petrograd, a central committee of the workers' movement was established in the form of the Petrograd Workers and Soldiers Soviet on 12 March 1917. This soviet appealed to workers and soldiers to send deputies to elect an Executive Committee.[69] Soviets elected one deputy for each 1,000 workers to sit on the Petrograd Soviet, or alternatively, one delegate for each company of soldiers.[70] A meeting of over 250 workers, soldiers, and intellectuals elected Nikolay Chkheidze as chairman and Alexander Kerensky as vice-chairman.

The Petrograd Soviet rejected participation in a Provisional Government with the Duma Committee, which consisted of Octobrists and Constitutional Democrats such as Foreign Minister Miliukov and Minister of War Aleksander Guchkov. Instead, the Petrograd Soviet presented the government with a list of demands as a condition of its support, which was signed on 15 March 1917.[71]

[64] Robert Service, *A History of Modern Russia from Nicholas II to Vladimir Putin* (Cambridge: Harvard University Press, 2005), 32.

[65] Ian Beckett, *The Great War* (London: Pearson/Longman, 2007), 523.

[66] David Mandel, 'The Factory Committee Movement in the Russian Revolution', in *Ours to Master and to Own*, ed. Ness and Azzellini (Chicago: Haymarket Books, 2011), 104–29.

[67] Leon Trotsky, *The History of the Russian Revolution, Vol. 1* (London: Victor Gollancz Ltd, 1932), 174.

[68] Rosenberg, *The History of Bolshevism*, 122.

[69] 'Provisional Executive Committee of the Soviet of Workers' Deputies, Proclamations. March 12, 1917', in *Documents of Russian History, 1914–1917*, ed. Frank Golder (New York: The Century Co., 1927), 285–6.

[70] 'Proclamation Calling for the Election of Workers' and Soldiers' Deputies to the Petrograd Soviet', in *The Russian Provisional Government: Documents Vol. 1*, ed. Robert Browder and Alexander Kerensky (Stanford: Stanford University Press, 1961), 70–1.

[71] 'Provisional Committee of the State Duma, Proclamations. March 3, 1917', in *Documents of Russian History, 1914–1917*, ed. Frank Golder (New York: The Century Co., 1927), 308–13.

Their demands consisted of a complete democratization of the state and the granting of civil and political freedoms. They called for an immediate general amnesty for all political prisoners and the abolition of restrictions and discriminations based on religious or national grounds. It was proposed that the hated police force of the Tsar would be turned into a national militia with elected officer subject to democratic controls. The workers also rallied against autocratic managerial despotism in the factories and desired greater freedom in the workplace.[72] Their top priorities included an eight-hour workday, improved work conditions, and a right of supervision over how factories were organized. In March, workers' demands did not extend to managing the technical or economic side of production, but workers did want to limit the power of management and to be able to negotiate organizational matters.[73]

In the first weeks of the Petrograd Soviet's existence the number of delegates grew to such an extent that by the end of March it had reached nearly 3,000.[74] Under such circumstances, it was difficult to organize efficient meetings. The sessions of the Soviet resembled mass demonstrations rather than functional meetings. The delegates decided to select a smaller council of about 600 members, which was composed of an equal number of workers and soldiers. This reduced number allowed for more business to be conducted, but the majority of decision-making still occurred in the Executive Committee, which from the very first days of the revolution was the key organizational body of the soviets. By early April, the Executive Committee consisted of forty-two members, so many that they created a special 'Bureau of the Executive Committee' with only seven members to deal with current and urgent business.[75] This Bureau was allowed to take independent political decisions in emergencies.

The executive organs of the soviets began to meet daily, while the plenary sessions for ordinary delegates became more sporadic. The business of the executive required an ever-growing team of administrative labourers, most of who had been clerks in old government departments. As the Executive Committee became a more efficient administrative machine, it began to organize independently from the rank and file soviet delegates. Carmen Sirianni argues that, 'effective power gravitated to executive committees and their even smaller bureau' throughout the system.[76] In theory, the delegates continued to hold the right to dismiss the Committee, guaranteeing that ultimate power remained in the lower soviets. Yet already in these early days a tension appeared between the soviets as revolutionary

[72] Mandel, 'The Factory Committee Movement in the Russian Revolution', 107. [73] Ibid.

[74] 'The Reduction of the Number of Deputies in the Soviet', in *The Russian Provisional Government: Documents Vol. 1*, ed. Robert Browder and Alexander Kerensky (Stanford: Stanford University Press, 1961), 78.

[75] 'The Executive Committee of the Petrograd Soviet', in *Documents of Russian History, 1914–1917*, ed. Frank Golder (New York: The Century Co., 1927), 288–90.

[76] Carmen Sirianni, *Workers Control and Socialist Democracy: the Soviet Experience* (London: Verso, 1982), 70.

organizations and their more permanent administrative functions. As institutions without a clear structure, constitution, or proper delegation of roles, the soviets were not ideally suited for administrative tasks. However, in the absence of a permanent central government or well-resourced parliamentary institutions, they began to take on some of the day-to-day tasks of provisions, supplies, and rebuilding. Large plenary sessions took on a merely symbolic function as they grew distant from real decision-making power.[77]

For all practical purposes, February to October was a period of dual power in which the Provisional Government could only make decisions that were agreed to by the Petrograd Soviet. Workers and soldiers recognized the soviets as the true authoritative institutions in the country and would only follow orders of the government that were not in contradiction with those of the Petrograd Soviet.[78] However, during the first months of the revolution the soviets left the majority of business to the Provisional Government and established an agreement that the soviets would be a 'controlling organ of revolutionary democracy'.[79] The Petrograd Soviet did not request any formal definition of its authority as members saw their role as guiding the revolution and protecting it against counter-revolutionary forces. They aimed to influence the government and ensure its actions were in accordance with the principles of the soviets' programme. As a result, the government instituted wide-ranging political freedoms to citizens including civil rights, the abolition of restrictions based upon nationality, religion and class, penal reform, freedom of speech, press and assembly, the release of political prisoners, and the calling of a constituent assembly.[80] The implementation of the soviets' programme was supervised by an 'Observation Committee' that was selected by the soviets to monitor government activities.[81] The committee was established to 'convey to the Provisional Government the revolutionary demands, to pressure the government to fulfil these demands, and to control government actions.'[82] Provincial soviets were instructed by Petrograd to 'in no way solely assume government functions'.[83] Members of the soviets preferred to surveil government actions rather than remove the government entirely.

[77] Ibid., 203.

[78] This was due to the first official decree of the Petrograd Workers and Soldiers Soviet, Order No. 1, which stated that orders of the Provisional Government were only to be followed by the workers and soldiers if they did not contradict those of the soviet. See John Boyd, 'The Origins of Order Number 1', *Soviet Studies* 19, no. 3 (1967), 359–72.

[79] 'Resolution of Support for the Provisional Government by the All-Russian Conference of Soviets', in *The Russian Revolution and the Soviet State 1917–1921: Documents*, ed. Martin McCauley (London: Macmillan Press, 1975), 26–7.

[80] 'Attitude of the Executive Committee of the Soviet on the Question of Participation in the Provisional Government', in *The Russian Provisional Government: Documents Vol. 1*, ed. Robert Browder and Alexander Kerensky (Stanford: Stanford University Press, 1961), 125–6.

[81] Ibid., 126. [82] Quoted in Anweiler, *The Soviets*, 130.

[83] 'Instruction to All Soviets of Workers and Soldiers Deputies', quoted in Anweiler, *The Soviets*, 130.

Debates at the All-Russian Congress of Soviets in June presented a division between the moderate and radical socialists.[84] The point of conflict related to the instability of a system of dual power. This could be resolved either through the dissolution of the Provisional Government and the assumption of sole power by the soviets or through the formation of a coalition government between socialists and moderates. The majority of delegates from the Mensheviks and Socialist Revolutionaries did not favour taking sole power and argued for joining the Provisional Government. They considered that complete soviet rule would alienate the peasantry and the bourgeoisie. The workers and soldiers organized in the councils represented only a small proportion of the total population. The moderate socialists argued that as the peasants and urban-dwellers were continuing to organize themselves in self-governing units, a national constituent assembly would be a more democratic indicator of the desires of the masses. At this point Russia was still largely an agrarian economy with a majority of peasants in the lower classes. The Bolsheviks, however, famously argued for Lenin's slogan of 'all power to the soviets' and the rejection of the bourgeois Provisional Government. With the Bolsheviks still in a small minority at this stage, the All-Russian Congress decided against the assumption of power by the soviets and in favour of the formation of a coalition government. The Bolsheviks rejected participation in this government, thus setting the scene for the next phase of the conflict.

This period of dual power raised what Trotsky called the 'paradox of the February Revolution'. The working classes overthrew the old regime but appeared unable or unwilling to govern themselves. In Trotsky's interpretation of this period of dual power, he argues that the workers' conditional support for the Provisional Government alongside the soviet system revealed an example of their lack of political consciousness. However, it is difficult to dismiss the attitudes of the workers during this period as simply a product of their naivety. Workers were responding to genuine concerns of the possible deleterious consequences of a complete takeover of administrative responsibilities. They preferred to preserve their hard-fought victories and extend these through pressure on the Provisional Government. Although the workers were distrustful of the propertied classes, there was little support for abolishing the Provisional Government and establishing a full council republic. As one meeting of metalworkers on 21 March 1917 near Petrograd resolved:

> All measures of the Provisional Government that destroy the remnants of the autocracy and strengthen the freedom of the people must be fully supported on

[84] Of the 1,090 delegates at the conference, 285 were Socialist Revolutionaries, 248 were Mensheviks and 105 were Bolsheviks. See 'Composition of the First All-Russian Congress of Soviets of Workers' and Soldiers' Deputies', in *Documents of Russian History, 1914–1917*, ed. Frank Golder (New York: The Century Co., 1927), 360–1.

> the part of democracy. All measures that lead to conciliation with the old regime and that are directed against the people must meet a most decisive protest and counteraction.[85]

Workers demanded a strict control of ministers within the government and the vigilant oversight of the implementation of the soviets' programme. However, it was not seen as necessary to transform the councils into bureaucratic organizations that would undertake governmental administrative duties.

Following a failed revolt in July, the Bolsheviks began agitating both legally and in clandestine for an armed uprising of the workers that would bring them to power. Through his study abroad, Lenin had resolved that the revolution must destroy the existing state institutions and create new ones. Combining Marx's text on the Paris Commune with his experiences of the 1905 Russian Revolution, he viewed the soviets as organs of revolutionary power that could be seized by the Bolsheviks to direct the revolution.[86] However, once the All-Russian Congress had refused to assume sole power, the Bolsheviks required a different course of action. 'All hope for peaceful development of the Russian revolution has definitely vanished', Lenin declared. 'The objective situation is either a victory of the military dictatorship . . . or victory, in a decisive battle of the workers, which is possible only as a powerful mass rising against the government and the bourgeoisie.'[87]

The Bolsheviks began to benefit from being the only party that was not compromised by its support for the failing Provisional Government. Their base grew as they became widely associated with the ideas of workers' power and support for the soviets. Stephen A. Smith has argued that during this period the Russian population also became more conscious of class affiliations symbolized by the growing use of the greeting 'comrade' rather than citizen.[88] This also highlights the development of the power of the soviets during this period and the dwindling of support for the Provisional Government. In October, the Bolshevik Party stood at the precipice of an important decision for armed insurrection. Lenin strongly advocated for the seizure of power and attempted to persuade the Bolshevik Central Committee to support an uprising. The Committee was at first hesitant but agreed on 5 November (Gregorian calendar) to an armed rebellion. This was carried out on 7 November 1917 when the newly formed Military Revolutionary Committee of the Petrograd Soviet ordered the occupation of key government buildings and an attack on the Winter Palace.[89]

[85] Quoted in David Mandel, *The Petrograd Workers and the fall of the Old Regime: From the February Revolution to the July Days, 1917* (London: The Macmillan Press, 1983), 67.

[86] Anweiler, *The Soviets*, 162.

[87] Vladimir I. Lenin, 'The Political Situation', in *Collected Works, Vol. 21*, 37.

[88] Stephen A. Smith, *The Russian Revolution: A Very Short Introduction* (Oxford: Oxford University Press, 2002), 31.

[89] Alexander Rabinowitch, 'The Bolsheviks Come to Power', in *The Russian Revolution: The Essential Readings*, ed. Martin A. Miller (Oxford: Blackwell Publishers, 2001), 104–46.

The traditional liberal interpretation of the October Revolution views it as a carefully plotted *coup d'état* orchestrated by Lenin and a handful of Bolshevik conspirators.[90] According to anti-communist liberal historian Richard Pipes, Lenin took advantage of the collapse of government and general instability by seizing power without the involvement and against the wishes of the majority of the population. Pipes emphasized the role of key leaders and the passivity of the masses in this process. Revisionists have challenged this interpretation by pointing to a number of complicating factors. The first is the wide degree of popular support the Bolsheviks enjoyed by October. During the course of 1917, the Bolsheviks attracted greater support from workers in the soviets due to their championing of the lower classes and their revolutionary agitation against the perceived failings of the Provisional Government.[91] Steadily growing their party from disaffected moderate socialists, soldiers, and peasants, the Bolshevik Party won 51 per cent of the seats of the dumas in Moscow in September compared with only 12 per cent three months earlier.[92] The Bolsheviks also gained majority support in a few of the metalworkers' factories and made substantial increases in their vote in other areas from February to October 1917. The idea that the Bolsheviks seized power solely through illegitimate and clandestine machinations underestimates their broad support amongst parts of the working class. However, even at the peak of their popularity in October no more than 5 per cent of workers were actual members of the Bolshevik Party and only 1.5 per cent of the Russian population were industrial workers.

A second key point of contention is the extent to which the liberal interpretation overlooks the important role played by ordinary workers. In the absence of a functional system of government, citizens across the country began to take matters into their own hands. Alexander Berkman contended that the October Revolution was a profound social revolution that 'radically transformed all the heretofore existing economic, political and social relations'.[93] Berkman claimed that 'for weeks and months prior to it, the actual Revolution had been going on all over Russia: the city proletariat was taking possession of the shops and factories, while the peasants expropriated the big estates and turned the land to their own use.'[94] The seizure of power in October was only successful because of the development of power in the soviets. By October,

[90] Richard Pipes, *A Concise History of the Russian Revolution* (New York: Knopf, 1995), 113.
[91] Mark D. Steinberg, ed., *Voices of Revolution* (New Haven: Yale University Press, 2001), 4.
[92] Oliver H. Radkey, *Russia Goes to the Polls: The Election of the Russian Constituent Assembly of 1917* (Ithaca: Cornell University Press, 1989), 53.
[93] Alexander Berkman, 'The Russian Tragedy', in *The Life of an Anarchist: The Alexander Berkman Reader*, ed. Gene Fellner (New York: Seven Stories Press, 1992), 236.
[94] Ibid.

> the central political issue was that of soviet power. It was popular support for this cause which doomed Kerensky and the Provisional Government and explains the ease with which armed resistance to the new order was overcome, even where (as in Moscow) it was more formidable than in the capital.[95]

When the Bolsheviks took power they did so in the name of the soviets and the working class. However, it was not long after the initial overthrow that the Bolshevik Party began centralizing power into its own hands. There was little support for armed action against the Provisional Government from the other socialist groups. Delegates to the Second All-Russian Congress of Soviets from the Menshevik Party and Right Socialist Revolutionaries stormed out of the meeting on 13 November 1917 in protest over the Bolshevik's actions. When the new Council of People's Commissars was elected as the new government its members were drawn exclusively from the Bolshevik Party. The other socialist parties attempted to work towards a new socialist government with a coalition of members from different socialist groups, but the Bolsheviks rejected this possibility. Even key members of the Bolshevik Central Committee were critical of this rejection, with five members resigning due to not wishing 'to bear responsibility for this fatal policy... which is carried out against the will of a large part of the proletariat and soldiers'.[96] Although the Bolsheviks had majority support within a few of the workers' soviets, in reality, their armed takeover quickly alienated potential allies and led to a minority government.

There is disagreement within the historical literature over Lenin's commitment to worker self-organization based on a dispute over whether support for the soviets was part of a deep ideological commitment or merely a tactical manoeuvre on the path to Bolshevik rule. The libertarian interpretation of Lenin is that he distrusted the unguided instincts of the masses, which he believed could serve as a bridge to reactionary political paths and economic and social chaos. Support for this reading comes in part from 'What is to be Done?' in which Lenin discussed the need for a vanguard party to direct the spontaneous impulses of the workers towards revolutionary activity.[97] On the other hand, Lenin also stressed the necessity of a mass uprising of workers in which the party would act as a leadership of the workers' movement, rather than replacing it. While there are quotations within his pre-revolutionary writings that support different interpretations, his actions following the revolution reveal a more centralist approach.

[95] Edward Acton, *Rethinking the Russian Revolution* (London: Bloomsbury Academic, 1990).

[96] Central Committee of the Russian Social-Democratic Labour Party, *The Bolsheviks and the October Revolution: Minutes of the Central Committee of the Russian Social Democratic Labour Party (Bolsheviks) August 1917–February 1918* (London: Pluto Press, 1974).

[97] Vladimir I. Lenin, 'What is to be Done?', in *Collected Work, Vol. 5* (Moscow: Foreign Languages Publishing House, 1961) 347–530. For criticisms of this interpretation see Lars T. Lih, *Lenin Rediscovered* (Leiden: Brill Academic Publishers, 2005).

During the pre-October period Lenin was supportive of worker initiatives at self-management, yet after the revolution he became more convinced on the need for unity:

> large-scale machine industry—which is precisely the material source, the productive source, the foundation of socialism—calls for absolute and strict unity of will... But how can strict unity of will be ensured? By thousands subordinating their will to the will of one.[98]

As soon as the councils presented a hindrance to the revolutionary seizure of power by the party, their autonomy from the Bolshevik Party was drastically reduced. The majority of council delegates from other socialist parties did not agree with Bolshevik one-party rule nor did they accept the illiberal measures the Bolsheviks began to apply in order to secure their position. To combat dissent, in December 1917 the Bolsheviks created a new brand of secret police called the *Cheka* who had the power to arrest any citizen and to inspect any institution. This police force penetrated all soviets and began a wave of terror against suspected counter-revolutionaries and dissidents. The remaining socialist parties still working within the soviets now faced even more difficult conditions. The secret police also clamped down on anarchist activity and shut down several left-wing newspapers and publications. Within a matter of months, the Bolsheviks had disenfranchised the soviets and established control over the central apparatuses of government.[99] On 14 June 1918, the Bolsheviks decided to expel all the Mensheviks and Right Socialist Revolutionaries from the soviets, further consolidating their one-party rule. In 1920, Lenin described the new situation:

> the dictatorship is exercised by the proletariat organized in the Soviets: the proletariat is guided by the Communist Party of the Bolsheviks... No important political or organizational question is decided by any state institution in our republic without the guidance of the party's Central Committee.[100]

The re-emergence of local, decentralized councils in Kronstadt in 1921 elicited a hostile reaction from the Bolsheviks. The Kronstadt sailors demanded direct democracy in accordance with the will of the people rather than a Bolshevik minority. They proclaimed that 'the Communist Party, which rules the country,

[98] Vladimir I. Lenin, 'The Immediate Tasks of the Soviet Government', in *Selected Works* (New York: International Publishers, 1971), 424.

[99] Paul Avrich, *Kronstadt 1921* (Princeton: Princeton University Press, 1970), 161. For a more detailed account of the Bolshevik seizure of power from the councils see Maurice Brinton, *The Bolsheviks and Workers' Control, 1917–1921* (London: Solidarity, 1970).

[100] Vladimir I. Lenin, '"Left-Wing" Communism: An Infantile Disorder', in *Collected Works, Vol. 31* (Moscow: Progress Publishers, 1965), 17–118.

has become separated from the masses, and shown itself unable to lead her from her state of general ruin.'[101] Both Lenin and Trotsky blamed the rebellion on the influence of foreign imperialist powers and dismissed it as a negligible challenge to Bolshevik rule. An examination of the demands of the Kronstadt sailors, however, reveals not the operation of foreign agents but a desire for 'new elections to the Soviet... on a fairer basis' that would lead to 'true representation of the labourers' and for a rejuvenation of the Soviet as 'an active and energetic organ'.[102] The criticisms were not directed at the soviet system as such but towards the Bolshevik control of this system through a dictatorial centralized party. Nevertheless, the rebellion stood as a challenge to Bolshevik rule and was ruthlessly put down. The final call of the Kronstadt delegates was 'all power to soviets and not to parties', before they were subdued by the Communist Party in March 1921.[103] By 1921, with the crushing of the Kronstadt sailors' rebellion, all semblance of rule by the soviets themselves had vanished and the party had assumed complete control.

The Union of Soviet Socialist Republics, created by the Bolsheviks as a one-party state, had little resemblance to the original council form or the hopes and aspirations of most council delegates at the beginning of the revolution. As Alexander Rabinowitch notes, when the councils arose they were 'genuinely democratic, embryonic organizations of popular self-rule' which channelled the desires of the dissatisfied lower classes of citizens for the 'creation of an egalitarian society and a democratic-socialist, multi-party political system'.[104] The position of the councils within the increasingly totalitarian one-party state was reduced to bureaucratized pillars of state power.[105] Even though the councils developed independently of Bolshevik ideology, they soon became incorporated within the communist state. Prior to this point, the councils were revolutionary organs of workers' power as part of a broad, popular democratic movement against tyranny. The Bolsheviks were able to pacify the democratic and anti-centralist forces in the councils and transform the self-government of elected factory committees and cooperatives into a centralized Bolshevik state.

Germany: The Councils Betrayed

The German councils, by contrast, are far less well known than their Russian counterparts. The later history of the collapse of the Weimar Republic and the rise

[101] Anonymous Pamphlet, 'To the Populace of the Fortress and Town of Kronstadt, Comrades and Citizens!', *Kronstadt Izvestia* Number 1, 3 March 1921.

[102] Ibid.

[103] Israel Getzler, *Kronstadt 1917–1921: The Fate of a Soviet Democracy* (Cambridge: Cambridge University Press, 1983), 240.

[104] Alexander Rabinowitch, *The Bolsheviks in Power: The First Year of Soviet Rule in Petrograd* (Bloomington and Indianapolis: Indiana University Press, 2007), x.

[105] Anweiler, *The Soviets*, 254.

of Nazism has tended to overshadow this ambiguous chapter in German history. Unlike many other revolts and revolutions of the twentieth century, the working class was the principal protagonist of the German Revolution.[106] The revolution occurred in a country with the strongest union movement in the world, which was made up of 2.5 million workers. German workers had been steeped in Marxist theory for two generations and the unions were deeply involved in shop-floor negotiations over pay and working conditions. While it is accurate to say that the council form developed relatively spontaneously in Germany, it was only possible due to the preparatory efforts of labour organizers over the previous decades.[107]

The origins of the development of workers' councils lie in the anti-war movement and the waves of mass strikes over the previous years. One such strike broke out in Berlin in June 1916, with strike committees organizing 55,000 workers and creating institutions that would provide an embryonic form for future workers' councils.[108] Fritz Wolffheim, a Hamburg labour organizer, published an article in *Arbeiterpolitik* (Workers' Politics) in March 1917 in which he argued for the creation of a federation of workers' councils across numerous different industries to lead strike actions.[109] Wolffheim had been influenced by his time editing publications for the American Industrial Workers of the World (IWW) and the activities of American IWW sailors at German ports. The labour unrest of the past decade had fuelled discussions of the need for a new form of organization, referred to as a unitary organization [*Einheitsorganization*], which would combine elements of the trade union and party.

Responding to deteriorating living conditions, a national wave of mass strikes broke out across Germany in April 1917, which gave rise to heightened revolutionary activity. In Leipzig, workers' councils were formed to coordinate activities of a strike across different industries, which were the first council institutions to appear in Germany.[110] To bypass the trade union leadership's ban on organizing strikes, workers relied on extensive networks throughout the factories in the form of factory delegate committees [*Arbeiterausschüsse*], which provided the initial outlines of later workers' councils. Another wave of national strikes was organized by the Revolutionary Shop Stewards [*Revolutionäre Obleute*]—a radical organization with extensive networks within the industrial factories—in January 1918. This involved a walkout by 400,000 metalworkers in Berlin, which quickly spread

[106] Hoffrogge, *Working-Class Politics in the German Revolution*, 5.

[107] Däumig, Ernst. 'The National Assembly Means the Councils' Death', in *All Power to the Councils! A Documentary History of the German Revolution of 1918–1919*, ed. Gabriel Kuhn (Oakland: PM Press, 2012), 42; John Gerber, *Anton Pannekoek and the Socialism of Workers' Self Emancipation, 1873–1960* (Dordrecht: Kluwer Academic Publishers, 1989), 108–32.

[108] Karl Korsch, *Revolutionary Theory*, ed. Douglas Kellner (Austin: University of Texas Press, 2013), 18.

[109] Darrow Schecter, *Radical Theories: Paths Beyond Marxism and Social Democracy* (Manchester: Manchester University Press, 1994), 79.

[110] Gerber, *Anton Pannekoek and the Socialism of Workers' Self Emancipation, 1873–1960*, 120.

nationwide and encompassed over one million workers, making it the largest demonstration in Germany up to that time.[111]

These waves of mass strikes set the scene for the dramatic events of November 1918. Renegades within the union movement were the main opposition to the First World War within Germany and began to step up their activities.[112] They mobilized workers, disrupted ammunition production, and attempted to bring Germany's war efforts to a halt. As the German armed forces showed the final signs of defeat by the Allies, a sailor's mutiny at Kiel spread across the country, leading to the abdication of the Kaiser and two separate declarations of a German republic on 9 November 1918. The first of the declarations was by Philipp Scheidemann of the Social Democratic Party of Germany (SPD), who declared Germany a republic from the Reichstag; the second was by revolutionary socialist, Karl Liebknecht of the Independent Social Democratic Party of Germany (USPD), who proclaimed Germany a free *socialist* republic from a balcony of the Berlin Royal Residence.[113] This situation was symptomatic of the contested political climate at the time and the number of competing claims to power and authority. Liebknecht, who had recently been released from jail and refounded the Spartacus League, was viewed as an erratic radical by the SPD.[114] In turn, the radical elements of the workers movement, including the USPD, the Spartacus League [*Spartakusbund*], and the Revolutionary Shop Stewards distrusted the SPD leadership who was attempting to obstruct the revolution. The future governmental form of the new German state would only finally be decided at the National Congress of Workers' and Soldiers' Councils [*Allgemeiner Kongreß der Arbeiter- und Soldatenräte*] in mid-December 1918.

Later that same evening, on 9 November 1918, the Stewards attempted to seize the initiative by announcing elections for workers' and soldiers' councils to be held the following day.[115] This group was the most organized and disciplined in the workers movement and made up the core of the organized sections of the councils. The Stewards had been planning a coup independently of the sailors' mutiny in Kiel and had been surprised by the abdication of the Kaiser and the pace of the revolution. The initial plans for the formation of workers' councils were hastily drawn up by Revolutionary Shop Steward Richard Müller. The brevity and ambiguity of Müller's proposal would later allow different parties to attempt to

[111] Ibid., 121.

[112] This opposition was formed in spite of the support of the war by the unions' leadership. The main organizers of the anti-war efforts were the Revolutionary Shop Stewards. Martin Comack, *Wild Socialism: Workers Councils in Revolutionary Berlin, 1918–1921* (Lanham: University Press of America, 2012), 31–3.

[113] Kuhn, ed., *All Power to the Councils!*, 27. Germany was officially called the Socialist Republic of Germany by the revolutionary councils during November and December 1918.

[114] The Spartacus League was originally a group within the USPD who split with them to form the German Communist Party on 31 December 1918.

[115] Arnold, *Rätebewegung und Rätetheorien in der Novemberrevolution*, 70; Gluckstein, *The Western Soviets: Workers' Councils versus Parliament, 1915–20*, 98–100.

impose their own designs on the council form. Upon hearing of plans for elections, the SPD sent speakers to the factories and barracks to influence the elections in favour of the SPD leadership.

In the confusion of elections the following day, council delegates in fact elected representatives to two political bodies: an interim cabinet for a provisional government and an Executive Council [*Vollzugsrat*]. Learning of the SPD's attempt to control the provisional government, the Stewards suggested the establishment of an 'Action Committee', [*Aktionsausschuss*] which they hoped would assist in controlling the conservative leanings of the provisional government.[116] Delegates at the meeting rejected the suggestion, but a compromise was reached to elect an Executive Council, which was, in theory, the highest ranked political organ in Germany.[117] The Executive Council, headed by Richard Müller, issued a declaration that the sovereignty and constituent power of the German people was represented by the councils and embodied (at least provisionally) in the Executive Council.[118] But to the great dismay of the Stewards, delegates voted in favour of an SPD dominated interim cabinet to be established as a provisional government in Berlin. The cabinet of six members, called the 'Council of People's Deputies' [*Rat der Volksbeauftragten*], formally recognized the councils as the source of its power, although the exact relationship remained unclear.[119] The Executive Council held the right to appoint and dismiss the six People's Deputies and demanded a right of control over the operation of the ministries.[120] But in practice, the Council of People's Deputies began to assume greater power and governmental functions and disregarded resolutions of the Executive Council, leading to an increasingly acrimonious relationship between the two.[121] During November and December 1918 open hostility was temporarily muted due to a strong public demand for unity across the working class.

[116] Eberhard Kolb, ed., *Quellen zur Geschichte der Rätebewegung in Deutschland 1918/1919, Band I: Der Zentralrat der deutschen sozialistischen Republik 19.12.1918–8.4.1919, Vom Ersten Zum Zweiten Rätekongress* (Leiden: E. J. Brill, 1968), xv.

[117] Rosa Luxemburg, 'Um den Vollzugsrat', in *Die Rote Fahne*, 26, 11 December 1918.

[118] Richard Müller, 'Speech to congress on 16 December 1918, Zentralrat der sozialistischen Republik Deutschlands', in *Allgemeiner Kongreß der Arbeiter- und Soldatenräte Deutschlands vom 16. bis 21. Dezember 1918 im Abgeordnetenhause zu Berlin. Stenographische Berichte* [Congress Report] (Berlin, 1919), 16–17.

[119] In negotiations between the Council of People's Deputies and the Executive Council on 22 November 1918 over a division of powers and duties it was agreed that 'the political power lies in the hands of the workers' and soldiers' councils in the German Socialist Republic. It is their duty to maintain and to expand the achievements of the revolution and to suppress the counterrevolution.' Although at this meeting it was agreed that the Council of People's Deputies would act as the executive body and the Executive Council would have a 'right of control', the basic powers and responsibilities of each organ were never formally set out. See 'Vereinbarung zwischen dem Rat der Volksbeauftragten und dem Vollzugsrat vom 22.11.1918', in *Die Deutsche Revolution 1918–1919: Dokumente*, ed. Gerhard A. Ritter and Susanne Miller (Hamburg: Hoffman und Campe Verlages, 1981), 119.

[120] Richard Müller, *Vom Kaiserreich zur Republik, Vol. 2* (Vienna: Malik, 1925), 146.

[121] Müller, 'Report by the Executive Council of the Workers' and Soldiers' Councils of Great Berlin', in Kuhn, ed., *All Power to the Councils!*, 37.

The composition of the Council of People's Deputies itself was indicative of the competing ambitions and tendencies that existed within the revolutionary movement. There was a political schism between the three SPD members and the three USPD members of the Council over the precise role of the workers' and soldiers' councils.[122] Even within the USPD there was a left-wing faction around the Revolutionary Shop Stewards and other radicals and a more moderate faction centred around Karl Kautsky, Rudolf Hilferding, and Hugo Haase. The more radical elements within the USPD favoured the establishment of the councils as permanent political and economic institutions, at least until more of the revolution's aims had been achieved.[123] In their conception, the councils should form the basis of a new executive power to be based in Berlin composed of directly recallable delegates. In the economic sphere, the USPD advocated for worker-managed factories under democratic control. At the very least, there was a strong desire among the radical elements of the revolution to create more facts on the ground before anything resembling nationwide elections could be considered. They wanted to destroy the power base of the old industrialists and officer class and transform the structures of German society. The fear was that in a capitalist society, democratic elections would be strongly biased in favour of the ruling elite. On the other side stood the SPD members led by their party leader, Friedrich Ebert. He considered the councils as merely temporary organs with only limited economic functions and preferred the immediate election of a constituent assembly to establish a parliamentary republic.[124] The SPD leadership thought that fundamental issues of constitutional law, the composition of the economic order, and the new structure of government should be decided after the election of a national assembly. In reality, they were sceptical of the chaotic and undisciplined nature of the councils and did not consider them as desirable alternatives to a parliamentary system. This disagreement led to one of the biggest questions of the National Congress of Workers' and Soldiers' Councils: the choice between parliamentary democracy and proletariat democracy, or otherwise stated, 'national elections or the council system.'[125]

The popular nature of the council movement represented a dramatic break with the previous theory and practice of the SPD in Germany. The general view

[122] Müller, 'Democracy or Dictatorship', 59.

[123] Tormin, *Zwischen Rätediktatur und sozialer Demokratie*, 59. In the early stages of the revolution the USPD believed that the councils might exist alongside a parliamentary democracy but from December 1918 onwards they became increasingly disillusioned with these prospects and preferred the replacement of parliamentary institutions with a council system. Ralph Haswell Lutz, *The German Revolution, 1918–1919* (Stanford: Stanford University Publications, 1922), 268. For a more in-depth analysis of the USPD's position and factions see Nicholas Vrousalis, 'Revolutionary Principles and Strategy in the November Revolution: The Case of the USPD', in *The German Revolution and Political Theory*, ed. Kets and Muldoon, 113–34.

[124] Hoffrogge, *Working-Class Politics in the German Revolution*, 74.

[125] This was the central point on the agenda of the National Congress of Workers' and Soldiers' Councils.

amongst the party leadership was that the councils were filled with poor unskilled labourers who knew nothing about socialism or revolution.[126] The SPD held a wait-and-see approach when it came to the revolution, which focused on improving German workers' living conditions and led to political passivity.[127] Throughout the war, the SPD leadership had attempted to control workers, make reasonable demands to government, and focus efforts on production. Rather than conceive socialism as a matter of top-down planning within state apparatuses, the councils embodied a more radical form of socialism consisting of mass participation from below.[128] Delegates were voted from within the factories and were directly accountable to their constituencies. The entire movement was based on the participation of ordinary workers and their continual pressure on leadership to fulfil key demands. The leadership of the SPD considered this form of organization irresponsible and subject to the whims of the masses who lacked the hard-headed realism of their leaders. There was also a general fear of the bolshevization of German politics and the threat of minority takeover. However, the German councils were not modelled after the Bolshevik council state. Indeed, the extreme measures that the Bolsheviks undertook throughout 1918 during the beginning of the 'Red Terror' tended to discredit the idea of a proletariat dictatorship.[129] Most of the German socialists were neither favourably disposed towards the Bolsheviks nor particularly impressed by the results they had achieved.

The split within the provisional government represented the precarious balance of power between revolutionary and conservative forces. In reality, a state of dual power persisted in Germany throughout November and December of 1918 between the councils and the old state bureaucracy, military command, and police force. As the latter offered no resistance to the councils, the whole structure tended to remain in place.[130] The conservative elements of the state were compelled to begrudgingly accept the de facto position of the councils. The bourgeoisie, industrialists, and organized unions were suspicious of the councils but were too timid to risk a direct confrontation.[131] The revolutionaries had perhaps naively underestimated the staying power of the bureaucratic apparatuses even after the revolution had taken place. Friedrich Ebert managed to insist that the overwhelming majority of personnel in these institutions should retain their positions and that

[126] Peter von Oertzen, *Betriebsräte in der Novemberrevolution* (Berlin: J. H. W. Dietz, 1976), 268–71.

[127] For a study of the SPD's politics of 'attentismus' see Dieter Groh, *Negative Integration und revolutionärer Attentismus. Die deutsche Sozialdemokratie am Vorabend des Ersten Weltkrieges* (Berlin: Propyläen, 1973).

[128] Comack, *Wild Socialism*, 1.

[129] Albert S. Lindemann, *The 'Red Years:' European Socialism Versus Bolshevism, 1919–1921* (Berkeley: University of California Press, 1974), 35–6; Däumig, 'The National Assembly Means the Councils' Death', 42.

[130] Tormin, *Zwischen Rätediktatur und sozialer Demokratie*, 89–90.

[131] Däumig, 'The Council Idea and Its Realization', 53.

council delegates should monitor them to ensure compliance with revolutionary objectives. Later, Richard Müller would complain how 'the entire political and economic life is the same, only that the workers' and soldiers' councils, embodied in the Executive Council, represent the sovereignty of the state.'[132] There was little thought within the SPD leadership of the democratization of the bureaucratic apparatus. They used their role within the council movement to protect the state machinery and allow it to retain much of its old character.

Even in the earlier stages of the revolution, conservative forces in the councils were already attempting to undermine them from within. Unknown to most council members at the time, late in the evening on 10 November 1918 a secret deal was struck between SPD leader Friedrich Ebert and head of the armed forces General Wilhelm Groener. According to this pact, the General guaranteed the military's support of the SPD against the councils so long as Ebert agreed to reinstate military discipline and restore the power of the officers.[133] Fearing the radicalization of the revolution along the lines of the Russian soviets, Ebert allied himself with the conservatives and old elites of the Empire in order to avoid a social revolution.[134] Groener and Ebert conducted nightly conversations on a secret telephone line keeping each other informed about daily events. As a result, real power in the council movement always remained with the SPD, since they were the only faction with whom the old conservative powers would negotiate.[135] Ebert aimed to win over the old elite to the SPD and form a ruling coalition against the radical elements of the councils.[136] Evidence suggests that he joined the revolution primarily to slow events down and control it. On the eve of the Emperor's abdication, Ebert complained that 'if the Emperor does not abdicate the social revolution is unavoidable. But I don't want it; indeed I hate it like sin.'[137] His participation in the Council of People's Deputies was a strategic play rather than any show of support for the council form or the ambitions of a social revolution. He was adamant that following the events of November, 'the victorious proletariat will not institute class rule.'[138]

The council movements called for an end to the war, the establishment of a republic, and the reorganization of the army, civil service, and workplaces. An

[132] Müller, speech to congress on 16 December 1918, *Conference Report*, 15–16.

[133] The primary source for this information is General Groener's memoirs. As there is no evidence to confirm the conversation form Friedrich Ebert's side the credibility of these memoirs has been doubted by critics. See 'General Groener über sein Bündnis mit Ebert vom 10.11.1918', in Ritter and Miller, eds., *Die Deutsche Revolution 1918–1919: Dokumente*, 98–9.

[134] Müller, 'Democracy or Dictatorship', 60.

[135] Müller, 'Report by the Executive Council of the Workers' and Soldiers' Councils of Great Berlin', 35.

[136] Haffner, *Die deutsche Revolution—1918/19*, 121.

[137] According to Prince Maximilian, Ebert stated this on 7 November, 1918. Prince Max von Baden, *Erinnerungen und Dokumente*, ed. Golo Mann (Stuttgart: Ernst Klett, 1968), 599.

[138] Friedrich Ebert, *Schriften, Aufzeichnungen, Reden, Vol. 2* (Dresden: Carl Reissner Verlag, 1926), 139.

indication of the desires and aspirations of the rank-and-file delegates of the councils can be gained from the speeches and voting that took place at the first National Congress of Workers' and Soldiers' Councils from 16 to 20 December 1918 to decide on the future of the German republic.[139] Plans for the congress were first spoken about on 10 November 1918 at the initial gathering of council delegates at Circus Busch.[140] The proceedings of the conference offer invaluable source material on the political perspectives of the delegates and the competing arguments that were staged within the councils. The 489 delegates of this so-called 'Parliament of the Revolution' were to decide on the future of the German state form and other central political issues such as the timeframe of national elections, socialization of industry, and the structure of the military.[141]

The most immediate demands of the soldiers were for a dismantling of the system of military hierarchy and discipline, including the abolition of all marks of rank, the election of officers by their men, and the takeover of military discipline and command by the councils. The Congress approved these measures through its affirmation of the radical 'Hamburg Points' that were introduced by the Hamburg soldiers' council and approved without dissent.[142] Friedrich Ebert did not openly oppose the points at this stage, although he would have known that they would have been entirely unacceptable to the military high command who supported him. Instead, he sought to influence the progression of events through his position as the Representative for Military Affairs on the Council of People's Delegates. In late December 1918, Ebert commissioned the formation of new voluntary units, which would later be used against the revolutionary forces. One of the contradictions of this period was that although delegates voted for the transformation of military hierarchy and discipline, in practice many of the troops still elected their old officers back to the same position. As a result, there was minimal structural change.[143] After the elections on 19 January 1919 the government declared the Hamburg points to be mere 'guidelines' and refused to change the fundamental structure of the army. By June 1919, soldiers' councils were no longer functioning in Germany and had been replaced by the establishment of a new army.[144]

On the morning of Friday, 20 December 1918, delegates of the congress debated measures for socializing the economy. Such a programme had already been announced by the provisional government in a declaration on 10 November

[139] The conference ran until 20 December 1918 rather than 21 December 1918 as is falsely stated even in the official conference report. For a comprehensive analysis of the conference see Roß, *Biographisches Handbuch der Reichsrätekongresse 1918/1919.*

[140] Rosenberg, *History of Bolshevism*, 41.

[141] Roß, *Biographisches Handbuch der Reichsrätekongresse 1918/1919*, 166. The phrase '*Revolutionsparlament*' comes from the SPD periodical, Vorwärts no. 345, morning edition on 16 December 1918.

[142] *Congress Report*, 346.

[143] Däumig, 'The National Assembly Means the Councils' Death', 47.

[144] Fowkes. ed. *The German Left and the Weimar Republic: A Selection of Documents*, 224.

1918, 'for the speedy and thorough socialization of the capitalist means of production.'[145] However, aside from appointing a 'Socialization Committee' to produce a report, the cautious interim government had been content with minor social reform measures rather than a change of relations between capital and labour.[146] From the revolutionary outbreak onwards, the word 'socialization' was at the forefront of national debate. In a 1919 pamphlet entitled 'What is Socialization?' leading German Marxist theorist and member of the Socialization Committee, Karl Korsch, describes socialization as a 'new regulation of production with the goal of replacing private capitalist economy with a socialist communal economy'.[147] This constituted a striving towards the democratic control of the means of production by workers who would determine production based on the needs of the community. For Korsch, socialization did not simply mean that workers would begin to run factories, as in the case of producers' associations, but that production would be brought under the ownership and control of the community as a whole. In Korsch's conception, this would entail a middle ground between the exploitation of capitalist production and the centralized planning of state socialism through a network of producer and consumer groups in civil society. Other individuals and groups within Germany's council movement had varied understandings of what was meant by socialization, but most of these entailed a form of social ownership of the means of production and worker management and control of key industries.[148]

Rudolf Hilferding opened proceedings on the final day of the conference by presenting a report from the Socialization Committee. Acknowledging the considerable difficulties that would be involved, he recommended socialization of the mines and parts of the coal industry, while approaching the socialization of other industries with more caution. He requested that agricultural production by peasant farms should be left for the time being, while industries in which capitalist cartels and trusts had produced particularly exploitative systems should be gradually socialized. The main practical difficulty facing the government was the shortage of capital and raw materials. The SPD leadership considered that the socialization of industry would further hamper an already crippled German economy. In a previous cabinet meeting, Gustav Bauer, SPD Minister for Labour, contended that socialization was likely to produce 'Russian conditions'

[145] 'Aufruf der Versammlung der Berliner Arbeiter- und Soldatenräte vom 10.11.1918', in *Die Deutsche Revolution 1918–1919: Dokumente*, ed. Ritter and Miller, 96–7.

[146] The Socialization Commission submitted its Preliminary Report on 15 February 1919, advising for the 'expropriation of State and private capital in mining'. The report was not seriously acted upon and by April 1919 the Commission disbanded citing opposition and obstruction from the Economics Ministry.

[147] Karl Korsch, 'What is Socialization? A Program of Practical Socialism', *New German Critique* 6 (1975), 60–81. For further discussion of socialization see also Rudolf Hilferding, 'Speech to Congress, 20 December 1918', *Congress Report*, 312–22.

[148] See Emil Frankel, 'The Status of "Socialization" in Germany', *Journal of Political Economy* 32, no. 1 (1924), 68–85.

of rationing and starvation.[149] Philipp Scheidemann maintained that socialization measures would scare away employers and hinder the creation of new jobs. The USPD delegates questioned whether full economic recovery was really a condition for socialization, but even left-wing delegates recognized the obstacles of socializing the economy in one country alone without international solidarity.[150] Yet, there was general optimism towards the idea of a gradual process of socialization, particularly from the miners who pushed for even more immediate steps to be taken.[151] In response to the question of pursuing socialist measures in one country alone, it was argued that if Germany started the process, other countries would follow and German socialization would help spread socialism abroad. Hilferding concluded the debate as follows: 'Germany is going this alone. But, party comrades, precisely that makes this task not only difficult but also promises that the solution will carry an extremely highly reward.'[152] Delegates voted with a clear majority in favour of the socialization of all industries that were 'ripe' for it, in particular, the mining industry.[153] The victory for the SPD was to formulate this resolution such that there arose no immediate actionable directives, allowing for the delay of any practical socialization measures.

On the issue of council democracy or national assembly, on the other hand, the majority of delegates were clearly not in favour of asserting the councils as a new state form. They were generally against the idea of establishing anything like the council dictatorship of Russia.[154] One of the most important consequences of the Congress was the scheduling of national elections for 19 January 1919, even earlier than first proposed, which placed Germany on track to become a parliamentary democratic republic. Ernst Däumig's recommendation of the continuation of the council system was voted down with a sizeable majority. The safer option, presented by SPD member Max Cohen, was to call for national elections to a new parliament. His reasoning was that without a clear majority the socialists would face substantial resistance from the bourgeoisie and risked a Bolshevik-style minority takeover and civil war. The negative experience of Russia played a large role in the minds of the delegates, as the German revolutionaries had always considered that a German revolution would necessarily be based on a proletarian majority. For many of the delegates who had either fought in the war or experienced other wartime hardships, the idea of experimenting with a largely hitherto

[149] Kolb, ed., *Quellen zur Geschichte der Rätebewegung in Deutschland 1918/1919, Band I: Der Zentralrat der deutschen sozialistischen Republik 19.12.1918–8.4.1919, Vom Ersten Zum Zweiten Rätekongress*, xxiii.

[150] Eduard Heimann, 'Die Sozialisierung', *Archiv für Sozialwissenschaft und Sozialpolitik* 45, no. 3 (1919), 527–90, 540.

[151] See Felix Bluhm, *'Die Massen sind aber nicht zu halten gewesen.' Zur Streik- und Sozialisierungsbewegung im Ruhrgebiet 1918/19* (Berlin: edition assemblage, 2014).

[152] Rudolf Hilferding, 'Closing address to congress, 20 December 1918', *Congress Report*, 341–4.

[153] Ibid., 344.

[154] Ulrich Kluge, *Die deutsche Revolution 1918–1919* (Frankfurt am Main: Suhrkamp, 1985), 59–60.

untested state form was an unattractive option. There was a widespread hope that the socialist goals of the revolution would be implemented from above by a socialist majority government following a national assembly. As a result, the congress voted in favour of Cohen's suggestion. Däumig warned that the councils would be signing their own death sentence by supporting a national vote, since the bourgeoisie would never allow the councils and parliament to exist side by side. He argued for a 'proletarian democracy expressed in the council system' that would be a more genuine expression of the will of the people than a bourgeois parliament.[155] Richard Müller also questioned the other delegates:

> Should the fate of the German Revolution be handed to a national assembly elected by every German adult—exploiter and exploited, revolutionary and counterrevolutionary alike—or should the proletariat, the armed workers and soldiers, keep and secure the political power in a council system, establish the dictatorship of the proletariat, and wrest the economic power from the bourgeoisie?[156]

Däumig's warnings proved accurate. Following a workers' revolt in early January 1919 the SPD and the army acted to violently repress the councils with the assistance of the reactionary *Freikorps*, returned soldiers still loyal to the officer class. The hastily assembled 'Revolutionary Committee' who had issued a call for the overthrow of the SPD government was little match for the well-organized and disciplined troops loyal to the government. The uprising was put down and a number of its leaders were killed in the process. With Luxemburg and Liebknecht murdered by the *Freikorps* and the councils undermined and powerless, a new parliament was elected and plans for more extensive social and political transformations were put on hold. The SPD won 165 of the 423 seats in the elections and continued to suppress the revolutionaries.

This new order was immediately challenged by a general strike movement in Berlin, the Ruhr district, and *Mitteldeutschland*, which was organized by the leaders of the councils.[157] The strikers continued demanding official recognition of the workers' councils in the new regime and pushed for the immediate socialization of industry. The government made some verbal concession to the strikers, but due to the fact that the strikes were not nationally coordinated, they were not able to put sufficient pressure on the government. In Berlin, the strikes only began in earnest as they were already ending in other parts of the country.[158]

[155] Däumig, 'The National Assembly Means the Councils' Death', 43.

[156] Müller, 'Democracy or Dictatorship', 59.

[157] For an analysis of this strike movement see Weipert, *Die Zweite Revolution. Rätebewegung in Berlin 1919/1920;* Lange, *Massenstreik und Schießbefehl—Generalstreik und Märzkämpfe in Berlin 1919.*

[158] Hoffrogge, *Working-Class Politics in the German Revolution*, 117.

The government brought an end to the strikes in Berlin in March 1919 through the use of heavy artillery in working-class districts of Berlin, resulting in over one thousand casualties.[159]

While it is clear from the councils' proclamations that their most immediate concerns were for the democratization of social and economic life, delegates could not see at the time that their support for a national assembly would lead to the defeat of these more important goals. The revolution ultimately failed to attain the workers' more pressing demand for the reorganization of the economy and military along the lines of a socialist democracy. During the first months of the revolution, the SPD leadership were able to outmanoeuvre their adversaries and impose their own narrative on the course of the revolution. In this way, they managed to prevent the realization of the more far-reaching demands of the radical elements of the councils.

The USPD had another rise in popularity in March 1920 as a result of the Kapp–Lüttwitz Putsch, a coup by right-wing officers which attempted to reverse the results of the 1918–19 Revolution and either reinstall the monarchy or promote other forms of right-wing authoritarianism. Although the civil government was initially forced to flee, the ministerial bureaucracy refused to cooperate with the new government. The SPD called for a general strike, as did the USPD and KPD, which led to 12 million workers bringing down the attempted coup on 17 March 1920. This led to the Ruhr uprising [*Ruhraufstand*] by disaffected workers in the Ruhr district in which local workers' councils attempted to seize political power through the general strike. Following the collapse of the Kapp–Lüttwitz Putsch, the German government sent its army to suppress the insurgency, which was carried out with significant cruelty and executions of members of the 'Red Ruhr Army'.[160]

Events transpired slightly differently in other German cities, where a number of 'council republics' were declared in Munich, Bremen, and Brunswick.[161] However, by 1921, the organizational form of the councils was largely defeated across Germany. It was left to intellectuals to debate different theoretical models after it had been vanquished as a true historical force.[162]

The revolutionary council movements transitioned to a constitutionally recognized 'works councils' [*Betriebsräte*] of the Weimar Republic.[163] Following the

[159] Jones, *Founding Weimar.*

[160] Weipert, *Die Zweite Revolution. Rätebewegung in Berlin 1919/1920.*

[161] See Allan Mitchell, *Revolution in Bayern 1918/1919. Die Eisner-Regierung und die Räterepublik* (München: Beck, 1967); Richard Grunberger, *Red Rising in Bavaria* (London: Arthur Barker, 1973).

[162] Gabriel Kuhn argues 'only after the revolution was the council system explored in more theoretical depth by authors like Otto Rühle, Karl Plättner, and Erich Mühsam.' Kuhn, ed., *All Power to the Councils!*, xiii. The term 'council communism' as distinguished from official communism came to be used in 1921.

[163] On the transition from a revolutionary council movement to the constitutionally recognized 'Works Councils' [*Betriebsräte*] of the Weimar Republic see Hoffrogge, *Working-Class Politics in the*

promulgation of the new Constitution in 1919, works councils were designated the task of representing workers of each enterprise in economic matters. Radical council delegates attempted to expand the scope and responsibilities of these works councils, but their proposals that the councils should be independent of enterprises (and unions) and be able to organize at a regional and national level failed to be enacted.[164] The most ambitious body in this period was the Works Council Central Committee [*Betriebsrätezentrale*], which became the new forum for the council movement after the suppression of the March 1919 uprising.[165] The law that governed works councils dictated that councils could represent workers' demands, but councils were given no power or control over production in the factories. There was a national economic council, but it had little influence or real power. Indicative of the hostile environment at the time, as the laws were being debated in parliament in Berlin, protests against the restrictions placed on the councils were dispersed with gunshots, leading to the deaths of forty-two people in the struggle. Richard Müller and other radical council delegates played a brief role in the initial meetings of the works councils but were unable to implement their ideas or exercise a decisive influence over the direction of these now ineffective organs.

This historical introduction to the council movements as they arose in Russia and Germany provides the backdrop against which I present a number of theoretical examinations of prominent theorists of the council movements. The ambiguous legacy of the council movements has, for the most part, led to this important period being overlooked in traditional histories of political thought. Less attention has been given to political theorists associated with the council movements and to their vision of political life. The following four chapters seek to recuperate aspects of this political thought in order to bring the significance of their political arguments back into view.

For theorists who saw a revolutionary potential in the council movements as the basis of a new post-capitalist order, one aspect of the councils stood out: the way they facilitated the self-action and self-rule of the masses. The councils formed the institutional basis of Anton Pannekoek's vision of a self-determining society in which the majority of citizens would become politically active and

German Revolution, 127–45. See also Boris Stern, *Works Council Movement in Germany* (Washington: Government Printing Office, 1925).

[164] Ralf Hoffrogge, 'From Unioinism to Workers' Councils: The Revolutionary Shop Stewards in Germany, 1914–1918', in *Ours to Master Ours to Own, Workers' Councils: Workers' Control from the Commune to the Present*, ed. Dario Azzellini and Immanuel Ness (Chicago: Haymarket Books, 2011), 99.

[165] Hoffrogge, *Working-Class Politics in the German Revolution*, 89–90. See also Weipert, *Die Zweite Revolution. Rätebewegung in Berlin 1919/1920* and Axel Weipert, 'The Central Office of Factory Councils in 1919–20: A Forgotten Chapter in the German Council Movement', *Historical Materialism* 27, no. 3 (2019), 141–56.

participate in processes of self-government and economic self-management.[166] Pannekoek understood the councils as a vehicle of the self-emancipation of the working class and an integral part of their struggle for freedom. Central to this new idea of a participatory socialism involving the active participation of the masses was a new conceptualization of political freedom understood as collective self-determination. Chapter two offers an articulation of such a conception of freedom and outlines its relationship to existing theoretical debates.

[166] Anton Pannekoek, *Workers' Councils*.

2
Freedom as Collective Self-Determination

The council movements struggled for the creation of a self-determining society in which citizens would play a more active role in the governance of political and economic institutions. At the heart of this struggle was a debate over the meaning of freedom and what it meant to live in a free society. The council movements did not simply frame their political arguments in terms of a demand for equality or justice. Rather, they sought to reclaim the language of freedom. They struggled for a freedom which did not require the enslavement of the many as a condition of the freedom of the few. They did not privilege the idea of freedom of contract and free competition over the lived experience of workers subject to the arbitrary power of their bosses and the vagaries of labour markets. Drawing on older notions of freedom as collective self-determination, theorists within the council movements combined a sensitivity to the exercise of arbitrary power with concerns for guaranteeing the rights of political participation and self-government. Following the development of industrial production and global capitalism, workers faced new threats of domination from concentrated economic power that rendered them passive and disempowered. In response to these developments, the council movements emphasized that freedom required the active participation of workers in processes of political self-government and self-management of the economy.

In this chapter, I examine a notion of freedom as collective self-determination, drawn primarily from the writings of Anton Pannekoek. This selection is based on the consideration that this ideal was explored more extensively in his writings than in any other council theorist. I nevertheless claim that this underlying conception was shared by other radical council theorists such as Rosa Luxemburg, Karl Korsch, Rirchard Müller, and Ernst Däumig, particularly those who were participatory socialists and valued the pedagogical dimensions of political struggle. But Pannekoek was especially attentive to the need for the development of a new anti-bureaucratic model of socialism and a participatory vision of revolutionary transformation. Pannekoek emphasized the connection between the development of revolutionary class consciousness and working-class organization in addition to the need for democratic participation in political institutions and workers' self-management of workplaces. He envisaged a 'new socialism of the labouring masses' which he distanced from a statist conception of socialism and associated with struggles for greater democratization and

Building Power to Change the World: The Political Thought of the German Council Movements. James Muldoon, Oxford University Press (2020). © James Muldoon. DOI: 10.1093/oso/9780198856627.003.0003

self-administration.[1] Drawing on Joseph Dietzgen's 'proletarian philosophy', Pannekoek put forward an ideal of political freedom as based on a vision of active and educated workers democratically managing their society.

For Pannekoek and the radical council theorists, freedom was viewed as an activity rather than a state or condition. Political freedom involved struggling against domination and participating in processes of self-governance. Pannekoek shared the concerns of republican political theorists for combatting structures of domination and the influence of foreign powers. Yet in contrast to certain republicans, he identified the bureaucratic state and free market economic relations as two of the principal sources of domination in modern society. He also believed that democratic participation was essential rather than auxiliary to a proper understanding of freedom. Collective self-determination required widespread and ongoing participation from broad sectors of the community and not merely the establishment of a protective structure of government. It was also important that such freedom was not achieved by a higher power or ruling social group. For Pannekoek, to be liberated by a vanguard revolutionary party or to have civil liberties legislated from above would be insufficient without the development of the political agency of ordinary citizens. To be free meant to actively participate in a political community, to play some direct role in shaping its laws and character; and to influence the direction of its ongoing transformation.

Freedom as collective self-determination was the highest good within the radical council theorists' constellation of values. Although these values also included solidarity, equality, and multifaceted human development, the underlying goal of their struggle for a socialist society was to expand the scope of human freedom. Pannekoek regularly expressed the idea of revolutionary action as a 'struggle for freedom', particularly in *Workers' Councils* and in his unpublished manuscript, 'The Workers' Way to Freedom.'[2] Similarly, for Karl Korsch, 'socialism, both in its ends and in its means, is a struggle to realize freedom.'[3] Gustav Landauer concurs that 'socialism is the means by which we want to reach and secure this freedom.'[4] The daily newspaper of the USPD, published between 1918 and 1922, was called *Freiheit* (freedom), indicating the centrality of this ideal to their struggle.

While radical council theorists demonstrated interest in specific freedoms such as freedom of the press, freedom of speech etc., their abiding concern was for the value of freedom as such. They recognized freedom's independent value, regardless of its relation to other goods, and started from an understanding that freedom

[1] Anton Pannekoek, 'Friedrich Adler', *Die Nieuwe Tijd* (1916), 640–7, 647.

[2] See Gerber, *Anton Pannekoek and the Socialism of Workers' Self-Emancipation 1873–1960*, 231.

[3] Quoted in Karl Korsch, *Karl Korsch: Revolutionary Theory*, ed. Douglas Kellner (Austin: University of Texas Press, 1977), 15.

[4] Gustav Landauer, *Revolution and Other Writings: A Political Reader*, ed. Gabriel Kuhn (Oakland: PM Press, 2010), 70.

had what Ian Carter has described as 'non-specific value' or value as such.[5] This is what Marx referred to as 'freedom without any specific name', which denoted how '[f]reedom of trade, freedom of property, of conscience, of the press, of the courts, are all species of one and the same genus.'[6]

I claim that freedom as collective self-determination can be contrasted with the two main conceptions of freedom in contemporary political theory today: the liberal ideal of freedom as non-interference and the republican ideal of freedom as non-domination. In his 1958 essay 'Two Concepts of Liberty', Isaiah Berlin distinguished a negative conception of liberty as non-interference from a positive conception of liberty as self-mastery, or rational and moral self-determination.[7] His essay defended a version of negative liberty, which he believed avoided the totalitarian dangers inherent in a positive conception of self-mastery and control.[8] His ideal of negative liberty was based on Hobbes' classic statement of the idea in which 'freedom signifies the absence of [external] opposition.'[9] Berlin modified the Hobbesian formula to define political liberty as 'the area within which a man can act unobstructed by others.'[10] Berlin's highly influential essay established for a generation of scholars the philosophical respectability of a negative view of liberty and the confusion and dangers inherent in a positive one.

These biases against the tradition of positive liberty have only been reinforced by the recent work of republican political theorist, Philip Pettit. Pettit argues that the positive/negative distinction has obscured a third valuable view of liberty as non-domination located within the republican tradition. Pettit understands the ideal of freedom as non-domination to consist of a particular status in which a person is secured against interference on an arbitrary basis.[11] For Pettit, domination occurs when one party has the capacity to arbitrarily interfere with and control the possible choices of another on the basis of an opinion or an interest not shared by the dominated party.[12] To be free, on this view, is to be free from the possibility of being subjected to the exercise of arbitrary power. Freedom in this sense is constituted by a republican regime of rightly ordered laws and norms that guard against possible arbitrary interference to which a person may be exposed.

[5] For a liberal defence of the non-specific value of freedom see Ian Carter, *A Measure of Freedom* (Oxford: Oxford University Press, 1999), 31–68. In contrast, John Rawls has stated that throughout the history of thinking about democracy 'the focus has been on achieving certain specific liberties.' John Rawls, *Political Liberalism*, 292.

[6] Karl Marx, 'On Freedom of the Press', *Rheinische Zeitung*, No. 139, Supplement, 19 May 1842. Available in Marx and Engels, *Collected Works Vol. 1*, 132–81.

[7] Ibid.

[8] His conception of negative liberty roughly corresponds to Constant's 'liberty of the moderns'. On the similarities between Constant and Berlin's accounts of negative liberty see Katrin Flikschuh, *Freedom: Contemporary Liberal Perspectives* (Cambridge: Polity Press, 2007), 16.

[9] Thomas Hobbes, *Leviathan* (Cambridge: Cambridge University Press, 2003), 145.

[10] Berlin, 'Two Concepts of Liberty', 122. The subtle difference between Hobbes and Berlin is that for Berlin unfreedom is brought about only where interference is caused by a human action rather than Hobbes' mechanistic account where any external impediment is a potential cause of unfreedom.

[11] Pettit, *Republicanism*, vii–viii.

[12] Ibid., 22.

As a passive condition rather than an act, exercise, or practice, it is based primarily on the presence of protective institutions.[13]

This ideal of freedom as collective self-determination captures important aspects of an attractive conception of freedom that are missed through a purely negative lens. My argument, therefore, is not that various negative accounts of freedom are incoherent or undesirable. On the contrary, the simplicity and intuitive appeal of negative liberty will ensure that it will always play a significant role in our understanding of freedom. Freedom as collective self-determination need not replace negative theories as the only true or real account of freedom. My claim, rather, is that this view of freedom adds something indispensable to our understanding of freedom *as a practice*, which is obscured from other perspectives. There is, therefore, an important place for freedom as collective self-determination alongside negative accounts if we hope to capture the full range and scope of freedom. This view of freedom, for example, resonates with a diverse collection of theorists and actors of social movements struggling for freedom who prioritize the view of freedom as a collective practice and constant struggle.[14]

The conception of freedom as collective self-determination developed in this chapter provides an avenue for reconsidering the positive liberty tradition in a manner that avoids some of the common pitfalls and weaknesses of previous accounts.[15] For example, Pannekoek was not committed to a one-track perfectionist account of human development, a fixed metaphysics of human beings, or an account that connects freedom with unattractive ideals of self-mastery or the rule of reason. By positive liberty I do not intend to defend an account concerned with the internal psychological limitations on human autonomy or a desire for one's actions to accord with a 'higher self' of virtue or reason. I am interested in a sociopolitical theory of liberty rather than a moral-psychological account of the conditions of human autonomy and free will.

The plan of the chapter is as follows. After tracing the historical origins of an ideal of freedom as collective self-determination, I develop a robust account of freedom as collective self-determination based on the writings of Pannekoek but also drawing from other radical council theorists. I highlight its most important characteristics and reveal points of contrast with other conceptions of freedom. I conclude by putting forward grounds for the intuitive appeal of this conception of freedom in gaining a richer and more applicable understanding of the role of freedom in political struggle.

[13] Pettit also stresses the importance of civil society and republican values in Pettit, *Republicanism*, 241–70.

[14] As I explain later in the chapter, this includes thinkers as diverse as Martin Luther King Jr, Mahatma Ghandi, Angela Davis, Nelson Mandela, Fannie Lou Hammer, and Mikhail Bakunin.

[15] Isaiah Berlin, 'Two Concepts of Liberty', in *Four Essays on Liberty* (Oxford: Oxford University Press, 1969).

The Origins of Freedom as Collective Self-Determination

The ideal of freedom as collective self-determination can be traced back to one of the oldest versions of active citizenship in the Athenian polis. To be free for an Athenian entailed directly participating in government through deliberation and decision-making. Citizenship provided citizens with admission to the public realm and an equal right to exercise political power in spite of differences in economic and social status. Liberty (*eleutheria*) in Athens had two sides and included both a 'freedom of the polis' in the public sense of participation in government and 'freedom within the polis', meaning personal liberties in the private sphere against domination.[16] A citizen enjoyed the freedom to participate in shaping the character of their community in addition to the freedom to live as they wished within the private sphere. The equation of *eleutheria* with lawlessness—and Athenian democracy with mob rule—was only made by democracy's critics such as Plato, Cicero, and the Roman tradition.[17] In contrast, the *libertas* of the Roman plebs did not involve rights of participation in government or an ability to address the assembly. A status of legal equality and having no master did not entail an 'extension of equality from legal to political or social rights, let alone equal access to office, voting, or debate'.[18]

This Greek idea of active citizenship was given its most coherent formulation in Aristotle's *Politics*, which argued for an idea of a citizen as an equal participant in ruling and being ruled in turn.[19] The Aristotelian 'republican' concept of active citizenship exercised a wide-ranging influence on civic humanist, classical republican, and communitarian writers prior to the current popularity of the neo-Roman republican conception of liberty as non-domination.[20] There are also deep resonances with Machiavelli's writings in *The Discourses on Livy* in which he argues that the active participation of the popular masses is a means towards counteracting domination by elites and maintaining a 'free way of life'.[21]

[16] Josiah Ober, *Mass and Elite in Democratic Athens: Rhetoric, Ideology, and the Power of the People* (Princeton NJ: Princeton University Press, 1989), 94. Mogens Herman Hansen, *The Athenian Democracy in the Age of Demosthenes: Structure, Principles, and Ideology* (Norman: University of Oklahoma Press, 1991), 79.

[17] Nadia Urbinati, 'Competing for Liberty: The Roman Critique of Democracy', *American Political Science Review* 106, no. 3 (2012), 607–21.

[18] Hanna Pitkin, 'Are Freedom and Liberty Twins?', *Political Theory* 16 (1988), 523–52, 534.

[19] Aristotle, *Politics*, ed. Ernest Barker, revised by Richard Stalley (Oxford: Oxford University Press, 1995). However, Aristotle was not a democrat nor did he call the power of citizens to participate in deliberation and decision-making their freedom.

[20] See J. G. A. Pocock, *The Republican Moment. Florentine Political Theory and the Atlantic Republican Tradition* (Princeton, NJ: Princeton University Press, 1975); Michael Sandel, *Democracy's Discontent. America in Search of a Public Philosophy* (Cambridge, MA: Harvard University Press, 1996).

[21] Niccolò Machiavelli, *The Discourses on Livy* (Chicago. The University of Chicago Press, 1996), 16–19.

This notion of freedom was most prominently revived in the modern era by Jean Jacques Rousseau. In Rousseau, the ideal of collective self-rule returned in the form of a self-determining political community in which all members engaged in deliberation over the common good within a sovereign assembly in order to determine a 'general will'. This Rousseauian image was influential over the early French socialists and was also prominent in the growing number of advocates for democratic government. Marx drew upon these democratic republican themes in his argument against the alienation of capitalist economic relations and the bureaucratic state. Marx believed that freedom was best realized in a free association of producers in which individuals could fully develop their manifold powers. According to Marx, 'free activity for the Communists is the creative manifestation of life arising from the free development of all abilities of the whole person.'[22] Freedom consisted in the possibility of a democratic collective determining its own affairs and for each individual to be able to flourish and self-actualize within that community.

In the nineteenth century, socialists reframed the classic ideal of a self-determining political community within a Marxist notion of revolutionary struggle and emancipation. The pursuit of collective self-determination involved a struggle against the dominating forces of capital and the state and the promotion of human flourishing. They drew on republican themes of collective control and participation in government, while recasting them in the language of revolutionary class struggle against capitalism. Radical socialists of the early twentieth century transformed the classic republican ideal of citizenship of a self-governing state into workers' mass action in an ongoing struggle against exploitation and domination for a free association of free producers. Among them was Anton Pannekoek, who was deeply engaged with the practical realities of revolutionary action and how organizational methods could best align with the ideals of a free society. As a result, he was critical of attempts to replace the free activity of the masses with the direction of a vanguard or parliamentary party and its leaders. It is this conception of freedom as collective self-determination that I will further outline below.

The Development of Anton Pannekoek's Ideas on Freedom

Pannekoek based his views of human freedom on his understanding of the Marxist historic-materialist method and the idea that human societies were in a constant state of social development. His political thought aimed at understanding and transforming the world through the development of a synthesis of Marx's and

[22] Karl Marx and Friedrich Engels, *Collected Works Vol. 5* (London: Lawrence and Wishart, 1976), 225.

Joseph Dietzgen's writings.[23] Dietzgen was a socialist philosopher who Pannekoek believed provided an important supplement to Marx's work through a theory of knowledge and human understanding. Attempting to develop these insights into a unified whole, Pannekoek employed both Dietzgenian and Marxist concepts to offer an account of a 'proletarian philosophy', which he thought made important advances on previous philosophical systems.[24] For Pannekoek, Dietzgen's system was a continuation and development of the systems of Kant and Hegel.

In Pannekoek's view, Kant's philosophy was 'the purest expression of bourgeois thought' in that its emphasis on 'free will' and an abstract idea of freedom corresponded to the ideas and aspirations of a rising bourgeoisie.[25] Pannekoek was critical of ideals of freedom prominent in German bourgeois circles that conceived of it in purely individualistic terms and which emphasized the individual's right to property and participation in the market as the highest form of freedom. He referred to such an understanding as a 'petty bourgeois freedom' and viewed this as an obstacle to revolutionary transformation. This kind of freedom was necessarily one-sided and incomplete and was part of 'the old illusions that middle class revolutions would bring freedom and equality to the entire population'.[26]

In contrast, Marx's worldview was materialist, which provided a different philosophical base. Pannekoek claimed that 'for the proletariat, it is material forces that govern the world, forces outside the scope of the individual; for the middle class, development depend on the creative force of the human mind.'[27] In Pannekoek's view 'the idea of freedom, as a political watchword, derives from middle class interest in free enterprise and free competition; but each class that uses it gives the idea a meaning of its own.'[28] The proletariat required its own understanding of freedom and how it could be achieved in a socialist society.

In addition to the philosophical foundations of Marx and Dietzgen, Pannekoek's point of departure was a sociological critique of the practical functioning of German social democracy.[29] Reflecting on the growing bureaucratism of the party and the growth of a privileged strata of elites within it, Pannekoek identified a tendency towards disempowering the membership base and taking decisions on their behalf. He felt that the leadership was naturally led towards more self-serving policies that ended up protecting the bureaucratic apparatus. Particularly in the period leading up to and during the First world War,

[23] Gerber, *Anton Pannekoek and the Socialism of Workers' Self-Emancipation 1873–1960*, 17.

[24] Pannekoek, 'The Position and Significance of J. Dietzgen's Philosophical Works', in Joseph Dietzgen, *The Positive Outcome of Philosophy* (Chicago, 1906), 21.

[25] Gerber, *Anton Pannekoek and the Socialism of Workers' Self-Emancipation 1873–1960*, 17.

[26] Pannekoek, 'Why Past Revolutionary Movements have Failed'.

[27] Pannekoek, *Die taktischen Differenzen der Arbeiterbewegung*, quoted in Bricianer, *Pannekoek and the Workers' Councils*, 111.

[28] Ibid.

[29] Gerber, *Anton Pannekoek and the Socialism of Workers' Self-Emancipation 1873–1960*, 128.

Pannekoek placed greater emphasis on the democratic nature of socialism and the idea that it was workers themselves who should be the primary agents of social transformation. In his criticisms of a statist conception of socialism, Pannekoek developed a more bottom-up idea of socialism as democratic participation in the economy and the self-administration of workplaces.[30] During this period, John Gerber notes how 'the struggle for democratization—in the form of struggles for greater democracy both within the existing state and in the new self-administering organs of proletarian struggle—would take on a new intensity and significance.'[31] Pannekoek sought to define this 'new socialism of the labouring masses', built on the capacity of workers for self-emancipation:

> The hope of socialism no longer lies in its gradualist and bourgeois side, the admirable socialist parties with their glittering speakers, their famous politicians, their noble feelings of human love, their nice programs, their good, proud, self-righteous workers. It lies instead in the dark poverty and misery of the masses, who, as they rebel against their misery, are hated, scorned, and persecuted as the enemies of state and society; out of their struggles and sacrifices will arise the full freedom of mankind.[32]

Conceptualizing Freedom as Collective Self-Determination

According to MacCallum's influential formulation, freedom necessarily involves three conceptual components:

> Whenever the freedom of some agent or agents is in question, it is always a freedom from some constraints or restriction on, interference with, or barring to doing, not doing, becoming, or not becoming something. Such freedom is thus always *of* an agent, *from* something, *to* do/become something . . . '*x* is (is not) free from *y* to do (not do, become, not become) *z*,' x ranges over agents, *y* ranges over such 'preventing conditions' as constraints, restrictions, interferences, and barriers, and *z* ranges over actions or conditions of character or circumstance.[33]

Pannekoek understood political freedom as a political community's ongoing struggle against forces of domination *and* experimentation with new practices and structures of governance. In this definition, *x*, individuals and the collective

[30] See for example Anton Pannekoek, 'Was ist Sozialismus?', *Lichtstrahlen* 11 (1915), 220–3.
[31] Gerber, *Anton Pannekoek and the Socialism of Workers' Self-Emancipation 1873–1960*, 130.
[32] Anton Pannekoek, 'De sociaaldemokracie en de oorlog', *De Nieuwe Tijd* (1915), 69–84, 137–51, 146.
[33] Gerald C. MacCallum, Jr, 'Negative and Positive Freedom', *The Philosophical Review* 76, no. 3 (1967), 312–34.

social body are free from *y*, forces and structures of domination (objective and ideological), *through*, *z*, performing actions that i) struggle against domination; and ii) develop and enhance a community's capacity for self-determination.

Note that there is a slight change in the formulation—from '*to*' to '*through*'—on account of the constitutive nature of action in this ideal of freedom. For most negative liberty theorists, it is sufficient that external impediments are eliminated such that an opportunity to act is open, whereas for Pannekoek freedom is constituted by actions against domination and actions that develop a community's capacity for collective self-determination. It could be argued that such a definition confuses liberation with freedom insofar as to struggle against domination means to not yet be free. However, Pannekoek considered both of these sets of actions as part of a single continuum of a struggle for freedom. In this sense, to seek to eliminate sources of domination was to take the first steps on a path to collective self-determination. Pannekoek considered that an emancipatory struggle would be one continuous process:

> The revolution by which the working class will win mastery and freedom, is not a single event of limited duration. It is a process of organization, of self-education, in which the workers gradually, now in progressing rise, then in steps and leaps, develop the force to vanquish the bourgeoisie, to destroy capitalism, and to build up their new system of collective production.[34]

The definition of 'x' includes individuals and the social collective because Pannekoek aimed for the reconciliation of an individual's personal liberties with the freedom of the community through an individual's participation in the collective self-determination of society. Pannekoek argued that in 'a body of self-determining people . . . everybody has to follow the decisions which he himself has taken part in making. But the full power always rests with the workers themselves.'[35] In this sense, each individual takes 'all the responsibilities as a self-relying individual amidst equal comrades'.[36] Karl Korsch referred to this as the importance of the 'creation of the conditions of intellectual freedom not only for "all" workers but for "each individual" worker'.[37] Freedom as collective self-determination could only be achieved when each individual was able to exercise their capacity for autonomy, creativity, and self-development within a self-governing community.

Radical council theorists also identified capitalist relations of production and the bureaucratic state as the primary sources of domination ('y') in workers lives. Marx emphasized this economic exchange rests upon an unequal social

[34] Anton Pannekoek, 'Workers' Councils', *International Council Correspondence* 2, no. 5 (1936).
[35] Pannekoek, 'Workers' Councils'. [36] Ibid.
[37] Karl Korsch, *Marxism and Philosophy* (London: Monthly Review Press, 1970), 142–3.

relationship between two classes of people with different structural positions corresponding to different amounts of power and mobility. 'The worker, whose only source of income is the sale of his labour-power', might be able to choose between different employers, but, Marx added, they 'cannot leave the whole class of buyers'.[38] In her interpretation, Rosa Luxemburg argued that this situation represented one of structural domination in which individually uncoordinated, cumulative but unintentional actions lead to a condition of unfreedom for workers forced to sell their labour. Due to the 'separation of labour-power from the means of production', the worker has no commodity to bring to the marketplace to exchange, nothing, that is, 'but to bring himself to market as a commodity, i.e. to bring his own labour-power'.[39]

These objective structures of domination were also supplemented by the control that capitalists exercised over cultural and ideological apparatuses. Through the ownership and control of the media, information services, and cultural institutions, capitalists could promote their own particular understanding of reality as the norm. Pannekoek argued:

> The ideas of the ruling class dominate society and permeate the minds of the exploited classes. They are fixed there, fundamentally, by the inner strength and necessity of the system of production; they are actually implanted there by education and propaganda, by the influence of school, church, press, literature, broadcasting and film.[40]

So long as a bourgeois mentality predominated, those '[m]inds submissive to the doctrines of the masters cannot hope to win freedom'.[41] It is for this reason that Pannekoek believed 'capitalism must be beaten theoretically before it can be beaten materially.'[42]

One tension in this definition of freedom as collective self-determination is that x is free 'through' doing z, while seemingly being constrained insofar as they *must* perform a specific action or set of actions, namely those which are properly self-determining. In other words, one could object that a consequence of this interpretation of freedom is that one is only free if one actively participates in a self-determining political community. What of those who are either unable or unwilling to participate? I do not think there is a straightforward and satisfying answer to this concern. Against this possible objection we could charitably read the notion of participation broadly to include a wide variety of possible activities in service of the community. But some notion of activity does appear essential to

[38] Karl Marx, 'Wage Labour and Capital', in *Collected Works, Vol. 9* (Moscow: International Publishers, 1977), 197–228, 210.

[39] Rosa Luxemburg, 'Introduction to Political Economy', in *The Complete Works of Rosa Luxemburg, Volume I: Economic Writings 1*, ed. Peter Hudis (London: Verso, 2013), 234.

[40] Pannekoek, *Workers' Councils.* [41] Ibid. [42] Ibid.

Pannekoek, which raises the troubling question of whether those more able to participate would be better able to actualize their freedom.

It could be claimed that Pannekoek's emphasis on mass action need not entail full participation from every member and that it would suffice for a community to be free if it contained a generally active and mobilized citizenry. There are points at which Pannekoek states that it is 'the majority of the population' who 'must manage the means of production' and where he distinguishes between the rule of 'some few eminent individuals' versus 'the character of the many'.[43] However, this remains a point of contention and has often been highlighted in negative liberty theorists' criticisms of positive liberty.[44] Although such objections are not fatal, it is a point at which some potentially troubling consequences of the account may have to be accepted. Namely, that freedom for Pannekoek appears intrinsically tied to notions of activity and participation in the self-governance of a political community.

The Importance of Participation and Direct Control

Collective self-determination for Pannekoek entailed widespread participation in processes of governance through which individuals could exercise direct control over the central institutions of society. He argued that this entailed a capacity to shape the underlying conditions of society, emphasizing the positive side of political freedom: 'The proletarian revolution is not simply the vanquishing of capitalist power. It is the rise of the whole working people out of dependence and ignorance into independence and clear consciousness of how to make their life.'[45] To throw off the forces of domination would be merely the first step in a process of the development of the collective capacity for self-determination. Pannekoek emphasized that '[d]emocracy means popular government, people's self-government. The popular masses themselves must administer their own affairs and determine them.'[46] The state and capitalist relations of production were theorized as sources of domination, but in order to practise freedom, citizens had to perform the positive role of participating directly in processes of self-government. Pannekoek highlighted the importance of direct control over political and economic institutions:

> The real freedom of the workers consists in their direct mastery over the means of production. The essence of the future free world community is not that the

[43] Ibid. [44] Berlin, 'Two Concepts of Liberty'. [45] Pannekoek, 'Workers' Councils'.
[46] Pannekoek, 'Social Democracy and Communism'.

> working masses get enough food, but they direct their work themselves, collectively.[47]

The possibility of this form of freedom resided in the capacity of all individuals for political activity and self-organization:

> Fighting for freedom is not letting your leaders think for you and decide, and following obediently behind them, or from time to time scolding them. Fighting for freedom is partaking to the full of one's capacity, thinking and deciding for oneself... it is the only way to freedom.... Freedom, the goal of the workers, means that they shall be able, man for man, to manage the world, to use and deal with the treasures of the earth, so as to make it a happy home for all.[48]

The key element is not simply to avoid the arbitrary exercise of power, but to collectively participate in practices of self-government.

Radical council theorists held a clear idea of the high demand this conception of freedom placed on citizens. Däumig envisioned it as 'a Germany whose affairs are really determined by active people doing more than running to the ballot box every two or three years'.[49] For him, this exacting ideal of freedom involved 'an economic system determined by the people' and 'a dedicated attempt to make and keep the German people politically active'.[50] He continued: 'we have to abandon the entire old administrative machinery, on the federal, regional, and municipal level. The German people have to get used to self-management instead of governance.'[51] Pannekoek also believed that a 'self-determining people' implied 'that everyone takes part in it, body and soul and brains; that everyone takes part in leadership as well as in action'.[52] In sum, political freedom as collective self-determination required individuals to actively participate in processes of self-governance in order to shape the character of their political community.

Pannekoek was sceptical of less immediate forms of control and ways in which power could be stripped from workers and given to administrative bodies. It could be asked why the right to take the government to court for violating one's rights wouldn't count as a form of control that could be as good as or superior to participation in a legislative council or governing a workplace. In other words, why the emphasis on direct forms of control and the participation of the majority in self-governing institutions? For Pannekoek, this was based on a fear of usurpation: if decision-making was delegated to institutions not in the immediate control of workers then they could become an alien power that would end up

[47] Pannekoek, 'The Failure of the Working Class'. [48] Pannekoek, *Workers' Councils*.

[49] Däumig, 'The National Assembly Means the Councils' Death', in Kuhn, ed., *All Power to the Councils*, 43.

[50] Ibid., 48. [51] Ibid. [52] Pannekoek, *Workers' Councils*.

controlling them. Pannekoek drew from his experiences of the bureaucratization of the SPD and with European parliamentary politics to form this opinion. As a result of this reflection, Pannekoek was adamant that workers should construct 'new forms of organisation in which they keep the powers of action in their own hands'.[53] He argued that workers had to understand the 'significance of self-action and self-rule' as 'the way to freedom'.[54] The institutions through which this self-rule should be organized had to allow workers immediate control over decision-making such as strike committees, workers' councils, and any other organization that did not allow a separate and semi-autonomous leadership to develop. The benefit, in Pannekoek's view, of a strike committee was that 'it is continually in touch with them and has to carry out the decisions of the strikers. Each delegate at every moment can be replaced by others; such a committee never becomes an independent power.'[55]

Political Action as Constitutive of Freedom

Freedom as collective self-determination is distinct from negative ideals of freedom because it emphasizes the importance of the mass action of ordinary citizens participating in a self-governing political community. It is an exercise concept of freedom which rests not merely on the capacity to act but on political action as the practice of freedom. Pannekoek offered two different types of arguments as to why political action was so essential to freedom: *constitutive* and *instrumental.* On the one hand, he argued that freedom required political action as one of its constitutive components and could not exist without it. On the other hand, political action was also seen as *instrumentally* valuable for freedom due to its ability to effectively secure the conditions for the exercise of freedom and develop and maintain a community's capacities for self-determination. I will explain Pannekoek's specific grounds for each belief in turn, beginning with the constitutive argument.

First, Pannekoek's argument that political action was constitutive of freedom can be distinguished from the stronger claim made by Hannah Arendt that action was *definitionally identical* to freedom in the sense that before and after action individuals were unfree, since 'to *be* free and to act are the same.'[56] For Pannekoek, freedom was a practice that required participation from individuals, but would not cease to exist the moment a particular action ended. Freedom was constituted by one's participation in and membership of a self-determining political community. Unlike in Arendt's phenomenologically inspired account of freedom, the focus of the analysis was less on the physical acts of speaking and deliberating in the public

[53] Pannekoek, 'General Remarks on the Question of Organisation'.
[54] Pannekoek, *Workers' Councils.* [55] Pannekoek, 'Workers' Councils'.
[56] Arendt, *Between Past and Future*, 153.

sphere, and more on the collective process of gaining control over the character and direction of public institutions. Pannekoek often conceptualized this process as a 'fight', 'struggle', or 'path' for achieving a 'society of freedom' with an 'abundance for all', indicating that his definition of freedom centred upon a 'process of organization, of self-education' in which workers aimed to overcome the forces of the bourgeoisie and also 'build up their new system of collective production'.[57] The final aim was the creation of a self-determining society based on democratic self-administration. Freedom persists in between specific instances of speech and action because it was conceived of as an ongoing process and collective struggle connected to the formation of such a self-determining society, rather than virtuosic action or an innate capacity for new beginnings.[58]

Pannekoek's claim that the political action of workers was constitutive of their freedom was a departure from what he considered the main form of socialism inherited from the nineteenth century in which socialism was synonymous with rational economic planning and a state-controlled economy. He was critical of such a 'statist'- and 'leader'-oriented understanding of socialism and contested the belief of certain workers' that 'by transferring government into the hands of these socialists they would assure their freedom.'[59] The locus of freedom, for Pannekoek, could be found not in the 'admirable socialist parties with their glittering speakers, their famous politicians, their noble feelings of human love, their nice programs', but rather in the actions of the masses.[60] It was 'out of their struggles and sacrifices' through which 'will arise the full freedom of mankind'.[61] Pannekoek looked to the 'political act of the organized working class, by which it operates directly and not through the medium of delegates'.[62] It was from 'independent action, from the fight for freedom, from revolt against the masters' that workers would achieve liberty. Such a conception of freedom was contained in one of Marx's statements that could have been the slogan of the radical council theorists: 'The emancipation of the working classes must be conquered by the working classes themselves.'[63]

To be free, for Pannekoek, meant to live autonomously under self-made rules and through participation in the general administration and governance of society. Pannekoek called for workers to be 'masters of the factories, masters of their own labor, to conduct it at their own will.'[64] At the heart of this view was an idea of conscious control and self-direction as outlined above. Pannekoek was adamant that workers' actual participation in the self-management of society was 'the only road to freedom', and that all other alternatives constituted 'dreams of imperfect

[57] Pannekoek, *Workers' Councils.*
[58] Arendt, *Between Past and Future*, 167.
[59] Pannekoek, *Workers' Councils.*
[60] Pannekoek, 'De sociaaldemokracie en de oorlog'.
[61] Ibid.
[62] Anton Pannekoek, 'Die Massenstreikdebatte', *Zeitungskorrespondenz*, 18 June 1910.
[63] Marx, 'General Rules of the International Workingmen's Association'.
[64] Pannekoek, *Workers' Councils.*

freedom'.[65] But if the only pathway was participation in processes of self-governance and citizens were hitherto accustomed to passivity and dependence, how could such an ideal be realized?

Political action was considered constitutive of freedom due to its *educative function*: freedom as collective self-determination was a capacity that had to be learnt and developed through action. For Pannekoek as well as other radical council theorists, the struggle for freedom was a precondition and element of freedom itself. Freedom was considered a practical exercise that required knowledge of the nature of different forms of domination in order for it to be adequately resisted. It also required an understanding of processes of self-governance that would be robust and egalitarian. By struggling against forces of domination and exercising capacities of self-rule in an embryonic form, workers could develop the practical skills of self-determination. Luxemburg was well aware of the important educative role of participation in political action: 'The working classes in every country only learn to fight in the course of their struggles.'[66] The stronger the movement for freedom, 'the more the enlightened masses of workers will take their own destinies, the leadership of their movement, and the determination of its direction into their own hands.'[67] Pannekoek echoed these sentiments:

> In our view, revolution is a *process*, the first stages of which we are now experiencing, for it is only by the struggle for power itself that the masses can be assembled, drilled and formed into an organization capable of taking power.[68]

Collective self-determination was not something that could be achieved overnight after generations of passivity and domination. As Luxemburg observed 'bourgeois class rule has no need of the political training and education of the entire mass of the people.'[69] Individuals had a very limited capacity to exercise control over the central political institutions in Imperial Germany. But in a socialist society, political education 'is the life element, the very air without which it is not able to exist'.[70] It was only through the experience of participating in self-governing communities, at the level of the strike, factory committee, and workers' councils, that individuals could change their attitudes, expand their ideological perspectives, and learn how to practise freedom. Yet as long as bourgeois mentalities maintain their hold, Pannekoek saw that 'the working class, lacking consciousness of its class position, acquiescing in exploitation as the normal condition of life, does not think of revolt and cannot fight. Minds submissive to the doctrines of the masters cannot hope to win freedom.'[71]

[65] Ibid. [66] Luxemburg, 'The Next Step'. [67] Luxemburg, 'The Junius Pamphlet'.
[68] Pannekoek, 'Marxist Theory and Revolutionary Tactics'.
[69] Luxemburg, 'The Russian Revolution'. [70] Ibid. [71] Pannekoek, *Workers' Councils*.

On an epistemological level, Pannekoek suggested that such knowledge could not be learnt theoretically, but had to be imparted through class struggle:

> this knowledge itself must be acquired in the hard school of experience, a harsh lived experience that shapes the mind in the full heat of combat... It is only through the practice of its struggles against capitalism... that the proletariat is transformed into a revolutionary class capable of conquering the capitalist system.[72]

The only way forward, according to Luxemburg, was through practical action, for workers must 'feel out the ground, try out, experiment, test now one way now another'.[73] Such experimentation would inevitably involve errors and mistakes. However, these mistakes must be made by the workers themselves rather than having their decision-making capacity usurped by the party leadership. Luxemburg argued that 'errors made by a truly revolutionary labor movement are historically infinitely more fruitful and more valuable than the infallibility of the best of all possible "central committees."'[74]

Political Action as Instrumental to Freedom

Pannekoek also considered that political action would be instrumentally valuable for freedom because it helped to secure the conditions for its exercise and to develop and maintain a community's capacity for collective self-determination. He believed that workers should take action themselves in order to create favourable conditions for the expansion of liberty. If freedom were won by another class, not only would workers not have the requisite skills and capacities to self-govern, but it would indicate a worrying balance of power favouring another group that could become oppressive. For Pannekoek, '[t]o be liberated by others, whose leadership is the essential part of the liberation, means the getting of new masters instead of the old ones.'[75] If workers were beholden to a party leadership or another social group then they would remain vulnerable to having their freedom taken away. Pannekoek argued:

> A political party cannot bring freedom, but, when it wins, only new forms of domination. Freedom can be won by the working masses only through their own organised action, by taking their lot into their own hands, in devoted exertion of

[72] Anton Pannekoek, 'Prinzip und Taktik', quoted in Serge Bricianer, *Pannekoek and the Workers' Councils* (Saint Louis: Telos Press, 1983), 241–2.
[73] Luxemburg, 'The Russian Revolution'.
[74] Luxemburg, 'Organisational Questions of the Russian Social Democracy'.
[75] Pannekoek, *Workers' Councils*.

> all their faculties, by directing and organising their fight and their work themselves by means of their councils.[76]

A secure freedom requires workers to develop their power without relying on the good favour of another social group. Pannekoek also considered that there was good reason to believe a class of officials would be ineffective at winning such a freedom:

> It is clear that the organisational forms of trade union and political party, inherited from the period of expanding capitalism, are useless here. They developed into instruments in the hands of leaders unable and unwilling to engage in revolutionary fight. Leaders cannot make revolutions: labour leaders abhor a proletarian revolution. For the revolutionary fights the workers need new forms of organisation in which they keep the powers of action in their own hands.[77]

For Pannekoek, a free society 'cannot be brought about by any superiority of some few eminent individuals whatever. It does not depend on the brains of the few, but on the character of the many.'[78]

A second way in which political action would further secure the conditions for freedom is through the creation and entrenching of widely supported cultural norms favouring self-determination. Pannekoek articulated this through the idea of freedom becoming the '"dominating life principle" of society'.[79] He noted the culturally transformative effects of participation in political action:

> The forces of solidarity and devotion hidden in them only wait for great fights to develop . . . Then even the most suppressed layers of the working class, who only hesitatingly join their comrades, wanting to lean upon their example, will soon feel the new forces of community growing also in themselves. Then they will perceive that the fight for freedom asks not only their adherence but the development of all their powers of self-activity and self-reliance.[80]

Pannekoek suggested that political action had a cumulative and expansive effect because the exercise of freedom is innately attractive for human beings and seeing it practised would encourage more to join in the struggle. In this respect, the exercise of freedom paves the way for the expansion of the conditions under which freedom can thrive.

[76] Anton Pannekoek, 'Theses On The Fight Of The Working Class Against Capitalism', *Southern Advocate for Workers' Councils* (1947), 33.
[77] Pannekoek, 'General Remarks on the Question of Organisation'.
[78] Pannekoek, *Workers' Councils*. [79] Ibid. [80] Ibid., 66.

Open and Creative Development

Radical council theorists avoided a common objection against theories of positive liberty insofar as they did not adhere to a questionable metaphysics of human beings or an objective conception of the good life. Instead, they supported a narrower conception of the *free* life, with an emphasis on the cultivation of the capacities and institutions required to support a self-determining society. Korsch was critical of a tendency of bourgeois thought to hold to a 'single track idea of "progress"' and believed that socialism would enable 'the universal development of free individuals in a free society'.[81] Radical council theorists adhered to a more open view of human perfectibility understood as the self-development of human beings without a specific goal in view, described by Condorcet as the 'indefinite perfectibility of the human race'.[82] Unlike for Aristotle and certain communitarians, freedom was not valued for its ability to actualize a fixed view of the *telos* of human beings or for its ability to make possible a set of specific virtues.[83] Pannekoek placed an emphasis on free and spontaneous activity, rather than acting in accordance with a prescribed model of human self-actualization. This notion of positive collective self-determination emphasized the openness of the future and the importance of creative acts of invention. Collective self-determination entailed the capacity to change the forms of revolutionary organization and the fundamental structures of the political community.

Workers' councils were valued for their open institutional structure and possibility for ongoing transformation. Cornelius Castoriadis described this aspect of council thought as 'the invention of new forms of organization, of struggle, or of life that in no way were contained in the previous state of affairs'.[84] This notion can also be found in many of the earlier radical council theorists who shared a philosophical anthropology of human beings as creative, productive, and expressive agents. They emphasized what Luxemburg called the 'positive creative spirit' of individuals and what Pannekoek described as the 'delight of glorious creative experience'.[85] This human creativity and inventiveness allowed ordinary workers to formulate revolutionary strategy and tactics themselves, which formed an integral part of their practices of freedom. Castoriadis explained that 'the growth of freedom within work, the development of the creative faculties of the producers, the creation of integrated and complete human communities, will be the paths

[81] Karl Korsch, *Karl Marx* (Leiden: Brill, 1930), 150.

[82] Marquis de Condorcet, *Sketch for a Historical Picture of the Progress of the Human Mind* (Westport, Connecticut: Hyperion Press, 1955), 142.

[83] See Alistair MacIntyre, *After Virtue: a Study in Moral Theory* (London: Duckworth, 1981).

[84] Cornelius Castoriadis, *Political and Social Writings Volume 2 1955–1960: From the Workers' Struggle Against Bureacracy to Revolution in the Age of Modern Capitalism* (Minneapolis: University of Minnesota Press, 1988), 264.

[85] Luxemburg, 'Organisational Questions of the Proletarian Revolution'; Pannekoek, *Workers' Councils*, 56.

along which socialist humanity will seek to find the meaning of its existence.'[86] Both Castoriadis and Pannekoek valued the councils not as the final form of a socialist society but as a means through which workers could exercise their own creativity and experiment with new practices and new organizational forms of collective self-determination.

Collective Self-Determination as a Political Ideal

We have seen that Pannekoek articulated a coherent account of freedom as collective self-determination, which differed markedly from liberal and neo-republican conceptions of freedom. We should value Pannekoek's conception of freedom as collective self-determination because it resonates with similar conceptions practised by other marginalized groups engaged in a struggle for the expansion of their freedom. Our understanding of freedom should be able to explain its profound value for those directly engaged in emancipatory political struggles.[87] Political theory should have particular relevance in the context of liberation movements and political conflict over the meaning and practice of freedom. In these circumstances, we would expect our understanding of freedom to explain the appeal and motivational force of specific articulations of liberty by drawing from the political vocabulary of actors themselves engaged in struggle.

Numerous theorists and actors struggling for the expansion of freedom throughout the twentieth and twenty-first centuries have shared similar ideas of freedom as collective self-determination: from workers' movements, black liberation movements, women's liberation movements, decolonization movements, and national independence movements. This is not to say that all emancipatory struggles have shared exactly the same understanding of freedom, but there is enough of a family resemblance between the political discourses of different freedom struggles to be considered politically significant. Political actors and radical theorists as diverse as Martin Luther King Jr, Mahatma Ghandi, Angela Davis, Nelson Mandela, Fannie Lou Hammer, and Mikhail Bakunin held similar intuitions about the nature of freedom. All these freedom fighters considered freedom as a collective experience based on human interdependence; part of an ongoing movement and struggle; and a practice that requires the participation of its members.

This understanding of freedom as a collective experience challenges the individualist liberal definition. It recognizes the social production of individuals and the necessity of their mutual reliance on one another. An individual's ability to

[86] Castoriadis, *Political and Social Writings Volume 2 1955–1960*, 132.

[87] John Christman, 'Freedom in Times of Struggle: Positive Liberty Again', *Analyse & Kritik* 1/2 (2015), 171–88, 173.

develop their capacities and to live a self-determining life in a community depends on their interaction with other individuals in cooperative projects. The radical council theorists strove for the abolition of private property and class antagonisms, which they hoped would lead to a society in which the 'free development of each is the condition for the free development of all'.[88] Friedrich Engels, one of the direct influences on the council movements, argued that 'society cannot free itself unless every individual is freed.'[89] Emancipation is reached only 'by offering each individual the opportunity to develop all his faculties, physical and mental, in all directions and exercise them to the full'.[90] This line of political thinking about freedom continues into twentieth-century emancipatory political thought. According to Dr Martin Luther King Jr, 'we are caught in an inescapable network of mutuality, tied in a single garment of destiny. Whatever affects one directly, affects all indirectly.'[91] This is based on a recognition of the mutual interdependence and interconnection of individuals within society. According to this view, the freedom of others in society is a necessary condition of an individual's personal freedom, such that each individual can only be truly free on account of the reciprocal freedom of others.

The exercise of this freedom was conceived as part of an ongoing collective struggle, which Nelson Mandela memorably phrased as the long walk to freedom. King expressed a similar sentiment: 'Change does not roll in on the wheels of inevitability, but comes through continuous struggle.'[92] Freedom in this conception is not a condition, but an ongoing collective journey. It requires individuals to act collectively as part of a mass movement. Angela Davis writes, 'Progressive struggles . . . are doomed to fail if they do not also attempt to develop a consciousness of the insidious promotion of capitalist individualism.'[93] In each case freedom is conceived of as an ongoing struggle of political collectives rather than a condition of the absence of arbitrary power. This temporal dimension of freedom as a journey and process was important to how these movements understood and experienced freedom. Freedom considered as a practice emphasizes the dynamic aspects of strategies of resistance, which are determined by prior relations of forces and seek to expand future capacities.

From the perspective of a negative liberty theorist such as Ian Carter or Matthew Kramer, it would be more accurate to say that freedom can be measured at each moment of the journey as the number of choices each individual can make in their particular circumstances. While such a measurement is possible, it is not

[88] Marx, *The Communist Manifesto*.

[89] Friedrich Engels, 'Antidühring', in Karl Marx and Friedrich Engels, *Collected Works, Vol 25* (London: Lawrence and Wishart, 1975–2001), 279.

[90] Ibid., p. 280.

[91] Martin Luther King Jr, 'Letter from a Birmingham Jail'.

[92] Martin Luther King Jr, '"Accessed The Death of Evil upon the Seashore," speech delivered at the Cathedral of St. John the Divine', New York City, 17 May 1956.

[93] Angela Davis, *Freedom is a Constant Struggle: Ferguson, Palestine and the Foundations of a Movement* (Chicago: Haymarket Books, 2016), 19.

consistent with the manner in which these actors spoke about or practised freedom. For those who had the biggest stake in the struggle, freedom was defined as a collective struggle against forces of domination and participation in a process of self-determination. The attempt to rebrand this struggle in the language of negative liberty, for example by the historical memory of the black freedom movement, as it was mainly referred to by participants in the struggle, as the civil rights movements, reveals an important erasure of a particular conception of freedom.[94] Angela Davis was critical of how the language of civil rights began to colonize the space of freedom, which negated the more positive aspects of the black freedom programme and its connection to issues of jobs, poverty, power inequalities, and self-determination.

A conception of freedom as collective self-determination remains an attractive ideal which speaks to a deep intuitive understanding of democracy as a system of self-rule in which people actively participate in processes of self-government. While the dominant electoral understanding of democracy consists of a set of institutional arrangements involving free and fair elections, there persists a deeper desire for active participation in shaping the conditions of our common lives. Margaret Canovan writes of an ever-present 'redemptive' face of democracy, one which emphasizes that democracy consists of 'government of the people, by the people, for the people'.[95] For Canovan, this ideal conception of self-government is in constant tension with the more pragmatic understanding of democracy as an institutional arrangement for the mediation of political conflict. Freedom as collective self-determination resonates with public aspirations for popular participation in politics and the desire for a more direct connection between citizens and institutions of governance. Although it remains an ideal that would be difficult to fully realize, the notion of revitalizing democracy through greater levels of citizen participation points to the ongoing relevance of freedom as collective self-determination.

[94] Ibid., 20.

[95] Margaret Canovan, 'Trust the People! Populism and the Two Faces of Democracy', *Political Studies* 47 (1999), 2–16.

3
Building Workers' Power

Leading up to the German Revolution, prominent theorists within the workers' movement engaged in debate about the question of power in their fight for freedom. Key participants in this debate considered a struggle for power against the bourgeoisie as one of their most important immediate goals. They believed a socialist revolution could only be achieved through a challenge to entrenched power structures and a fundamental shift in the balance of wealth and power between classes. Creating lasting social change required building workers' power through independent workers' organizations and the development of workers' political agency. This chapter claims that the distribution of power in society was of central importance to these theorists, but that differences existed between those who advocated 'organization' (Kautsky) and those who advocated 'mobilization' (Luxemburg, Pannekoek) as the most effective method of developing the independent power of the working class. In this chapter, I theorize these two methods of political struggle through an analysis of the sources of political power, the role of unorganized workers, the dynamics of political struggle, and the desirability of parliamentary activity. An analysis of these debates helps shed light on their different approaches to political struggle of political actors during the Revolution.

In the early months of the German Revolution, the USPD was divided between radical and moderate factions on questions of revolutionary principles and strategy. These differences between the radicals (Spartacus League, Revolutionary Shop Stewards) and the Marxist 'centrists' (the right-wing of the USPD: Kautsky, Hilferding, Haase, and Breitscheid) can be traced back to a series of polemics leading up to the war, which brought to the surface new tensions and disagreements within the SPD (the USPD was founded in 1917). To understand the different positions that were adopted towards the councils it is useful to examine how debates over strategy shaped theorists' outlooks during the 1910–18 period. Members of the USPD were the main supporters of a permanent role for the councils in a future German socialist society. Even the moderate faction acknowledged the importance of the councils and saw a valuable role for them in a post-capitalist society. Although Kautsky could not be considered a 'councilist' in the traditional sense of the term, he was a key participant in public debates over the role of the councils which shaped the contours of discussion at the National Congress of Workers' and Soldiers' Councils in December 1918. His position as a leading theoretician of the right-wing of the USPD and role in debates with Luxemburg and Pannekoek justify his inclusion in this chapter in

Building Power to Change the World: The Political Thought of the German Council Movements. James Muldoon, Oxford University Press (2020). © James Muldoon. DOI: 10.1093/oso/9780198856627.003.0004

order to outline the development of strategic debates within the German workers' movement leading up to the revolution.

A common theme shared by all parties to this debate was the centrality of building workers' power as a necessary step to political transformation. These theorists understood power as the capacity to shape the public sphere through collective action, which involved a competition between different classes over the exercise of this capacity. They considered there to be three main sources of power for workers: material resources, strategic knowledge, and organizational capacity. In the first category, workers had the advantage of their greater numerical size and their position as essential components of the production process. Their weakness in this area was their relative lack of resources, weapons and institutional positions of power and authority. The second main source of power was workers' ideological development and their understanding of their oppression. Ideological backwardness was a major limitation of the council movements because of the continued dominance of bourgeois modes of thought. Finally, workers could overcome certain deficiencies in a lack of material resources through superior organization and discipline. These theorists believed it would be crucial for workers to develop greater relational capacity and strong networks that would enable collective action.

According to Kautsky's organization method, workers' power was most effectively developed, sustained, and exercised by well-funded, mass-member workers' organizations led by a centrally organized workers' party. The central feature of this strategy was the gradual development of independent worker-controlled organizations as the primary source of workers' power. Contrary to Luxemburg and Pannekoek's criticisms, this was not a 'parliamentary only' tactic, since it accorded an important role to street demonstrations and political agitation. However, it did conceive of parliament as the central site of political struggle and an important indicator of working-class power. For Kautsky, the most desirable method for the conquest of political power was through the attainment of a majority in parliament, which would lead to a final struggle with the bourgeoisie and a qualitative shift in the relation of forces between the two classes. He considered that a revolutionary situation could not be concocted by a minority of the population but could only arise through sufficient economic development and the support of the majority. As the timing of the arrival of a revolutionary situation could not be predicted in advance, the task of a workers' organization was to continually grow its strength through new members and parliamentary positions.

Workers' power, in this sense, could be measured through parliamentary seats, members' fees, and the capacity to call large-scale street demonstrations. With the workers' organizations as the central result of the accumulated victories of decades of struggle, Kautsky was cautious of engaging in actions that could provoke state repression and put the organizational structure in jeopardy. Underpinning this strategy of caution and restraint was a fear of a return to the repression of socialist organizations during the 1878–90 anti-socialist laws. Kautsky also believed that the German state and bourgeoisie were much stronger and better organized than in Russia, which increased the need for patience and the further development of working-class forces. He wished to avoid the excesses of the revolutions of the eighteenth and nineteenth centuries and believed that a more mature workers' movement could undertake a transition to a socialist society in a more peaceful and controlled manner.

Following this gradualist approach to the development of power in organizations, Kautsky ruled out any shortcuts to power through a sudden burst of revolutionary activity. He viewed the unorganized masses who were not members of socialist organizations with suspicion since they would be an unknown quantity in political struggle. Workers' organizations fulfilled a pedagogical function by providing long-term training and discipline to workers, which transformed their character and provided them with the necessary skills and habits for a socialist society. For Kautsky, unorganized workers suddenly caught up in mass action could not be relied upon for disciplined and unified action.

Alternative methods for developing workers' power were put forward by Rosa Luxemburg and Anton Pannekoek in a sharp polemic against Kautsky in a series of articles from 1910 to 1912. While Luxemburg and Pannekoek stressed different factors in their respective positions, they both saw themselves as advocating on behalf of the Left faction of the SPD in favour of more radical tactics and revolutionary action. For the Left, workers' power was most effectively developed through the direct activity of the masses in strikes and other forms of revolutionary struggle. Parliamentary elections were peripheral to the main activity of educating and organizing workers for class struggle. What truly mattered was workers' organization, class consciousness, and readiness to fight for their class interests. A strong workers' party was still essential to Pannekoek and Luxemburg, but for different reasons. The task of the party leadership was to support the revolutionary initiative of the masses and provide a unifying framework for workers during heightened political activity rather than acting as a directive body for political actions. The leadership should cultivate the inventiveness of the masses and help articulate the tactics and strategies arising from below.

Luxemburg and Pannekoek placed a greater emphasis on the subjective factors of political struggle and saw the true power of the workers as based in the development of their revolutionary consciousness rather than a formal organizational structure. Membership of a formal organization was not a decisive factor because power was located in the development of the political capacities of the masses. Both members and non-members of socialist organizations could participate in political action and receive pedagogical benefits. When Pannekoek and Luxemburg spoke about political activity they also considered the confrontational actions of strikes and demonstrations as superior to the bureaucratic training of party-related activities. Workers were more likely to develop a sharper awareness of class antagonisms through direct participation in class struggle against the bourgeoisie.

Luxemburg and Pannekoek were both critical of Kautsky's cautious approach and his rejection of the mass strike as an appropriate political tactic for the struggle for universal suffrage in Germany. They believed that the mass strike and other mass political actions enabled many new workers to be exposed to class struggle and that these had the potential for vastly increasing the number of workers engaged in political action. During a mass strike, workers across all industries could be motivated to mobilize in the streets and take action. They were sceptical of Kautsky's position that power could be incrementally built and stored through organization-building. For them, it had to be developed through clashes with the bourgeoisie. What Kautsky neglected, for the radicals, was that the power of the capitalist class had to be eroded through direct assaults on its main sources. There was no way in which workers' power could be gradually developed in a vacuum without confronting the bourgeoisie in political struggle. They highlighted a paradox in Kautsky's strategy of attrition: the larger the workers' movement became and the closer it was to its final goal, the more risk adverse it would need to be to preserve these hard-won gains. While Kautsky believed that the 1912 Reichstag elections would prove to be a significant and near decisive blow to the ruling class, he recommended no escalation in the struggle and a cautious approach to extralegal activity. They considered this passivity stifling for the revolutionary initiative of the masses, which would ultimately hinder the growth of workers' power.

In this chapter, I explain how these theorists conceptualized challenging the structural power of the bourgeoisie and shifting the balance of power between social classes. I outline three major sources of power for workers as theorized by Pannekoek and how the proletariat could maximize its opportunities to develop each aspect. I then contrast two different strategies for building workers' power and reveal the strengths and limitations of each approach.

The Road to Power

In a report by the Executive Council of the Workers' and Soldiers' Councils of Great Berlin, Richard Müller reminded delegates, '[a]ll political questions remain, in the end, questions of power.'[1] The question of the distribution of power in society was of central importance to council theorists and featured prominently as a major theme in their writings. Pannekoek believed that the value of specific

[1] Richard Müller, 'Speech given by Müller at the first General Congress of the Workers' and Soldiers' Councils of Germany, December 16, 1918', 31.

tactics such as parliamentarianism, trade unionism, and workplace agitation should be assessed from one central consideration: 'Here is the criterion for every form of action, for tactics and methods of fight, for forms of organization: do they enhance the power of the workers?'[2] For Pannekoek, the long-term ambition of creating a more just and egalitarian society must be preceded by a preliminary goal: 'the immediate objective of the class struggle is to increase the social power of the proletariat.'[3] Kautsky concurred with this view and considered that socialist strategy:

> begins with the assumption that the war against the present state and the present society must be waged in such a way as to constantly strengthen the proletariat and weaken its enemies... [it is] served by anything that disorganizes our enemies and undermines their authority and combativity, just as anything that contributes to organizing the proletariat, that widens its horizons and combativity increases the confidence of the popular masses in their organizations.[4]

The political thought of *Wilhelmine* Germany was dominated by a pervasive sense of power politics. Following the downfall of idealism in the aftermath of the failures of the 1848 revolutions, there was a turn away from the construction of abstract constitutional frameworks based on normative principles and a return to analyses of factual power relations. Realist approaches to politics began to flourish which attempted to examine more closely the nature of political power both in the national and international arenas. Authors such as August Ludwig von Rochau, Adolf Lasson, and Heinrich von Treitschke developed new visions of politics which supported Bismarck's ideal of German political unification and aggressive foreign policy. The military was a strong tool for social integration and 'penetrated the whole society with military values, ideas of honour, and the military manner of thinking and acting'.[5] While *Realpolitik* was initially developed as a defence of a conservative political ideology, it came to influence the workers' movement and its conceptions of the primacy of revolutionary strategy and the necessity of political conflict for achieving the goals of the movement. It was from within this era that the early Marxist-influenced workers' movement developed their political strategies.

This conception of the importance of an analysis of power relations was in opposition to those in Germany who argued for shifting people's views based on

[2] Pannekoek, *Workers' Councils.*

[3] Anton Pannekoek, *Die taktischen Differenzen der Arbeiterbewegung* (Hamburg: Erdmann Dubber, 1909), 13. Partially reprinted in Serge Bricianer, *Pannekoek and the Workers' Councils* (Saint Louis: Telos Press, 1983).

[4] Karl Kautsky, 'Eine Neue Strategie'. Quoted in Salvadori, *Karl Kautsky and the Socialist Revolution 1880–1938*, 145.

[5] Hans-Ulrich Wehler, *Das Deutsche Kaiserreich 1871 bis 1918* (Göttingen: Vandenhoeck u. Ruprecht, 1988), 158.

appealing to higher moral principles of cooperation and collective interest. From this perspective, it was hoped that reforms could be achieved by those in power voluntarily adopting new norms through the influence of democratic and ethical ideals without any recourse to coercion and violence. For thinkers such as Friedrich Förster, 'pedagogic' strategies were preferred to 'militaristic' ones as a method of breaking not only with the existing order, but also with previous modes of political conflict and power politics.[6] Förster argued that by depicting politics as a struggle for power, the workers' movement reduced civil life to a 'sphere of animality', and obscured the 'reality of the other life'.[7] He believed that the intensification of the conflict would only lead to increasing levels of violence and civil war. He doubted whether socialists could create a society based on peaceful cooperation and solidarity through the use of class struggle.[8] The workers' movement would be forced to adopt the techniques of power politics and would inevitably come to resemble their adversaries.[9]

Radical socialists, on the other hand, believed that social relations could only be transformed through a fundamental shift in the balance of power between classes. Luxemburg emphasized that 'political power, however, is for us socialists only a means. The end for which we must use this power is the fundamental transformation of the entire economic relations.'[10] They were concerned with the capacity for the ruling bourgeois minority to dominate workers through their control over resources, people, and ideas. They were acutely aware of the vast inequalities of power due to the position workers occupied in the production process, their lack of economic resources, their undeveloped sense of class consciousness and relative disorganization. Due to this fundamental imbalance in power between classes, the council movements sought to counteract the dominance of the bourgeoisie through undermining their opponents' primary sources of power and building workers' capacity for collective action. The development of workers' power would enable them to enact important social reforms and to push through an emancipatory political programme.

Although differences existed between them, theorists within the council movements tended to understand power as the capacity to shape the public sphere through collective action, which entailed an acknowledgement of the conflictual and consensual dimensions of power. Their conception of power included an antagonistic element due to the importance of class struggle and a fundamental clash of interests in their political analysis. Council theorists were aware of the decisive control that the bourgeoisie exercised over the state, economy, and society and realized they would have to confront this power head on. Yet power also

[6] Förster, *Weltpolitik und Weltgewissen.* [7] Ibid., 6, 14.

[8] Albert Dikovich, 'Heroismus und Sorge um das Selbst. 1919 im Lichte der frühen politisch-ethischen Schriften György Lukács', in *Die Ungarische Räterepublik 1919 in Lebensgeschichten und Literatur*, ed. Albert Dikovich and Edward Saunder (Vienna, 2017), 121–44.

[9] Förster, *Weltpolitik und Weltgewissen*, 144. [10] Luxemburg, 'The Socialization of Society'.

consisted of an important cooperative dimension: building workers' power involved the development of workers' ability to self-govern as a result of greater resources, knowledge, and organizational capacities. It was a creative and transformative power exercised through self-management in the production process and self-determination in social relations.

Amongst the complex debates in the literature on the nature of political power, two contrasting views stand out: power as domination ('power over'), whose proponents include Max Weber, Robert Dahl, and Steven Lukes; and power as empowerment ('power to'), presented by Hannah Arendt, Talcot Parsons, and Antonio Negri.[11] The definition of 'power over' proposed by Dahl, following Weber's classic formulation is: 'A has power over B to the extent that he can get B to do something that B would not otherwise do.'[12] While Dahl proposed a non-evaluative understanding of power, which remains neutral as to the moral evaluation of its use, Lukes believed the exercise of power over contains an intrinsically negative element because it implies an action contrary to a subject's interests. While 'power over' is not necessarily reducible to domination, this is usually how it is characterized in debates.[13] Hannah Arendt, on the other hand, defined power as a relational capacity for collective action, something that 'springs up between men when they act together and vanishes the moment they disperse', which, it has been argued, could simply refer to a different aspect of social reality than Lukes' three dimensions of power.[14] Antonio Negri differentiated *potestas* or 'power over', 'power in its fixed, institutional or "constituted form"' from *potentia* or 'capacity', 'power in its fluid, dynamic or "constitutive" form'.[15] Inspired by Spinoza, Negri considered *potentia* as a materialist power that mobilized itself through democratic revolutions and the living labour of the multitude, which would be lost and consumed within a constitutional system.

Although council theorists did not employ the terms 'power to' and 'power over', it is evident from the context of their writings that they were concerned with

[11] Max Weber, *Economy and Society: An Outline of an Interpretative Sociology, Vol. 1* (Berkeley and Los Angeles: University of California Press, 1978); Robert A., Dahl, 'The concept of power', *Behavioral Science* 2 (1957), 201–15; Steven Lukes, *Power: A Radical View.* 2nd ed. (Basingstoke: Palgrave Macmillan, 2005); Hannah Arendt, 'On Violence', in *Crises of the Republic* (New York, NY: Harcourt Brace Jovanovich, 1972); Talcott Parsons, 'On the concept of power', *Proceedings of the American Philosophical Society* 107 (1963), 232–62; Antonio Negri, *Insurgencies: Constituent Power and the Modern State* (Minneapolis: University of Minnesota Press. 1999).

[12] Dahl, 'The concept of power', 202–3.

[13] For an alternative account, Pamela Pansardi conceives of the debate as consisting of an underlying account of 'power to' as the ability of an agent to achieve one's ends and 'power over' as a subset of this, involving a second agent in the achievement of the first agent's aims. Pamela Pansardi 'Power to and power over: two distinct concepts of power?', *Journal of Political Power* 5, no. 1 (2012), 73–89.

[14] Hannah Arendt, *The Human Condition* (Chicago: The University of Chicago Press, 1998), 200. Mark Haugaard, 'Power: a "family resemblance" concept', *European Journal of Cultural Studies* 13, no. 4 (2010), 1–20.

[15] Antonio Negri, *Subversive Spinoza* (Manchester: Manchester University Press, 2008).

both of these aspects of power. Their primary goal in political struggle was to build the strength and power of workers in order to reduce relations of domination in society. There are instances in the council theorists' writings in which they are concerned primarily with power as a zero-sum struggle between two antagonistic social classes. Their analyses of the nature of the bourgeoisie's power was often framed in antagonistic terms of how this power could be challenged and overcome. Council theorists had no illusions about the threat the bourgeoisie posed to their political programme and the extent to which they would try to resist it. Luxemburg acknowledged that the ruling class would 'mobilize heaven and hell against the proletariat', which meant that the proletariat would require power to enact their programme:

> It is sheer insanity to believe that capitalists would goodhumoredly obey the socialist verdict of a parliament or of a national assembly, that they would calmly renounce property, profit, the right to exploit. All ruling classes fought to the end, with tenacious energy, to preserve their privileges.[16]

As the workers' movements aimed to dismantle the capacity of the bourgeoisie to extract wealth from the labour of workers, they could expect to be met with profound resistance. Luxemburg and the council theorists did not pretend that this could be achieved without conflict and a confrontation of physical force. This is why the radical council theorists advocated disbanding the military and arming a workers' militia. For Luxemburg:

> The violence of the bourgeois counterrevolution must be confronted with the revolutionary violence of the proletariat. Against the attacks, insinuations, and rumors of the bourgeoisie must stand the inflexible clarity of purpose, vigilance, and ever ready activity of the proletarian mass. Against the threatened dangers of the counter-revolution, the arming of the people and disarming of the ruling classes. Against the parliamentary obstructionist maneuvers of the bourgeoisie, the active organization of the mass of workers and soldiers. Against the omnipresence, the thousand means of power of bourgeois society, the concentrated, compact, and fully developed power of the working class.[17]

In the face of 'frantic attempts to re-establish their system of exploitation through blood and slaughter', workers would require the strength to repress counter-revolutionary forces.[18] Yet herein lay a profound difficulty for the council theorists. While the revolution needed to defend itself, it also sought to restructure society according to principles which were diametrically opposed to those of class

[16] Luxemburg, 'What Does the Spartacus League Want?'.
[17] Ibid.
[18] Luxemburg, 'Our Program and the Political Situation'.

domination. The aim of the council movements was not simply to gain power and take over the instruments of the state for their own benefit. They took seriously Marx's realization that 'workers could not simply seize the power of the state.'[19] Their goal was not a reversal of places such that the proletariat would replace the bourgeoisie as a dominating class in society. Pannekoek noted that 'capitalism cannot be annihilated by a change in the commanding persons; but only by the abolition of commanding.'[20]

Their understanding of power was more multifaceted than the classic Weberian definition of power as unilateral domination, i.e. control over the actions of another.[21] Workers sought to develop their power to counteract the domination of the bourgeoisie and institute a classless society in which economic assets would be collectively managed and society would be democratically organized. For the council theorists, the emancipation of the working class should bring about an end to the exploitation and domination inherent in capitalist relations of production. The proletariat's power would be employed for the purpose of an emancipatory programme in which all individuals could participate in the collective self-determination of society. While this would entailed the repression of forces that sought to maintain relationships of domination in society, the ultimate goal was to develop workers' capacities for self-determination. In this sense, council theorists often employed the terms 'strength', 'capacity', 'energy', and the 'self-activity' of workers to emphasize that at the basis of a self-determining society was not a dominating power but a creative and cooperative capacity of collective action.

Three Sources of Power

Council theorists were attentive to different sources of power and sought to devise strategies for how they could be developed. One account that succinctly captures the main concerns of the council movement theorists is an early work by Pannekoek, *Tactical Differences in the Workers' Movement*.[22] Pannekoek theorized three main sources of power for workers: material resources, strategic knowledge, and organizational capacity.[23] Although there were differences between council theorists, Kautsky approvingly quoted Pannekoek's analysis of these three sources of power and shared a similar basic understanding. They agreed that it was through a growth in material resources, ideological awareness, and greater levels of organization that the working class could develop its power.[24] In

[19] Karl Marx, 'The Civil War in France'.

[20] Anton Pannekoek, 'The Failures of the Working Class'.

[21] Weber defines power as 'the probability that one actor within a social relationship will be in position to carry out his own will despite resistance'. Weber, *Economy and Society*, 53.

[22] Pannekoek, *Die taktischen Differenzen der Arbeiterbewegung*. [23] Ibid., 19.

[24] Kautsky, 'Die neue Taktik'.

the first category, workers had the advantage of their greater numerical size and their position as an essential component of the production process. Their weakness in this area was their relative lack of resources, weapons, and positions of institutional authority. The second main source of power referred to workers' ideological development. For Pannekoek, ideological backwardness was the major limitation of the German workers' movement because of the continued dominance of bourgeois modes of thought. It would only be through a greater understanding of their oppression in capitalist society and the development of a new proletarian culture that workers could build this aspect of their power. Finally, workers could overcome certain deficiencies in a lack of material power through superior organization and discipline. It would be crucial for workers to develop greater relational capacity and strong networks that would enable collective action. This required workers to develop organizations to enhance their agency and experience in political struggle.

The first source of power for the bourgeoisie was their position as the dominant class in society, which granted them control over material and economic resources. Gorter believed that at the centre of the bourgeoisie's material power stood its control of banking capital. This was because 'West-European (and American) society and State have become one big, thoroughly organized whole, which is entirely controlled, moved and regulated by banking capital.'[25] He described this capital as 'the blood, flowing through the entire body, and nourishing all its branches'.[26] It provided the bourgeoisie with resources extracted from the labour of the workers. It also united other smaller classes against the proletariat in defence of the small gains they received from it. Control over capital also placed the bourgeoisie in a position of command over industry and production. For Pannekoek, the bourgeoisie's 'strength comes from the fact that it leads in all the principal branches of production', allowing it to continue to benefit from surplus value.[27] The ownership and control over the vast majority of society's wealth placed the bourgeoisie in a strategically enviable position, which the workers could only overcome with great effort.

Yet in terms of material power, the workers held two distinct advantages. The first was size. By sheer number the proletariat was much larger than the bourgeoisie and appeared to be growing in size. To capitalize on this advantage it was imperative that the workers themselves be involved in mass actions rather than just relying on the actions of their leaders. Second, the workers occupied an indispensable position in the production process. They supplied the labour through which surplus value was created. Without the workers, the whole system would break down and could be brought to a halt through mass strikes. Workers were the essential element, which could operate by itself in a self-determining

[25] Gorter, 'Open Letter to Comrade Lenin'. [26] Ibid.
[27] Bricianer, *Pannekoek and the Workers' Councils*, 77.

society rendering the role of factory owners redundant. In political struggle, workers could draw upon these structural advantages and use them in their favour.

However, without a clear understanding of their oppression and the will power and tactical know-how to fight, workers would endure the domination of their oppressors. Kautsky considered that 'what the proletariat lacks is a consciousness of its own strength.'[28] For Pannekoek, 'class consciousness alone enables this vast, muscular, inert body to bestir itself into life and activity.'[29] Herman Gorter, a leading theoretician in the Dutch Left, concurred that it was not the sheer number of the proletariat that would prove decisive, 'its power [was] based above all on its quality.'[30] Pannekoek saw that 'the bourgeoisie possessed another hidden source of power', the 'ideological hold over the proletariat' because 'the proletarian masses were still completely governed by a bourgeois mentality.'[31] The greatest source of strength for the bourgeoisie was not its dominance of political and economic institutions but its ideological control over culture. This can be related to Lukes' third dimension of power: an ideological power of shaping workers' values, identities, and desires in a manner which leads them to acquiesce in their own domination.[32] The proletariat's embrace of bourgeois ideas and structures of thinking meant that even when workers possessed sufficient material power and gained a tactical advantage in the German Revolution, they failed to institute workers' control over production. As a result, for Pannekoek, a material uprising against the bourgeoisie must be preceded by a struggle against bourgeois mentalities and the creation of a new proletarian culture: 'Spiritual emancipation, self-thought is the precondition for material liberation, for self-action.'[33]

For Pannekoek, the development of the proletariat's spiritual power required two elements: theory and ideology. Together they provided workers with a knowledge of capitalist oppression, an understanding of the importance of solidarity, and a belief in their capacity for self-determination. Ideology arose out of the daily experience of workers, which provides them with an immediate understanding of their oppression in capitalist relations of production. Ideology formed the basis of class consciousness, but it must be further developed to serve a revolutionary purpose. From an immediate knowledge of the material conditions of their lives, workers must construct a mental picture of a new self-determined society in which they would self-manage production. Theory is what allowed them to turn 'blind, instinctive social actions into conscious well-thought-out social

[28] Kautsky, *The Road to Power*.
[29] Pannekoek, *Die taktischen Differenzen der Arbeiterbewegung*, 17.
[30] Gorter, 'Open Letter to Comrade Lenin'.
[31] Pannekoek, 'World Revolution and Communist Tactics'.
[32] Lukes, *Power: A Radical View*, 27.
[33] Pannekoek, 'Bildungsarbeit', *Zeitungskorrespondenz* (135) 3 September 1910. Quoted in John Gerber, *Anton Pannekoek and the Socialism of Workers' Self-Emancipation*, 1873–1960 (Dordrecht: Kluwer Academic Publishers, 1989) 57.

actions'.[34] It enabled workers to 'rise from unconscious drives to fully conscious, purpose-minded men'.[35] Pannekoek believed that 'our power lies in the deep understanding of the laborers for every detail of capitalism, in other words in the socialistic knowledge, in the theory of socialism.'[36] The process of the development of revolutionary consciousness began with knowledge of capitalist exploitation and developed through an interplay of economic development and working-class activity.

Pannekoek believed that a widespread cultural transformation would be necessary to achieve this aim. The development of class consciousness would proceed step by step through 'waging a relentless battle against the traditional ideas to which the ruling classes are clinging'.[37] Ultimately, 'the workers see themselves changed into new men with new habits, into men who feel closely united with their comrades as integral parts of a body animated by one and the same will.'[38] This would be constituted by a 'spirit of proletarian morality, of solidarity, of the feeling of belonging to a class', and motivated by 'the conviction that collective interest must take precedence over personal interests'.[39] In a proletarian culture, issues such as the promotion of education, healthcare, measures to alleviate poverty and suffering would all be of primary concern. In order to achieve this, workers must struggle against the role of traditional ideas left over from past systems of thought and deeply engrained bourgeois mentalities, which ran contrary to the spirit and consciousness needed for revolutionary activity. Finally, workers would 'form a community that is increasingly close-knit, and therefore capable of taking on the administration of society as a whole'.[40]

The third, and potentially most important, source of power in addition to material and ideological power was organizational capacity. Pannekoek noted that 'as long as a class remains splintered in distinct units, each one having a different objective, they cannot pretend to exercise the least power.... organization unifies these disparate wills and roots them in a single will, that of the masses henceforth endowed with cohesion.'[41] It was for this reason that Pannekoek considered organization 'the chief principle in the working class fight for emancipation'.[42] Working-class organization referred to the institutional structures and patterns of behaviour that facilitated workers to act collectively and enabled them to counteract the entrenched power of the bourgeoisie. It concerned how workers could form lasting bonds, engage in deliberation and debate, coordinate actions, and pursue a common goal. Pannekoek noted that ideological development was

[34] Pannekoek, *Die taktischen Differenzen der Arbeiterbewegung*, 25. [35] Ibid., 132.
[36] Pannekoek, 'Socialism and Religion'.
[37] Pannekoek, *The Position and Significance of J. Dietzgan's Philosophical Works*, 12–13.
[38] Pannekoek, *Die taktischen Differenzen der Arbeiterbewegung*, 94. [39] Ibid., 76.
[40] Pannekoek, 'Party and Working Class'.
[41] Pannekoek, *Die taktischen Differenzen der Arbeiterbewegung*, 18.
[42] Pannekoek, 'General Remarks on the Question of Organization'.

not enough: 'however knowledge is used, it is insufficient when the power to act is missing. What can the thinking head do without a strong arm to carry out what is thought?'[43] This required strong organizations capable of creating the conditions that enabled workers to act collectively. Yet on the question of organization, a significant difference emerged between the radicals and Kautsky.

The Meaning of Organization

Kautsky thought that the main task for socialists should be developing workers' power through strengthening its organizations. He described this programme as 'building up the organization, the conquest of all positions of power, which we are capable of seizing and holding through our own strength, the study of state and society and enlightenment of the masses'.[44] The central worker-led organizations were the party, the unions, and the press. It was important that these were worker-controlled institutions that retained an independence from bourgeois elements. Kautsky also considered that these 'real concrete organizations' consisted in formal structures with decision-making rules, fee-paying members, and an accountable leadership hierarchy. These institutions would play a central role in educating workers in class politics and would also enable them to pool resources and coordinate actions. An elected leadership that is democratically accountable to its members was essential in ensuring that 'the goals and methods of struggle at least generally, if not always in detail, are set by the mass.'[45] Without formal organizations, the leaders that emerged in revolutionary situations remained institutionally unaccountable. The formal aspects of the organization were essential to Kautsky to ensure the legitimacy of decisions and the accountability of its leadership. The economic resources gathered through membership fees also provided an important source of the organization's power that could be used to support workers in political struggle. Kautsky contended:

> One of the main effects that the organization has on the character of the worker consists in the confidence on the material support of the collectivity, which the individual finds. This support finds a very strong expression in the resources which the unions muster and collect for emergencies and the struggle.[46]

If the state were provoked to arrest the leaders, seize the funds, and outlaw an organization, this would cripple the workers' movement and deal a potentially fatal blow to the struggle. Without these formal structures, workers would no longer be able to act through the same democratically established rules and

[43] Pannekoek, *Die taktischen Differenzen der Arbeiterbewegung*, 18.
[44] Kautsky, 'Die Aktion der Masse'. [45] Ibid. [46] Kautsky, 'Die neue Taktik'.

procedures and would have to resort to secretive meetings of a small minority. While this was not the historical reality during the banning of the SPD in Germany during the late nineteenth century, it did appear to be one of Kautsky's grave concerns.

The central disagreement between Kautsky and Pannekoek was whether the formal or spiritual dimensions of an organization should be considered as primary. Both parties were agreed that one important function of an organization was the development of working-class consciousness. For Kautsky, organizations would enable 'teaching the workers how to use the powers arising at any given stage of economic development in the most effective manner and by preventing the waste of those powers'.[47] But Pannekoek went further still. He considered that the essence of organization was the transformation in the character of workers and that the term 'organization' best described the habits of discipline, solidarity, and self-sacrifice that workers learnt through political struggle. 'But what transforms a great number of people into an organization?' asked Pannekoek, 'Discipline.'[48] It was discipline, 'the cement of organization', which Pannekoek argued would form 'the spiritual bond which creates an energetic, compact mass out of hitherto scattered units.'[49] Kautsky disagreed with this emphasis, contending that 'the organization revolutionizes the character of the proletarian. But this revolution is surely the *effect* and not the *essence* of the organization.'[50]

In the polemic, each theorist accused the other of only recognizing one element of the dialectic relationship between formal organization and the development of working-class consciousness. However, when viewed from a less partial perspective, it can be seen that both parties acknowledged the relationship between organization and consciousness but disagreed on the relative emphasis on each pole. Pannekoek argued that 'there is no disagreement between us as to the need for the workers to equip themselves as well as possible with powerful centralized associations that have adequate funds at their disposal.'[51] But for Pannekoek it was 'the spirit of organization' that was the 'active principle which alone endows the framework of organization with life and energy'.[52] He considered that attacks by the government on workers' organization could only 'destroy the external form, but not its internal essence'. Pannekoek argued that Kautsky ignored the class character of workers' organizations, which, unlike other apolitical associations, instilled in workers an inner sense of solidarity that could not be broken through dismantling their rules and statutes. Due to the development of habitual practices, 'the masses in which this spirit dwells will always regroup themselves in new organizations.'[53] For Pannekoek, there was little risk in pursuing more aggressive

[47] Kautsky, *The Road to Power*.
[48] Pannekoek, *Die taktischen Differenzen der Arbeiterbewegung*, 18. [49] Ibid.
[50] Kautsky, 'Die neue Taktik'. [51] Pannekoek, 'Marxist Theory and Revolutionary Tactics'.
[52] Ibid. [53] Ibid.

strategies because the workers' movement could be reconstituted following any frontal assaults by government forces.

On this point, it could be argued that Pannekoek underestimated the importance of both the material element of economic resources and the formal element of leadership structures and decision-making processes. A seizure of the funds of the workers' organization could constitute a significant blow that could prevent the workers' movement from employing professional organizers, printing newspapers, supporting striking workers, and paying for general organizational expenses. If prominent experienced leaders were imprisoned, it would take time and energy to train new ones. If the unions and workers' parties were outlawed, the very methods of the workers' movement of open organizing, large public assemblies, and accountable leadership structures would be ineffective. But what real risk was there of such a turn of events?

In the early twentieth century, the government could have moved towards more naked methods of repression that had been employed in suppressing previous working-class movements in the nineteenth century. Pannekoek argued that the working class could adapt to such repression, but there was a certain idealism in his position that workers could spontaneously regroup into new organizations and have the same organized levels of power as before. Kautsky's fears were based on the possibility that power developed within workers' organizations could be depleted through government attacks. Pannekoek mistakenly assumed that the workers' movement had such a formless character that any decrease in its economic resources would ultimately prove inconsequential. Even well-disciplined and trained individuals require resources, coordination, and formal structures to act effectively in anything more than a single street demonstration. Yet in Pannekoek's defence, it could be argued that the history of the Anti-Socialists Laws proves the opposite point and that the SPD thrived in the 1880s even with the direct repression of the state. The history of the workers' movement, Pannekoek could argue, proves the flexibility of workers even in the face of overt oppression.

Kautsky considered that workers organized in formal organizations such as a party and unions were vastly superior as a political force to unorganized workers participating in mass actions. Without a formal organization, a mass of workers gathered for a street demonstration could not accomplish any positive political steps such as formulating strategies, making democratic decisions, or creating new laws and institutions. Mass actions were important as part of the workers' movement, but they were most useful for 'the removal of despised persons or institutions' and other acts of resistance.[54] For the more positive work of long-term organizing and political struggle, formal organizations were necessary.

[54] Kautsky, 'Die Aktion der Masse'.

He also considered that such a long-term political struggle should be led by democratically elected leaders of a workers' party. Such leaders in Kautsky's conception would play a decisive role in the formulation of strategies and the direction of the movement. The masses could participate through deliberation and debate in workers' assemblies and through electing leaders, but the party members should adhere to strict discipline in political action. It was only through establishing a unified position and acting in a coordinated manner that the workers' movement could exercise its power against their better resourced capitalist opponents.

Rosa Luxemburg challenged this conception of the role of the workers' organization in her argument for the use of militant mass strikes in the Prussian struggle for universal suffrage in 1910. She argued that the tentativeness of the leadership was holding the masses back and would lead to their disillusionment and the collapse of political action. For Luxemburg:

> A party, such as German Social Democracy, which upholds the principle of organization and party discipline in an unprecedented manner virtually eliminates the initiative of the unorganized masses and their spontaneous and, as it were, improvised ability to act—which until now has been an important and often decisive factor in all great political struggles.[55]

The major problem of the Social Democratic Party in Germany was its tendency to view the masses as a passive force that could be directed and controlled by the party leadership. For Luxemburg, the role of the organization should be to foster the 'growing self-activity, self-determination and initiative' of the masses and to increase their capacity for political action.[56] Luxemburg diagnosed the problem of the inevitable bureaucratization of large organizations in which leaders have a 'strongly developed feeling of responsibility that unquestionably has a strongly paralysing effect on initiative and determination'.[57] The party and unions should not be in charge of educating and commanding the masses, but rather should be facilitating action through the exercise of its leadership. For Luxemburg, the most ideal party executive would be one that functioned as 'the most obedient, most prompt and most precise tool of the will of the entire party.'[58] Luxemburg recognized that 'campaigns of the party on this scale require uniformity and unity in order to be most effective.' But it should respond to the initiative of the base and help cultivate their actions. There was still an important role for a party leadership, which remained the 'most enlightened and conscious vanguard of the proletariat'.[59] Yet their role was different from what the SPD party and union leaders were used to: 'the task of Social democracy consists, not in the preparation

[55] Luxemburg, 'The Next Step'. [56] Luxemburg, 'Mass Action'. [57] Ibid. [58] Ibid.
[59] Luxemburg, 'The Mass Strike'.

or technical leadership of the strike, but in the political leadership of the movement as a whole.'[60]

Organization and Political Struggle

In addition to debates on the nature and role of workers' organizations, theorists disagreed on the relationship between organization and political struggle. The essential contribution of Luxemburg and Pannekoek was that the strength of the workers' movement could only be developed through its active participation in revolutionary class struggle. For Luxemburg, 'strong organizations prove themselves only in bitter struggles', which indicated their power in action and enabled the inclusion of previously inactive layers of workers in struggle. According to this conception, organization was a product of struggle, rather than struggle only being possible with a sufficiently developed organization. For Pannekoek, 'it is only by the struggle for power itself that the masses can be assembled, drilled and formed into an organization capable of taking power.'[61] While Kautsky emphasized the threat of open political struggle for existing workers' organizations, Luxemburg and Pannekoek highlighted the risk of inactivity and stagnation. To fail to lead the masses and to fall behind their radical demands would be equally disastrous for the workers' movement as it would lead to widespread disillusionment and cynicism. While mass action posed a risk of state repression and the discouragement of some workers, 'the great action will arouse new groups of the proletariat and will bring the organization's ideas into new circles.'[62]

Kautsky believed that the strength of the workers' movement lay in its capacity to organize and pose an alternative to bourgeois authority rather than in its ability to disrupt production through strikes. Before the working class could engage in a decisive struggle against the bourgeoisie, workers would need to develop their organization through other political activities. Kautsky believed that building workers' organizations, agitation for reforms, and participation in parliamentary activity all assisted with the development of workers' consciousness. Workers should only engage in a mass strike when they had a sufficient level of democratic organization to be able to pose an alternative to the authority of capitalists following the seizure of political power. If organized workers did not constitute a majority of the population—measured by parliamentary support—then attempting to seize power would constitute a minority takeover. This, Kautsky believed, would be an irresponsible shortcut to power and would possibly lead to a civil war and repressive measures against dissenting minorities. Once the workers' organization had developed sufficiently to gain majority support, it would be able

[60] Ibid. [61] Pannekoek, 'Marxist Theory and Revolutionary Tactics'.
[62] Luxemburg, 'The Next Step'.

to legislate socialist measures through parliament and resort to extralegal forms of force only if the bourgeoisie attempted to resist these measures. Kautsky's idea was for the gradual and incremental development of power to occur through a rise in members, votes, and resources. In Kautsky's eyes, more aggressive tactics posed a risk to this vision through a gamble on an exponential increase in power, which put all of the hard-won organizing of the previous decades in danger.

Underlying these distinctive conceptions of struggle lay different analyses of the revolutionary situation. For Luxemburg and Pannekoek, the Russian Revolution of 1905 signalled the intensification of conflict between the proletariat and capitalists and the beginning of a new phase of heightened activity. Luxemburg considered the method of the mass strike as universally applicable and rejected Kautsky's claim of distinctive conditions in the West, which made the use of the mass strike unadvisable. Luxemburg also claimed that the German government and capitalist class was much weaker than Kautsky believed and that the workers' movement needed to increase the pressure through more adversarial tactics. For Kautsky, because the workers' movement still lacked a majority in parliament, the SPD should focus its energies on the parliamentary elections of 1912. Commencing a mass strike prior to these elections risked raising expectations of further gains that could not be met and lead to a depression in the SPD's vote share. Kautsky believed that gains in parliamentary seats would significantly increase the power of workers and change the situation between the parties. He argued that the election would lead to 'a powerful leap forward' and that 'in a few years we will gain the absolute majority of the votes cast.'[63] The danger was that socialists would 'be led astray by impatience' and adopt more drastic methods that would raise workers' expectations and potentially provoke an armed confrontation with the state.

Because the workers were not yet strong enough to assault the capitalist state in a full frontal attack, Kautsky advocated a 'strategy of attrition' in which the workers' movement would 'not go forward directly to the decisive struggle, but prepares it for a long time, and only begins it when it knows that its opponent is sufficiently weakened'.[64] In the meantime, the proletariat should strive 'to gradually wear them out by continual exhaustion and threats and to consistently reduce their resistance and paralyse them'.[65] When the forces of the working class have been sufficiently prepared and a favourable situation presented itself, the workers' movement would then switch to a strategy of overthrow in order to seize political power. This called for a distinction between two forms of political activity: during the attrition phase workers' should struggle for reforms and carry out agitation through trade union and parliamentary activity, while during the overthrow the mass strike could be deployed. Kautsky did not believe that a period

[63] Kautsky, 'Was Nun?'. [64] Ibid. [65] Ibid.

of mass strikes would be possible under existing conditions in Germany. For him, a mass strike could only be employed as:

> a one-time event into which the entire proletariat of the Reich enters with its entire strength; as a struggle to the death; as a struggle which either overthrows our enemies, or smashes—or at least cripples—the totality of our organizations and our entire strength for years on end.[66]

Kautsky qualified this by adding that the mass strike would follow a period of mass actions and rising class antagonisms, but with the mass strike used as the final weapon in the seizure of political power. Kautsky's logic overlooked the possibility of large unexpected events rupturing the day-to-day routine of meetings and parliamentary activity and creating an explosion of mass activity that could provide resources for the movement. The fear that taking part in such activity could blow up in the faces of the socialists and lead them to lose everything deterred him from being open to more antagonistic strategies:

> The worst defeat would be...if we summoned the proletariat to the political mass strike and it did not respond to the appeal by an overwhelming majority.... We would nip in the bud all the promising seeds being nurtured in the coming Reichstag elections if, without it being necessary we provoked struggles which brought us heavy defeats.[67]

There is a problem with the internal consistency of Kautsky's argument stemming from the artificial separation of a period of steady growth in the power of the working class and the final overthrow of the bourgeoisie. The means Kautsky sought to employ for building workers' power did not allow the workers' movement to take advantage of moments of upsurge in political activity by adopting more aggressive tactics that could grow the movement. Nor did they include important political activities that would be necessary to radicalize workers and deplete the power of the capitalists. Luxemburg wondered how the great mass of the proletariat that had not yet been organized by the SPD could be reached without the heightening of conflict and the expansion of political struggle:

> how are they suddenly, with one leap, to be ready for a 'final' mass strike 'to the death' unless a preceding period of tempestuous mass struggles, demonstration strikes, partial mass strikes, giant economic struggles, etc., loosens them little by little from their paralysis, their slavish obedience, their fragmentation, and incorporates them among the followers of Social Democracy?[68]

[66] Ibid. [67] Ibid. [68] Luxemburg, 'Theory and Practice'.

For Luxemburg, Kautsky's privileging of trade union and parliamentary activity had not provided an adequate strategy to obtain majority support for socialism and to reach a moment of overthrow. The danger in doing too little was that the movement would not develop properly and the organized sections of the movement would not be able to take in increasingly larger sections of the unorganized workers.

Kautsky also neglected strategies through which the workers' movement could weaken the power of the bourgeoisie. His strategy involved a gradual increase in the workers' power through parliamentary activity, but he had little to say about how the bourgeoisie's power would be diminished rather than both parties simply increasing their strength. The mobilization theory of Pannekoek and Luxemburg, which placed a greater emphasis on open hostilities, sought to show the necessity of 'the most potent forms of action', which would be aimed at 'liquidating the powers of coercion available to the enemy and building up our own strength'.[69] Pannekoek offered the example of a large street demonstration as an illustration in which the police had to abandon their attempts to prevent the demonstration due to its enormous size. He viewed this as the first moments of the state's incapacity to assert its authority and control over the workers' movement. Effective forms of action had to consider how workers' strength could be increased, but also how it could sap the organizational capacity and authority of the capitalist class.

In many respects, Luxemburg and Pannekoek put forward a more robust political strategy of increasing pressure and agitation based on the idea of the revolution as a permanent and ongoing process of political struggle. Pannekoek noted that 'revolution is a *process*, the first stages of which we are now experiencing.'[70] As a result, there could be no withholding of forces until a later more suitable moment. The role of the workers' party should be to lead the struggle forward and to intensify the conflict through mass actions and offensive tactics. Luxemburg eloquently described the proper role of the workers' party in such conditions:

> a real mass action in the grand style can only be kindled and at length maintained when treated, not as a dry practice piece played to the time of, the party leadership's baton, but as a great class struggle in which all significant economic conflicts must be utilized to the full and all forces which arouse the masses must be guided into the vortex of the movement, and in which one doesn't shun a mounting intensification of the situation and decisive struggles, but goes to meet them with resolute, consistent tactics.[71]

[69] Pannekoek, 'Marxist Theory and Revolutionary Tactics'. [70] Ibid.
[71] Luxemburg, 'Theory and Practice'.

Pannekoek also insisted that such struggle should not be seen as divided between a preparatory and final stage. Every action should be assessed on its own merit based on the prevailing conditions and be viewed as part of a single unfolding revolutionary process. Instead of waiting for a final victory, action had to be taken in the present to build towards the growth of the workers' movement and the intensification of the class conflict: 'Each assault by the proletariat upon the individual effects of capitalism means a weakening of the power of capital, a strengthening of our own power and a step further in the process of revolution.'[72] Pannekoek and Luxemburg developed an approach which emphasized the intensifying logic of political struggle and the capacity to further mobilize unorganized workers as part of the revolutionary process. Although this theory also relied upon a strong role for a central leadership, this could be considered a 'mobilization' theory due to the importance of the revolutionary activity of the masses and the significant role that would be played by previously unorganized workers mobilized through the struggle. This was a major point of contention between Luxemburg and Kautsky both during the mass strike debates and the revolutionary events of 1918/19. Luxemburg believed that the base of support for socialism could be greatly expanded during times of revolutionary activity due to the pedagogic function of participating in political action. She argued that a few months of participating in a mass action was more effective than years of bureaucratic meetings and party activities. For Luxemburg, 'mass demonstrations have their own logic and their own psychology... They must be intensified, concentrated and must take on new and more effective forms.'[73] For Luxemburg, the best defence was a good offence. The workers' movement needed to push forward in their campaigns and not let off the pressure or allow their adversaries to believe that workers would step down after concessions were made. In terms of the immediate campaign for universal suffrage, she argued that 'a vigorous and successful mass offensive on the question of suffrage will be the best and most secure guarantee of the right to vote in the Reichstag elections.'[74]

Pannekoek and Luxemburg both argued for the importance of unorganized workers in political struggle. The campaign should not be restricted to party members, as it should be ready to expand to include workers who would be politicized in the course of the struggle. As the campaign develops, those who are implicated in the struggle broadens such that the campaign becomes an opportunity to spread socialism in a short period of time to a much larger segment of the population. Pannekoek argued that during these periods of heightened activity it is not party membership but class consciousness that is the decisive factor. The aim of political struggle is to extend this class character of the masses to broader sections of the working class through a strategy of mass mobilization.

[72] Pannekoek, 'Marxist Theory and Revolutionary Tactics'.
[73] Luxemburg, 'Theory and Practice'. [74] Ibid.

For Pannekoek, a spirit of solidarity and discipline were produced through political struggle rather than membership of a socialist organization:

> this transformation of human nature in the proletariat is primarily the effect of the conditions under which the workers live, trained as they are to act collectively by the shared experience of exploitation in the same factory, and secondarily a *product of class struggle*, that is to say militant action on the part of the organization; it would be difficult to argue that such activities as electing committees and counting subscriptions make much contribution in this respect.[75]

Kautsky considered that the unorganized masses would add an unpredictable element into the conflict. As they could not be controlled by the party leadership this could result in an escalating confrontation and the destruction the workers' movement. Pannekoek replied that the unorganized masses would take their cues from the organized and through a logic of intensification would develop class consciousness through their revolutionary activity. The radicals had faith in the self-developmental cycle of revolutionary action and its capacity to educate and cultivate the masses.

The Political Agency of the Masses

Luxemburg and Pannekoek advocated for the workers' party to increase the political capacity of the masses as one of the primary means to enhance the power of the workers' movement. Rather than emphasize the importance of parliamentary activity, they considered that it was the workers themselves who should be the central agents of political change and administrators of a self-determining society. They were critical of all forms of substitutionism that placed more emphasis on the role of experts, leaders, and bureaucrats who would act on behalf of the workers. Real power lay in a mobilized and class-conscious mass movement rather than winning seats in a bourgeois parliament. The most important task for the workers' movement was to train and mobilize the masses and cultivate their political agency. For Kautsky, there were limits to what could be achieved purely through mass actions. Institutional positions within parliament were important for developing his vision of the transition to a socialist society. While both sides of the debate considered some parliamentary activity to be important alongside mass action, they differed in their emphasis. As part of this debate, Pannekoek went one step further than Luxemburg in his criticisms of parliamentary activity and his attack on the state, which was one of the earliest

[75] Pannekoek, 'Marxist Theory and Revolutionary Tactics'.

statements of a more radical critique of the state as an organization of the bourgeoisie.

Due to the importance he placed on bureaucratic and administrative skills, Kautsky tended to valorize the pedagogic benefits of activity within the party. For Kautsky, a socialist society should be structured in a way that maximized the potential capacity of workers to participate in processes of self-governance. Yet he still considered that important positions would be filled by responsible bureaucrats and party experts. He recognized that the transition to a socialist society would require an institutional structure to support processes of administration and decision-making. A new society could not be built on the basis of mass demonstrations alone.

Luxemburg and Pannekoek believed that a more important source of power was in the workers' capacity to initiate mass actions without the authorization of party leadership. They held a different vision of a socialist future in which all citizens would be active in administering a self-determining society. Their view of power corresponded to a more active and militant political strategy of increasingly powerful mass actions aimed at crippling the power of the bourgeoisie. Luxemburg considered that the power of the workers' movement 'lies not in parliament, nor in parliamentary manoeuvres and back-room string-pulling, but outside in the mass of 44 million people'.[76] Following the Reichstag elections, Luxemburg advocated a return to mass actions and street demonstrations to further strengthen the workers' movement following their electoral success:

> our party can create for itself a position of real power in parliament only if it applies thoroughgoing, vigorous and resolute battle tactics. As the strongest party by far in the Reich, we are obliged to change over to the offensive all along the line, thus making the interests and demands of the millions standing behind us the focus of political life.[77]

Luxemburg never advocated boycotting parliamentary elections and shared Kautsky's belief that they were an important element of political struggle. But her view of political power led her to a different emphasis on the role of parliament. For Luxemburg, electoral campaigning was only ever a means to the end of mass mobilization and building the fighting spirit of workers. She never considered parliamentary positions to be important ends in themselves since parliament was a bourgeois institution, which would be replaced in a socialist revolution.

Pannekoek also believed that 'parliamentary activity and action by the masses were not incompatible with each other', but maintained that mass action provided

[76] Luxemburg, 'What Now?'.

[77] Pannekoek, 'Marxist Theory and Revolutionary Tactics'.

the workers' movement 'with a new, broader basis'.[78] In Pannekoek's formulation, mass action acted as '*a corrective to parliamentary action*' by applying pressure on representatives to act in accordance with the will of the masses: 'Fear of the consequences of the masses' indignation often induces the class holding parliamentary power to make concessions which the masses would not otherwise have obtained.'[79] In a similar position to Luxemburg, Pannekoek also emphasized that political power lay in the mobilized workers rather than in the institutions of parliament, which he considered 'of secondary importance' for 'the crucial determinant force lies outside.'[80]

On account of his theory that real political power lay in a mobilized and class-conscious workers' movement, Pannekoek argued that the primary role of the workers' party should be to develop the political capacities and facilitate the actions of the masses. He criticized Kautsky for his focus on the party restraining the activity of the masses and reducing their potential for spontaneous action. He believed that to emphasize this negative function would ultimately lead to a decrease in power. Pannekoek insisted that 'the party actually has a duty to *instigate* revolutionary action, because it is the bearer of an important part of the masses' capacity for action.'[81] The party's role was to enhance the revolutionary activity of the masses by building their capacity for political agency.

The State

A final major difference between the radicals and Kautsky was the question of the role of the state in class conflict. On this point, it was Pannekoek rather than Luxemburg who developed a detailed socialist critique of the state as a powerful organization of the bourgeoisie, which would need to be smashed as part of the struggle between the two classes. Kautsky, as we will see in chapter four, believed that elements of the state could be transformed into an instrument subordinated to the people's will and did not call for its complete elimination. Yet for the radicals, the end goal was an overcoming of the state as a prelude to the development of other self-determining institutions in a socialist society.

Pannekoek viewed the state as 'the combat organization of the bourgeoisie'.[82] With the state and its apparatuses, the bourgeoisie exercised command over the army, police, and officials, which further increased the potency of its raw material power. For Pannekoek, workers 'cannot defeat capitalism unless it first defeats this powerful organization'.[83] Particularly later in his life, Pannekoek tended to view the state as an inherently repressive institution: 'The state power is not a simple neutral object in the class struggle; it is a weapon and a fortress of the bourgeoisie,

[78] Ibid. [79] Ibid. [80] Ibid. [81] Ibid.
[82] Pannekoek, 'Class Struggle and Nation'. [83] Ibid.

the strongest support, without which the bourgeoisie could never retain its place.'[84] As a result, 'the conquest of political hegemony is not a struggle for State power; it is a struggle against State power.'[85] The goal of a workers' revolution is the dismantling of the state apparatus. Pannekoek wrote,

> The content of this revolution is the destruction and dissolution of the instruments of power of the state with the aid of the instruments of power of the proletariat... The struggle will cease only when, as the result of it, the state organization is completely destroyed. The organization of the majority will then have demonstrated its superiority by destroying the organization of the ruling minority.[86]

At various points in his life, Pannekoek advocated for different institutions as appropriate organizational forms of the working class. He believed that such institutions could not be 'the invention of theory', but must be 'built up spontaneously by the working class itself'.[87] In his later work, Pannekoek became sceptical of forms of parliamentarianism, trade unionism, and political parties due to their disempowering effect on the political activity of the masses, yet in earlier writings, Pannekoek did not reject these organizational forms outright. They could be useful in a variety of functions for increasing class consciousness and organizational strength. But insofar as party leaders took power from the masses and discouraged their activity, these forms needed to be superseded. Pannekoek believed 'the workers need new forms of organization in which they keep the powers of action in their own hands.'[88] He continued, '[i]t is clear that the organizational forms of trade union and political party, inherited from the period of expanding capitalism, are useless here. They developed into instruments in the hands of leaders unable and unwilling to engage in revolutionary fight.'[89] As the class struggle intensified it would become more of a direct struggle between the two classes and so would require open confrontation best carried out in the form of mass strikes and street demonstrations.

In contrast, Kautsky did not consider it necessary to completely eliminate the institutions of the state as he believed they could be transformed by the workers as part of the political struggle. In Kautsky's view, following the conquest of political power and the dominance of the working class 'the incipient socialist community will assimilate the political forms surviving in the period of transition from capitalism to socialism.'[90] The administrative structure that would carry out the

[84] Pannekoek, 'Imperialism and the Tasks of the Proletariat', *Kommunist* 1/2 (Geneva: 1915), 75.
[85] Pannekoek, 'Class Struggle and Nation'.
[86] Pannekoek, 'Mass Action and Revolution', *Die Neue Zeit* 30 (1912), 2.
[87] Pannekoek, 'General Remarks on the Question of Organization'. [88] Ibid. [89] Ibid.
[90] Kautsky, *The Labour Revolution*.

complex economic tasks in a socialist society would resemble certain aspects of a state:

> Whether the community of the future will continue to be called a State or not is essentially a question of terminology.... to many people the State has come to mean a sovereign community. When an oriental despotism and a democratic republic, rigidly centralized France and the loose federation of the British Empire, may all be called by the same name of 'State,' it is really not a matter of great moment to refuse this name to the Socialist community.[91]

This aspect of Kautsky's political programme will be examined in more detail in chapter four, where I outline Kautsky's programme of a democratic transformation of the institutions of the state, which he envisioned alongside a democratization of the economy.

Most of these debates within the SPD occurred before the outbreak of the war and the onset of revolution in Russia and Germany. However, the underlying positions of the theorists represented disagreements over revolutionary strategy which would inform their debates during the revolution. Differences in political strategy between the radicals and the Marxist centre reflected real differences in their final objectives. The following two chapters will examine in more detail key aspects of Rosa Luxemburg and Karl Kautsky's visions for a post-capitalist society. In her final years, Luxemburg wrote several texts in which she addressed the organization of a socialist society in greater detail than at any other point in her life.[92] Kautsky also developed a socialist action programme concerning the immediate steps that would need to be taken during the revolution to institute practical measures towards socialism.[93] He had a clear conception of the necessary political processes and institutional arrangements that would be needed as the revolution progressed. While significant disagreement existed between the two thinkers on questions of both strategy and institutional goals, examining their writings during this revolutionary period helps provide greater substance to the competing ideologies that existed within the council movements.

[91] Ibid.
[92] Luxemburg, 'The Socialization of Society'; Luxemburg, 'Our Program and the Political Situation'.
[93] Kautsky, 'Guidelines for a Socialist Action Program'.

4
Socialist Republicanism

The primary opposition between socialist groups during the German Revolution was the debate over the appropriate institutional form of the future German state: parliamentary republic or council system. On the one hand, the Ebert–Scheidemann leadership of the SPD advocated for the calling of a national constituent assembly to ensure the speedy transition to a parliamentary republic with little change to the economic and social order. They believed that following the abdication of the Kaiser and the declaration of a republic, 'the liberation of the people was completed.'[1] Their programme was for a parliament elected by all citizens with equal political rights, freedom of assembly, freedom of association, freedom of speech, and reforms to employment law. They opposed the transformation of other authority structures in the army, government bureaucracy, and workplace, directing all current civil servants in a declaration on 9 November 1918 to remain in their posts.[2] They also deferred the question of socialization indefinitely and stated that in the short term, 'property must be protected from arbitrary usurpation.'[3]

On the other hand, vocal advocates for a council system such as the Revolutionary Shop Stewards and the Spartacus League argued for the elimination of all parliaments, courts, and bureaucracies. They considered that 'appointees of the workers' and soldiers' council must take charge of all military and civil administration and positions of authority.'[4] They also called for the immediate socialization of the economy and the institution of workers' control over workplaces. While the Spartacus League never produced detailed plans for the council system, the Revolutionary Shop Stewards published outlines of the institutional structure of a workers' council system in their newspaper, *Der Arbeiter-Rat* [The Workers' Council] in addition to other booklets.[5] This conception of a 'pure'

[1] 'Declaration of Friedrich Ebert, Philipp Scheidemann and Otto Landsberg on 9 November 1918', in *The German Revolution and the Debate on Soviet Power*, ed. John Riddell (New York: Anchor Foundation, 1986), 44.

[2] Jones, *Founding Weimar*, 15.

[3] 'Declaration of Friedrich Ebert, Philipp Scheidemann and Otto Landsberg on 9 November 1918', 44.

[4] 'Organise the Power Anew from Below', *Die Rote Fahne*, 10 November 1918, in *The German Revolution and the Debate on Soviet Power*, ed. John Riddell (New York: Anchor Foundation, 1986), 57.

[5] A reconstruction of this theory can be found in Hoffrogge, *Working-Class Politics in the German Revolution*, 108–17.

Building Power to Change the World: The Political Thought of the German Council Movements. James Muldoon, Oxford University Press (2020). © James Muldoon. DOI: 10.1093/oso/9780198856627.003.0005

council system in which the working class exercised power became an influential model for future theories of workers' councils.

However, the framework of 'Council System or National Assembly' has obscured other possible ideals of democratization and socialization from historical view. Following a wave of scholarship that arose in the 1960s but which has not been greatly developed since this time, historians have investigated whether other revolutionary paths could have been possible during November 1918.[6] In support of a thesis first put forward by historian Arthur Rosenberg, Peter von Oertzen has claimed that 'the only real alternative to bourgeois democracy was not "Bolshevism" but a social democracy supported by the councils.'[7] Summarizing the results of these debates, Helga Grebing concluded that there were a number of possibilities in early November: 'First, partial socialization, second, establishment of the economic councils system, third, use of the democratic potential of the workers' and soldiers' councils to democratize administration, fourth possibly also utilization of approaches for the democratization of the army.'[8]

Following this line of research, this chapter examines the political programme of Karl Kautsky, a leading theoretician of the German Social Democratic Party and arguably the most influential Marxist of his era. Kautsky put forward a vision of a socialist republicanism that sought to chart a middle course between the two opposed forces of the Revolution. However, Kautsky had alienated the leadership of the SPD through his anti-war position, which resulted in his dismissal as editor of *Die Neue Zeit* in 1917. But this did little to gain him sympathy with the radical Left who considered him too cautious and conservative. Belonging to an isolated Marxist 'centre' (the right wing of the USPD: Hilferding, Breitscheid, and Haase), Kautsky exercised little practical influence over political events in 1918–19.[9] Yet, he produced several important pamphlets and articles in which he argued for a strategy that cut across the two opposing positions of the workers' councils/national assembly divide. For Kautsky, it was 'not a question of national assembly or workers' councils, but *both*'.[10] Kautsky's programme combined elements from the two dominant approaches and recommended a pathway of democratization and socialization that relied on the coexistence of a parliament and workers' councils.

[6] Kolb, *Die Arbeiterräte in der deutschen Innenpolitik 1918–1919*; Oertzen, *Betriebsräte in der Novemberrevolution*. More recently, see Lange *Massenstreik und Schießbefehl: Generalstreik und Märzkämpfe in Berlin 1919*; Weipert, *Die Zweite Revolution*.

[7] Oertzen, *Betriebsräte in der Novemberrevolution*, 67.

[8] Helga Grebing, 'Konservative Republik oder soziale Demokratie? Zur Bewertung der Novemberrevolution in der neueren deutschen Historiographie', in *Vom Kaiserreich zur Republik*, ed. Eberhard Kolb (Köln, 1972), 397.

[9] Kautsky was appointed under-secretary of State in the Foreign Office and was kept busy by the minutiae of government.

[10] Kautsky, 'National Assembly and Council Assembly', 101.

I claim that Kautsky's political position during the German Revolution could be characterized as a socialist republicanism that called for the radical transformation of the state and society. Kautsky proposed a detailed socialist strategy during the revolution based on an analysis that German society was ripe for socialist transformation and that concrete steps should be immediately taken towards socialization. I challenge the view that Kautsky advocated a political quietism during the revolution and that his programme amounted to bourgeois reformism. A proper analysis of Kautsky's political writings during this period has been clouded by his status as a Marxist heretic and his perceived proximity to the SPD on practical political questions. However, Kautsky's socialist action programme can be radically distinguished from the position of the leadership of the SPD. While one may accuse Kautsky of political naivety, he remained a staunch advocate of socialist transformation prior to and during the revolution.

Kautsky understood democracy and socialism as the twin goals of a socialist revolution. Not only was democracy an important political form for the struggle of the working class, but the establishment of a democratic republic was viewed as the institutional basis for the creation of a full socialist republic. In his earlier writings, democracy was primarily envisaged as a strategic means of socialist struggle. Yet, the experience of the Russian Revolution led Kautsky to appreciate the independent value of political democracy for its protection of civil liberties and political rights. In the German Revolution, Kautsky considered democracy as a political form in which the proletariat could develop its power and as the institutional basis for the realization of socialism.

Kautsky admired certain aspects of the Paris Commune and was inspired by Marx's writing on this political form. However, he disagreed with Lenin that a new proletarian state should be constructed based on the model of the Commune. It was not the unified legislative and executive powers of Marx's scheme that inspired Kautsky, but rather Marx's underlying idea of the reconfiguration of the state apparatus from an alien element situated above society to a direct expression of the people's will. Kautsky believed that this could best be achieved through a radically decentralized state with a parliament elected by universal suffrage and vigorously patrolled by an organized and educated citizenry. This administrative apparatus would provide the basis for plans to socialize the economy after careful planning and preparation through a scheme of coordination between workers, consumers, and representatives from the state. In the international arena, representatives of this socialist republic would be sent on peaceful missions to spread the principles of democracy, socialism, and international solidarity across the world through the cultivation of a peaceful league of nations.

For clarity, I have summarized Kautsky's main strategic aims during the first months of the German Revolution. The essential objectives for Kautsky were the following:

1. establishment of political democracy as a necessary precondition for socialist transformation and as the political basis for a future socialist society;
2. protection of civil and political rights such as freedom of speech, association, and the press, with political violence necessary only as a defensive measure against counter-revolutionary forces;
3. transformation of the bourgeois state into a decentralized administrative apparatus through the negation of its militaristic and oppressive characteristics;
4. establishment of a legislature as the supreme power over the bureaucracy through free elections to a constituent assembly with universal suffrage;
5. institutionalization of workers' councils as permanent centres for the mobilization of workers to ensure parliament was vigorously patrolled by an organized citizenry;
6. socialization of all industries at a steady pace following careful planning and with an emphasis on reviving and increasing production;
7. internationalization of democracy and socialism through championing these principles in international relations with other states.

Kautsky also stressed the importance of the political unity of the working class in action and called for the re-establishment of civil order and industrial production as essential to revolutionary activity. For Kautsky, the dictatorship of the proletariat could only be the rule of a working-class majority through parliamentary means without the use of terror. Kautsky viewed his socialist action programme as a practical expression of how the Erfurt Programme could be implemented during the revolution. Of chief importance to Kautsky was not to push the revolution in the most radical direction, but to stabilize a new socialist society based on the creation of an institutional framework which would be seen as legitimate by all citizens. He considered that establishing a parliamentary majority for socialists based on universal suffrage would be the most secure basis for the socialist transformation of society. It was this commitment to a politics of socialization *and* gradualism that distinguished him from both the SPD and the supporters of a pure council system. Kautsky believed that revolutionary paths were possible other 'than those made with powder and dynamite'.[11] The German Revolution, Kautsky hoped, would usher in a new period of socialist transformations using more peaceful methods than the violent revolutions of the nineteenth century.

[11] Kautsky, *The Labour Revolution.*

The 'Renegade' Kautsky

Gary Steenson has argued that during his time Kautsky was 'the most important theorist of Marxism in the world', who 'did more to popularize Marxism in western Europe than any other intellectual'.[12] Yet today, the 'Pope of Marxism', widely recognized during his time as the legitimate heir to Marx and Engels, remains a relatively neglected theorist and has been largely ignored as an independent figure for historical study.[13] Only a handful of book-length publications have appeared in the past three decades on his work. The majority of his writings remain untranslated in the International Institute of Social History in Amsterdam.[14] Of those who have studied him, the appraisal of his work has been mainly negative. The dominant view of Marxists is that Kautsky was not an exceptionally original Marxist theorist and ultimately betrayed the basic principles of Marxism.[15]

There is an amusing story told by Karl Kautsky's grandson that new acquaintances have occasionally been under the impression that his grandfather's forename was Renegade.[16] Such has been the pervasive influence of a negative portrait of Kautsky and his interpretation of Marxism. Of the many examples, three critical assessments stand out. The first is Lenin's vehement attack against Kautsky whose theories of democracy, the state, and socialist revolution Lenin perceived as 'a complete renunciation precisely of those revolutionary foundations of Marxism that this writer defended for decades.'[17] Lenin's central claim was that by 1914 the Marxist author of *The Road to Power*, which Lenin still greatly admired, had changed his position from his pre-war writings and now represented a form of liberal bourgeois opportunism.[18] For Lenin, Kautsky's failure to agitate at the outbreak of war, his criticisms of a soviet republic and his illusions of parliamentarism and a non-violent revolution were all based on an abandonment of Marxist principles and a collapse into bourgeois politics.

A second prominent criticism is that Kautsky constructed a crude and mechanistic vulgarization of Marxism that rested on an economic determinism and

[12] Gary P. Steenson, *Karl Kautsky, 1854–1938: Marxism in the classical years* (Pittsburgh: University of Pittsburgh Press 1991), 3.

[13] For the most recent overview of this literature see Ben Lewis, ed., *Karl Kautsky on Democracy and Republicanism* (Leiden: Brill, 2018), 9–50. For the most succinct analysis of Kautsky's life and works see Massimo Salvadori, *Karl Kautsky and the Socialist Revolution 1880–1938* (London: Verso, 1990). See also James Muldoon, 'Reclaiming the Best of Karl Kautsky', *Jacobin*, 5 February 2019.

[14] The repository is available online at: http://search.socialhistory.org/Record/ARCH00712/ArchiveContentList#1980

[15] Salvadori, *Kautsky and the Socialist Revolution 1854–1938*, 9–10.

[16] Kautsky, *Karl Kautsky: Marxism, Revolution and Democracy*, (New Jersey: Transaction, 1994) 45.

[17] Lenin, *The Proletarian Revolution and the Renegade Kautsky.*

[18] See Lars T. Lih, 'Lenin and Kautsky: The final Chapter', *International Socialist Review* 58 (May–June 2008).

Darwinian evolutionism. This view is widely shared by critics across the spectrum of Western Marxism. The point was famously argued by neo-Hegelian Marxists such as Georg Lukács and Karl Korsch in the early 1920s in an attempt to criticize the fatalism and determinism of the politics of the Second International and to revive a more dialectic, activist, and revolutionary philosophy of Marx.[19] According to this view, Kautsky supported a 'biologically or technologically deterministic version of historical materialism' that held a providential faith in the inevitable coming of the revolution due to the forward march of economic development.[20] The failures of the Second International were reflected in Kautsky's political philosophy, which was interpreted as the official doctrine of the party and representative of a broad *Weltanschauung* shared by many socialists of the age.[21]

Third, prominent historian, Erich Matthias, has argued that Kautsky's radical political writings were a mere façade for his advocacy of a politics of passivity within the SPD.[22] He coined the term 'Kautskyism' to describe this variety of Marxism that professed revolutionary principles but was responsible for political inactivity and a gradual incorporation of the SPD into the German Empire. For Matthias, while Kautsky remained in appearance a Marxist writer, in fact he advocated for a bourgeois 'ideology of integration' into capitalist society. This view was also presented by Karl Korsch who argued that through Kautsky's philosophy, 'the Social Democratic movement *had been transformed from a revolutionary class struggle movement into a political and social reform movement.*'[23] This criticism of Kautsky's combination of revolutionary principles with a 'wait and see' politics has been widely shared by many socialist critics.[24] Dick Geary has argued when it came to practical politics, Kautsky 'failed to combine a genuinely revolutionary prognosis with the advocacy of any form of concrete action'.[25] As a result, there arose certain 'ambiguities of his theories and not least the distinction between a revolutionary analysis and an almost total silence on the issue of tactics'.[26] For Geary and many other critics, Kautsky had little to say about

[19] For the neo-Hegelian interpretation of Kautsky see Jules Townshend, 'Reassessing Kautsky's Marxism', *Political Studies* 37, no. 4 (1989), 659–64. See also Georg Lukács, *Lenin: A Study on the Unity of his Thought* (Cambridge: MIT Press, 1971); Korsch, *Marxism, and Philosophy and Other Essays*. For Kautsky's response to Korsch see Ben Lewis's recent translation, Karl Kautsky 'A Destroyer of Vulgar Marxism', *Platypus Review* 43 (February 2012).

[20] Matt Perry, *Marxism and History* (London: Palgrave Macmillan, 2002), 22.

[21] See Walter Holzheuer, *Karl Kautskys Werk als Weltanschauung* (Munchex C. H. Beck, 1972).

[22] Erich Matthias, 'Kautsky und der Kautskyanismus', in *Marxismusstudien*, ed. Iring Festcher (Tubingen: Mohr, 1957), 151–97.

[23] Karl Korsch, 'The Passing of Marxian Orthodoxy: Bernstein-Kautsky-Luxemburg-Lenin', *International Council Correspondence* 3, nos. 11&12 (December 1937).

[24] Dieter Groh, *Negative Integration und revolutionärer Attentismus* (GmbH: Ullstein, 1973); Alex Callinicos, *Social Theory: A Historical Introduction* (London: Polity Press, 1999), 112; Ernesto Laclau and Chantal Mouffe, *Hegemony and Socialist Strategy: Towards a Radical Democratic Politics* (London: Verso, 1985), 3.

[25] Geary, *Karl Kautsky*, 71.

[26] Ibid., 85.

practical strategy for revolutionary transformation, which led to inactivity and political quietism.

While there is some truth to each of these claims, they are an unrepresentative characterization of Kautsky's political theory which leads to a need for a reassessment of his work. Massimo Salvadori published an important study which challenged Kautsky's renegade status by persuasively arguing that while certain aspects of his politics changed over the years, there was a remarkably consistent set of core theses, which remained stable even across his alleged transformation from a revolutionary to a reformist.[27] Salvadori argued that on the issues of the democratic republic, the state, and his critique of minority dictatorship, Kautsky's positions developed within a consistent framework.[28] While there was a shift in Kautsky's thinking that occurred through his dispute with Rosa Luxemburg from around 1910 and continued to evolve during the war, it is misleading to suggest this amounted to a radical break from his earlier positions in *The Class Struggle* and *The Road to Power*. Kautsky himself denied any break with Marxism. He considered that his work had 'the definitive stamp of a consistent Marxism . . . written strictly according to the Marxist method'. While he had to 'bury several illusions' and 'recognise and correct several errors', Kautsky believed he remained 'an incorrigible Marxist'.[29]

Recent scholarship has also disputed the claim of Kautsky as a deterministic and evolutionist thinker. Paul Blackledge has contended that Kautsky articulated a sophisticated and powerful dialectical theory of history that was highly influential over a whole generation of Marxists.[30] In this view, Kautsky emphasized economic considerations and believed that capitalist development would lead to mounting contradictions, but this was not according to a consistent and progressive evolution with working-class victory as an inevitable end point. Kautsky was able to separate Darwinian theory of natural evolution from the study of human societies, which operated according to different patterns. Kautsky's connection to Lenin has also recently been reassessed by Lars T. Lih who has convincingly argued that Kautsky's earlier work was the basis for Lenin's political theory. This theory calls into question the neo-Hegelian interpretation of Lenin's alleged rejection of Kautsky's political philosophy.[31]

[27] Salvadori, *Kautsky and the Socialist Revolution 1854–1938*. See also Gilcher-Holtey, *Das Mandat des Intellektuellen. Karl Kautsky und die Sozialdemokratie.*

[28] For Salvadori, 'Kautsky maintained a "consistent" conception of the modern state, of the role of parliament, of the function of the political and civil liberties bequeathed by bourgeois liberalism, of the indispensability of a centralized bureaucratic-administrative apparatus, and of the importance of political democracy as an instrument for assuring knowledge of society and ascertaining the will of its citizens.' Salvadori, *Kautsky and the Socialist Revolution 1854–1938*, 12–13.

[29] Karl Kautsky, 'The Development of a Marxist', in Ben Lewis, ed., *Karl Kautsky on Democracy and Republicanism*, 298, 322.

[30] Paul Blackledge, 'Karl Kautsky and Marxist Historiography', *Science & Society* 70, no. 3 (2006), 337–59.

[31] Lars T. Lih, *Lenin Rediscovered: 'What Is to Be Done?' in Context*. The Lenin–Kautsky relationship studied in this work builds on Kautsky, *Karl Kautsky: Marxism, Revolution and Democracy.*

However, there has been little challenge to the negative view of Kautsky's political tactics and strategies, particularly leading up to and during the German Revolution. One prominent exception is Daniel Gaido and Richard B. Day, who have returned to Kautsky's earlier writings on the 1905 Russian Revolution and highlighted Kautsky's concerns with concrete issues of political strategy in order to contest the view of Kautsky as a 'pseudo revolutionary' and political quietist.[32] Yet like other writers analysing Kautsky from a Leninist perspective, their positive reappraisal of Kautsky has remained limited to the pre-1914 period. In his study of the 'centrist' Marxists around Karl Kautsky, Mike Macnair presented a number of 'core principled understandings about strategy' that emerged from Kautsky's writings, but he too is influenced by Lenin's renegade thesis and holds that Kautsky fostered 'the illusion of taking hold of and using the existing bureaucratic coercive state'.[33]

Ben Lewis has done the most recent work to challenge received opinions on Karl Kautsky through the translation of a number of Kautsky's important articles with perceptive commentary on the question of democratic republicanism and socialist strategy during the Revolution.[34] Lewis has brought to light Kautsky's writings on the French Revolution of 1848 and the Paris Commune in order to show that in 1905 Kautsky defended a form of the dictatorship of the proletariat along the lines of the Paris Commune and was critical of the weaknesses of the French bourgeois republic of 1848. However, Lewis has been less convinced of Kautsky's credentials during 1918 and has approvingly cited a number of Grigory Zinoviev's criticisms of Kautsky's 'Guidelines for a Socialist Action Programme' concerning Kautsky's strategies for socialist transformation. The conclusion has been that 'on every possible question, Kautsky puts forward the programme of the bourgeoisie, not the working class.'[35]

Building on these important contributions to the study of Kautsky's work, but questioning some of their central assumptions, the interpretation of Kautsky offered here proposes that Kautsky developed a socialist republicanism which involved the radical transformation of the state and the democratization of politics, the economy, and society.

[32] Daniel Gaido and Richard B. Day, eds., *Witnesses to Permanent Revolution: The Documentary Record* (Leiden: Brill, 2009).

[33] Mike Macnair, *Revolutionary Strategy: Marxism and the Challenge of Left Unity* (London: November Publications, 2008), 159.

[34] Lewis, *Karl Kautsky on Democracy and Republicanism*; Ben Lewis, 'Kautsky: From Erfurt to Charlottenburg', *Weekly Worker*, 10 November 2011, 5–7; Karl Kautsky, '"A Destroyer of Vulgar Marxism": Review of Karl Korsch's "Marxism and Philosophy" by Karl Kautsky', *Platypus Review* 43 (2012), 2–4; Karl Kautsky, 'Driving the Revolution Forward', originally published as 'Das Weitertreiben der Revolution', *Freiheit* No. 79, 29 December 1918.

[35] Grigory Zinoviev, 'Die Sozialdemokratie als Werkzeug der Reaktion', *Die Kommunistische Internationale* 2 (1919). Quoted in Lewis, 'Kautsky: From Erfurt to Charlottenburg'.

Political Democracy and Civil Rights

In Kautsky's 'Guidelines for a Socialist Action Programme', he argued that '[t]he democratic republic is the indispensable political basis of the new commonwealth we wish to construct. We must hold steadfastly to the democratic republic; we must consistently develop it in all directions.'[36] The centrality of democracy to this programme in no way represents a drastic departure from Kautsky's previous positions, but rather encapsulates a number of key points that Kautsky held consistently throughout most of his life. He understood political democracy as a form of rule by the majority with equal political and civil rights for all citizens. It was the most adequate form of government for the development of the working class, since it permitted workers to develop powerful worker-led organizations, struggle for economic and political demands, agitate more effectively, and gain important political experience. In Kautsky's vision, the establishment of a political democracy was the first step towards the conquest of political power by workers. Democratic institutions would increase the power of workers, while elections would also enable them to have a more reliable barometer of their growing strength without resort to violent conflict. In the pre-1914 period, Kautsky's recommendation of a 'democratic path to socialism' can be interpreted primarily as a method of political struggle. It is only later that he is more attentive to democracy as a valuable end in itself as part of the institutional framework of a transitional state towards socialism.

In the early 1880s, Kautsky was interested in democracy on instrumental grounds and considered that democratic elections 'have a primarily propagandistic purpose'.[37] However, in Kautsky's commentary on the Erfurt Programme, political democracy figured as the most adequate form within which the proletariat could conduct the class struggle and as a first step towards a new socialist order. For Kautsky, 'the universal ballot is to be regarded as one of the conditions prerequisite to a sound development of the proletariat.' He contended that '[w]ithout political rights, the working class cannot carry on its economic struggles and develop its economic organization.'[38] The more the working class developed, the more it required basic political rights to communicate and to organize. Kautsky described protections like freedom of the press and freedom of association as 'the light and air of the labor movement.'[39]

Political democracy aided in the development of the working class in two specific ways. Structurally, it facilitated the growth of the workers' movement by securing the conditions for the legal functioning of working-class institutions.

[36] Kautsky, 'Guidelines for a Socialist Action Programme'.
[37] Karl Kautsky, 'Wahlen und Attentate', *Der Sozialdemokrat* 23 (5 June 1881), 4.
[38] Kautsky, 'The Class Struggle'. [39] Ibid.

Political rights enabled socialists to organize as a party, to campaign openly, and to operate through unions, a free press, and political assemblies. Secondly, democracy was important due to the educative function of political participation on workers.[40] Kautsky contended:

> [t]his very participation of the proletariat proves to be the most effective means of shaking up the hitherto indifferent divisions of the proletariat and giving them hope and confidence. It is the most powerful lever that can be utilized to raise the proletariat out of its economic, social and moral degradation.[41]

The emphasis in the Erfurt Programme is on democracy's strategic importance as a form within which the working class could further develop its political power. Kautsky avoided the question of whether democracy would be an adequate state form for the realization of socialist objectives. Rather, he argued that parliamentary action would be an essential aspect of working-class struggle and that a victory for democracy would implicitly strengthen the position of the working class.

This position was reinforced and expanded upon in *The Road to Power*. Kautsky reiterated that a democratic republic is 'the only form of the state in which Socialism can be realized', and that political rights available in democratic states 'place weapons in the hands of the proletariat'.[42] Kautsky also added another crucial advantage: the open competition possible in a political democracy was able to 'shed a light upon the relative strength of the various parties and classes and upon the spirit that animates them'.[43] This would facilitate a sharper awareness of class identity and antagonisms, but it also strengthened the 'peaceful methods of conducting the class struggle' due to a greater awareness on each side of the strength of their forces and an unwillingness to risk direct military confrontation.[44] As he later put it, '[d]emocracy is a barometer which permits the strength and the political intelligence of the working class to be measured.'[45] Kautsky noted that it was impossible to say what the coming class struggle would look like, but the greater the strength of democratic institutions, the more likely 'economic, legislative and moral pressure' will take precedence over military force. Democracy was also considered necessary to ensure the mass character of the class struggle because it enabled it to be undertaken in the open without the resort to secret committees. Without this there could be a perversion of the movement and the dominance of small sects over the mass of workers.

This conception of the strategic value of political democracy to the class struggle undertook a shift after the war. First, Kautsky expanded his definition

[40] Kautsky, 'The Social Revolution'.
[41] Kautsky, 'The Class Struggle'.
[42] Kautsky, 'The Road to Power'.
[43] Ibid.
[44] Ibid.
[45] Kautsky, *The Labour Revolution*.

of democracy to include not simply universal suffrage, majority rule, and political rights, but also a greater emphasis on the protection of minorities and the political participation of citizens.[46] Political democracy also gained new significance as a valuable end in itself and as an indispensable part of the construction of a new socialist society. In a reflection on the February Revolution in Russia, Kautsky proposed a new conceptualization of the relationship between socialism and democracy:

> There are two things that the proletariat urgently needs: democracy and socialism. Democracy means extensive freedoms and political rights for the mass of the people and transforming the institutions of state and municipal administration into mere tools of the people. And then socialism, which means transforming private production for the market into social—i.e. state, municipal or cooperative—production for the needs of society. Both require the proletariat in equal measure. Social production without democracy could become one of the most onerous shackles. Democracy without socialism does nothing to abate the proletariat's economic dependency.

Democracy still figured as 'the most secure basis for mass proletarian mobilization', but it was now positioned as a political goal of a socialist republic, which was as essential to a future socialist order as socialism itself. Kautsky repeated this formulation of the twin goals of democracy and socialism in a number of subsequent texts such as *Demokratie oder Diktatur* and *The Dictatorship of the Proletariat*. In previous formulations, democracy was not granted the same prominence alongside socialism as an end in itself. But in 1918, following the Bolshevik capture of power, Kautsky wanted to emphasize that democracy was not merely one possible path to socialism that might be dropped if seen as a hindrance but rather should be considered an essential element of a future socialist society. He insisted 'democracy and socialism do not differ in the sense that one is a means and one an end; both are means to the same end... For us, socialism is unthinkable without democracy.'[47]

The term democracy is not frequently deployed by Kautsky in his earlier writings. He was more likely to speak of universal suffrage or the value of specific political freedoms in class struggle. However, in *The Dictatorship of the Proletariat*, Kautsky evidenced a greater appreciation of the 'effects' of democracy in producing a culture of civility and respect for minorities:

> The deeper the roots which a democracy has struck, and the longer it has lasted and influenced political customs, the more effective is the minority, and the more

[46] Kautsky, *The Dictatorship of the Proletariat*. [47] Ibid.

> successfully it can oppose the pretensions of any party which seeks to remain in power at all costs.[48]

This emphasis on democracy should not be interpreted as stating that bourgeois democracy is compatible with socialism or is a valid end point of political struggle. Kautsky distinguished between democracy as a form of government and capitalism as the rule of a particular class. Against socialists who viewed changes in forms of government as of little consequence, Kautsky underlined the advantages of a democratic form of government to the proletariat. He also envisaged the proletariat as the most consistent and steadfast defenders of democracy. However, Kautsky knew well that political democracy would not eliminate the economic domination of the bourgeoisie. It therefore constituted a necessary but not sufficient condition for a socialist republic. Kautsky agreed with the Bolsheviks regarding the importance of extending bourgeois democracy into the economic sphere. The difference was that Kautsky's 'conclusion was simply that mere democracy is *insufficient* and not that it is *detestable*'.[49] Democracy was important for establishing a political system of majority rule and also for protecting civil and political rights through a system of law.

In addition, Kautsky advocated a respect for civil and political rights such as freedom of speech, association, and the press, which he considered should be defended even during periods of revolutionary transformation. As we have seen, civil and political rights were a central pillar of Kautsky's conception of political democracy and formed part of the institutional basis of a new socialist society. In 'Guidelines for a Socialist Action Programme', Kautsky remarked: 'It goes without saying that the democratic rights that have been won—such as the freedom of the press, assembly and association—should be defended.'[50] An important exception to this, of course, was the right to private property, which would be overturned in a socialist society by a move towards collective ownership. Productive economic assets and large estates would be acquisitioned from capitalists to be collectively managed by democratically organized institutions. But even here, Kautsky argued that the most just and economically efficient form of socialist transformation would involve compensation for acquisitions. This was justified on grounds of equal treatment, but seemed to be more important for strategic reasons of raising economic productivity and preventing quick sell-offs and acts of economic sabotage. Kautsky never wavered on the importance of the protection of civil and political rights, including under a capitalist system, in a transition state, and in a future socialist society. Along with political democracy, civil and political rights would become a hallmark of Kautsky's conception of the democratic path to socialism.

48 Ibid. 49 Kautsky, *Demokratie oder Diktatur*, 209.
50 Kautsky, 'Guidelines for a Socialist Action Programme'.

In Kautsky's writings, civil and political rights were often opposed to the political instrumentalization of terror. His relentless criticisms of Lenin and the Bolsheviks from 1917 concerned a dispute over justifications for the use of force and violence in conducting class struggle. Kautsky's consistent principle on the question of violence was that it should only be adopted as a defensive strategy against the possibility of the ruling class overthrowing democracy. In *The Road to Power*, Kautsky argued 'we are neither supporters of legality at any price, not revolutionaries at any price. We know that we cannot create historical situations at will and that our tactics must confirm to these situations.'[51] For Kautsky, the question of the level of violence in the revolution would ultimately be decided by the response of the ruling class to losing political power. Neither Kautsky nor Luxemburg were under any illusions that the ruling class would give up without a fight. Kautsky agreed that 'one must reckon with attempts of the ruling classes to nullify by violence the realization of democracy by the rising class.'[52] However, in his opinion, this only leant greater force to the need to defend democratic rights. He reasoned that the stark opposition between the violence of the bourgeoisie and the discipline of the workers would further motivate workers in defence of democracy. Kautsky became more optimistic that conditions were developing in a way that would lead to less violent outcomes than in the bourgeois revolutions of the past. While in his earlier years he considered that 'the popular socialist state can be erected only through a violent overthrow', by the time he wrote his commentary on the Erfurt Programme he acknowledged that '[s]uch an overthrow can assume the most diverse forms, depending on the conditions in which it occurs. In no way is it fated to be necessarily linked to acts of violence and bloodshed.'[53] After 1917, Kautsky had come to believe that '[d]emocracy makes it possible for this revolution to be peaceful, bloodless, and without coercion.'[54]

Kautsky offered three main reasons why a violent revolution should be avoided by socialists. The first was 'the colossal superiority of the weapons of the present standing armies, as compared with the weapons in the possession of civilians' which 'makes any resistance of the latter practically doomed to failure from the beginning'.[55] Workers were better advised to organize under democratic conditions until the military became unreliable supporters of the government and turned to the side of the workers. The second reason was offered in a lesser known text written during the first months of the revolution, '*Was will die deutsche sozialistische Republik*'. In this pamphlet, Kautsky counterposed the 'methods of violence' with the 'methods of democracy', arguing that socialists should strive to conduct social struggle solely through the latter. He underscored the self-defeating character of the use of violence by either side due to its tendency

[51] Kautsky, *The Road to Power.* [52] Kautsky, *The Dictatorship of the Proletariat.*
[53] Kautsky, *Der Sozialdemokrat*; Kautsky, *The Class Struggle.*
[54] Kautsky, *The Labour Revolution.* [55] Kautsky, *Road to Power.*

to provoke reprisals, debase political life, and lead to civil war. Attentive to the importance of establishing the political legitimacy of the new regime, Kautsky believed that entrenching democratic norms of non-violent solutions to political conflict would be essential to stabilizing the new order and avoiding further divisions. Third, Kautsky opposed violence in political struggle because he viewed minority takeover as an illegitimate shortcut of socialist organizing that would lead to a deformed revolution and civil war. Kautsky believed that the proletariat would seize political power when they could obtain a parliamentary majority and exercise power through socialist legislation: 'By dictatorship of the proletariat we can mean nothing other than the rule of the proletariat on the basis of democracy.'[56] He considered this to be a correct interpretation of Marx and Engels' use of this phrase. In Kautsky's opinion, the dictatorship of which Marx wrote was nothing other than the majority rule of the proletariat through parliamentary means over the hitherto ruling class as it abolished conditions of exploitation and established the foundations of a new socialist society through legislation. For Kautsky, the resort to violence as a path to power was an admission that it could not be obtained through consent and therefore represented an illegitimate minority takeover.

Transformation of the State

Certain Marxist critics of Kautsky have contended that he was unable to conceive of political transformation outside of the framework of the bourgeois state. Along these lines, Mike Macnair has argued that what 'distinguished the centre [Kautsky's] tendency from post-1917 communists most fundamentally was the belief that the working class could take over and use the existing capitalist state bureaucratic apparatus'.[57] However, as will be shown, this interpretation misses the nuances of Kautsky's proposal during the German Revolution to radically transform the autocratic state into a socialist republic. While Kautsky rejected the Bolshevik conception of the complete replacement of the state with an alternative council system, he proposed dissolving the most oppressive military and bureaucratic aspects of the state and refashioning other elements for the purposes of a socialist society.

Kautsky's 'renegade' status has led many of his critics to overlook the radical nature of these proposals or to misinterpret them based on the presumption that Kautsky was seeking an alliance with the SPD and therefore shared substantive aspects of their political programme. I contend that Kautsky's proposals were significantly more radical than those of the SPD and were in substance much

[56] Kautsky, *Demokratie oder Diktatur*, 47.

[57] Macnair, *Revolutionary Strategy*, 58.

closer to the Spartacists than either party would have admitted. Kautsky was naive in certain aspects of his analysis of the political situation and in mistaking the true intentions of the Ebert–Scheidemann party leaders. But this, I will argue, was a result of a lack of insight into the motives of the SPD rather than the bourgeois nature of his programme. His overwhelming desire to work towards working-class unity in action led him to overestimate the truly socialist forces within the SPD and to misjudge the extent to which they desired genuine social transformation.

Kautsky's starting point in the 'Guidelines for a Socialist Action Programme' was Marx's analysis of the Paris Commune. For critics who assert that Kautsky had by this point become a liberal who had abandoned Marx's lessons, it is worth noting that Kautsky in fact begins his analysis by quoting Marx:

> I say that the next attempt of the French Revolution will be no longer, as before, to transfer the bureaucratic-military machine from one hand to another, but to smash it, and this is essential for every real people's revolution on the continent.[58]

Despite the qualifications we will see that Kautsky placed on this phrase, he still took this to be a valid interpretation for present conditions. Nevertheless, certain interpreters of Kautsky have viewed this programme as a duplicitous move in which 'he was exploiting the respect and high standing he had rightfully earned in the workers' movement to seek unprincipled unity with the SPD.'[59] Ben Lewis quotes the Bolshevik leader Grigory Zinoviev, arguing that Kautsky was wrong to claim that the working class had already '*come to power*' and established a democratic republic in Germany following the events of early November 1918. According to Lewis, Kautsky falsely asserted that the SPD-USPD coalition was a working-class government that had achieved the necessary reforms to constitute a democratic republic. However, after comparing the *Guidelines* to other writings of the period, there is strong evidence that this interpretation is based on a misunderstanding of the text. Kautsky did claim that the workers had 'conquered political power', but this was merely to say that the old regime had collapsed and a provisional government consisting of representatives from working-class parties had been installed. Kautsky did not intend to argue that the limited number of reforms in the early days of the revolution was sufficient for the constitution of a desirable democratic (or socialist) republic.

In 'Driving the Revolution Forward', Kautsky clarified his position: 'The military autocracy, which has hitherto stood in the way of all social progress, has been overthrown, but the old administrative and governmental apparatus continues to function in the state and in the army.' It would be important to go further in order

[58] Marx, 'The Civil War in France'. [59] Lewis, 'Kautsky: From Erfurt to Charlottenburg'.

not to 'restrict the revolution to a temporary change of roles'. In a passage which helps illuminate the radical nature of Kautsky's political programme, he claimed:

> The state mechanism that has existed until now must be completely refashioned [*völlig umgestaltet*]. The bureaucracy must be stripped of its power and many of its functions, and must be placed under the supervision/control of the democratic representatives of the people in the municipality, the provinces, the states and the nation.[60]

Kautsky noted that '*[t]here can be no doubt that the revolution has not yet come to an end, and that it is in its infancy both politically and socially.*'[61] The power structures of the old autocratic regime based around the industrialists, Junkers, and senior military officials had been temporarily obstructed. But he acknowledged the danger they still posed and argued emphatically that '[t]he return of the rule of these elements must be prevented under all circumstances.'[62] He asserted that '[t]he transformation of Germany into a democratic republic must not be confined to the disappearance of a few dynasties. It must penetrate the entire spirit of the government in all its details.'[63]

This still leaves the question of which transformations Kautsky considered desirable for Germany during this period. His attitude to state transformation can be discerned from the following passage in which Kautsky contrasted his position with that of the Spartacus League and the right wing of the SPD:

> The two extremes can be characterised in the following way. The one extreme has not yet completely freed itself of bourgeois thinking, placing much confidence in the bourgeois world, and overestimating its inner strength. In turn, the other extreme looks at the bourgeois world with an utter lack of comprehension, regarding it as the (last) refuge of scoundrels. They flout its intellectual and economic achievements and believe that the proletariat is able to immediately take over all political and economic functions previously carried out by the bourgeois authorities—without any specialist knowledge and any preparation. Between these two extremes we find those who have studied and understood the bourgeois world, who approach it independently and critically, but who also appreciate its achievements and the difficulties involved in the task of replacing it with a higher social order.[64]

It can be seen from this argument that Kautsky attempted to plot a middle course. Firstly, Kautsky did not consider it desirable or realistic to replace administrative

[60] Kautsky, 'Driving the Revolution Forward'. [61] Ibid.
[62] Kautsky, 'Was will die deutsche sozialistische Republik?'.
[63] Kautsky, 'Driving the Revolution Forward'. [64] Ibid.

apparatuses with a completely alternative 'anti-bureaucratic' system based on a council model. He argued that the councils did not lend themselves well to undertaking complex administrative tasks and that the technical sophistication of coordinating a modern industrial economy required some form of administrative apparatus with technical experts for its implementation. Yet, the existing highly militaristic and bureaucratic apparatus was an oppressive tool of the ruling class and had to be transformed in order to become an effective instrument of working-class emancipation. The question was how existing institutions could be adequately refigured to minimize the element of domination and to guarantee workers' control over decision-making.

The central transformations Kautsky proposed were drawn from Marx's analysis of the Paris Commune: the dissolution of the standing army, the abolition of the dominance of the officer corps in the state and army, and the subordination of the government bureaucracy to a national assembly of delegates elected through universal suffrage. In addition to the establishment of a people's militia, Kautsky also proposed extensive rights of self-government to local administrations and the handing over of certain powers such as policing, taxation, and housing to smaller municipal bodies. Even at a glance, it is clear that this plan is a long way from simply capturing the existing state apparatus and using it for socialist purposes. Yet Kautsky rejected other aspects of Marx's analysis of the Paris Commune. How did he justify this position?

Kautsky appealed to a distinction he contended could be found in Marx's writing between two different forms of the state. Revisiting Marx's *The Eighteenth Brumaire*, Kautsky found that Marx spoke explicitly about smashing a 'bureaucratic-military machine' [*bureaukratisch-militärische Maschinerie*], rather than a democratic republic. As a result, Kautsky claimed 'Marx rejected only a particular form of this apparatus, the *bureaucratic militaristic,* which reached its exceptionally highest expression in the Second French Republic.'[65] When he applied this analysis to the German situation, Kautsky distinguished between a coercive 'military autocracy', which should be abolished, and a technical administrative apparatus, which would need to be refigured as a necessary element of a future socialist society. In line with this interpretation, Kautsky opposed the takeover of the military and police by a socialist government and any attempt to use this 'previous means of rule ... in a socialist manner'.[66] He called for the 'dissolution of these institutions', which entailed the elimination of a standing army, the creation of a people's militia, and the transfer of police powers to local authorities. He also attempted to break up the centralized bureaucratic power of

[65] Kautsky, *Die proletarische Revolution und ihr Programm*, 118 (my translation).
[66] Karl Kautsky, 'The Republic and Social Democracy in France (1905)', in *Karl Kautsky on Democracy and Republicanism*, ed. Ben Lewis (Leiden: Brill, 2019), 192.

the state, which was used to maintain a tight control over citizens. For this task, the Paris Commune offered an important precedent:

> Only socialism can put an end to this by means of an order such as the one the Paris Commune started to create: that is, by means of the most comprehensive expansion of self-government, the popular election of all officials and the subordination of all members of representative bodies to the control and discipline of the organised people.[67]

However, there were elements of the Paris Commune that Kautsky no longer considered applicable. In 1918, Kautsky merely passed over the clear differences between his position and Marx's analysis of the Paris Commune. But it would have been obvious to all that Kautsky's proposals were in direct contradiction with Marx's analysis that the Commune was 'not a parliament, but a working institution, and united in itself both executive and legislative power'.[68] In his dispute with Lenin, Kautsky was willing to directly address these inconsistencies and provide a more detailed analysis and update of Marx's arguments.

Ben Lewis has argued that Kautsky betrayed his 'original commitment to "smashing the state" and replacing it with something along the lines of the Paris Commune of 1871'.[69] This is based on the position, put forward by Lars T. Lih, that Kautsky 'subscribed to the Commune ideal . . . and used it as a foundation of a scathing critique of the existing "bourgeois republic" in France'.[70] However, as much as Kautsky admired certain aspects of the Paris Commune, he never viewed it as an appropriate model for modern Germany. He argued that a technical-administrative apparatus could not be completely 'smashed', but rather should be subordinated to a people's assembly through which administrators would be subject to control by representatives of the people elected through universal suffrage. His plans to transform the state were inspired by Marx's ideal that '[f]reedom consists in converting the state from an organ standing above society into one completely subordinate to it', rather than a conception of a state with some unique proletarian character.[71] Kautsky's transformation of the state followed the spirit of Marx's writings on the Paris Commune insofar as it aimed at the creation of a non-dominating and self-determining collective association: 'While the merely repressive organs of the old governmental power were to be amputated, its legitimate functions were to be wrested from an authority usurping pre-eminence over society itself, and restored to the responsible agents of society.'[72] Kautsky envisaged a German socialist republic, but one appropriate for its

[67] Ibid., 259. [68] Marx, 'The Civil War in France'.
[69] Lewis, 'Kautsky: From Erfurt to Charlottenburg'.
[70] Lars T. Lih, 'The book that didn't bark', *Weekly Worker* 863, 27 April 2011.
[71] Marx, *Critique of Gotha Programme.* [72] Marx, 'The Civil War in France'.

stage of economic and social development without 'indiscriminately applying templates drawn from the past, and from other countries, to the Germany of today'.[73]

As a result, Kautsky rejected Lenin's argument that the correct interpretation of Marx led to support for the creation of an entirely new 'proletarian' state based on the model of the Paris Commune. Instead, Kautsky argued that the most essential aspect of the Paris Commune was its implementation of universal suffrage and struggle against militarism and autocracy. He believed three specific aspects of Marx's analysis were no longer relevant to twentieth-century European conditions. First, the abolition of the separation of powers would be a backwards step. He argued that a single body with unified executive and legislative power posed a threat to civil liberties: 'the danger arises that the executive power will become all-powerful relative to the population.'[74] The Russian Revolution resulted in a new absolute power without any check which tolerated no opposition and became the exact phenomenon of a state above society that Marx initially criticized. Kautsky also emphasized the different tasks of an executive and legislative body. In a parliamentary body, different perspectives and interests could be brought to bear on an issue, while unity was required of an executive in administering the laws. As a result, Kautsky concluded that the executive and legislative institutions performed separate tasks and should be kept apart. Second, the idea of recallable delegates was suited to an earlier era with less organized party formations. In the twentieth century, delegates from highly organized mass parties owed allegiance to their party and could be controlled through party discipline. There was nothing to suggest that the function of immediate recall would provide any greater proletarian character to a representative body, and it could be subject to abuse by local interests. Finally, a workers' wage, Kautsky suggested, would also not be adequate to attract individuals with the necessary expertise to become state officials. Although it would be important to eliminate all of the special privileges of the bureaucracy so that they did not constitute a separate class above society, Kautsky considered that their pay could reflect their professional role.

Kautsky also adopted a more federalist perspective to the organization of administrative institutions, which rejected the centralized view of the Jacobin faction within the Paris Commune: 'It is completely mistaken to presume—following the Jacobin tradition—that the centralization of administration would allow a revolutionary Paris to rule France more easily than with an extensive self-government of the municipalities.'[75] Rather than centralize powers in order to rule more efficiently, Kautsky argued for the radical decentralization of the German Empire by 'immediately granting the right of extensive self-government (within the framework of state laws) to the municipalities, administrative districts and

[73] Kautsky, 'Driving the Revolution Forward'. [74] Kautsky, *The Labour Revolution.*

[75] Kautsky, 'The Republic and Social Democracy in France (1905)', 192.

provinces'.[76] In 'Driving the Revolution Forward', Kautsky argued for the break-up of the state of Prussia into three smaller regions. At the same time, he argued that all of the smaller regional governments of the old German Empire should be combined in a federal system with a central administrative body. Kautsky's plans for the socialization of the economy relied upon large-scale administrative systems that would be coordinated across regions in order to avoid domination by local interests and ensure rational production based on the needs of society as a whole. The power of this political framework would reside in a legislative parliament elected through universal suffrage initially by a constituent national assembly.

Kautsky's position stands opposed to the future path taken by the Ebert–Scheidemann government. When Kautsky argued that '*[i]n this understanding of driving the revolution forward, we agree with the Majority Socialists (SPD)*', he was quite mistaken.[77] His idealistic position that 'only ignorance and division amongst the workers could delay the coming of socialism in the democratic republic' ignored the complete lack of political will on the part of the SPD leadership to undertake any form of socialization or fundamental restructuring of society.[78] Kautsky often spoke of the difference between the minority and majority socialists as a 'difference in revolutionary tempo', but it was not simply the pace of change that was at stake.[79] Although the Council of People's Representatives publicly declared, 'the government... sees its mission as implementing the socialist programme',[80] behind the scenes, the SPD was working to preserve the state structure and hold off any effective measures for the democratization of the army and bureaucracy. The USPD executive committee claimed the joint government was 'thoroughly transforming all aspects of public life, and eliminating all power positions of the propertied minority that has ruled up to now'.[81] However, such attempts would come to nothing. The USPD misjudged the situation when they declared: 'The people broke the power of the army officers, the control of the Junker caste in the administration, and the command of the capitalist clique over public life.'[82] In spite of Kautsky's plans for widespread democratization, the army, government administration, and economic elite all retained their power and privileged positions within German society.

76 Kautsky, 'Guidelines for a Socialist Action Programme'.
77 Kautsky, 'Driving the Revolution Forward'.
78 Kautsky, 'Was will die deutsche sozialistische Republik?'.
79 Kautsky, 'Driving the Revolution Forward'.
80 'Declaration of the Council of People's Representatives, 12 November 1918', in *The German Revolution and the Debate on Soviet Power*, ed. John Riddell (New York: Anchor Foundation, 1986), 53.
81 'Declaration of the Executive Committee of the Independent Social Democratic Party of Germany, 12 November 1918', in *The German Revolution and the Debate on Soviet Power*, ed. John Riddell (New York: Anchor Foundation, 1986), 55.
82 Ibid.

Parliament and the National Assembly

Kautsky considered that participating in elections and parliamentary activity was an essential aspect of proletarian class struggle. He was persuaded that socialists could win a majority of seats in parliament and obtain majority support for socialism. In the German Revolution, he argued for the establishment of a parliament through a national assembly based on universal suffrage as part of proposed transformations to the structure of the state. In Kautsky's plan, the parliament, which he hoped would be filled with a majority of socialist representatives, would be the centre of political authority in a socialist republic.

Kautsky has been viewed as the main representative of the 'parliamentary path' to socialism and as a result he has been criticized as a supporter of 'bourgeois parliamentarism'. Hal Draper, for example, considered that Kautsky defended parliamentarism 'as if it could be realized only in the existing bourgeois forms'.[83] Draper argued that Kautsky's support for this bourgeois form of representative politics prevented him from siding with Luxemburg and the Revolutionary Shop Stewards during the German Revolution. Kautsky did advocate for the establishment of a parliamentary system during the revolution, but it was not accompanied by a liberal system of private property and hence can be distinguished from liberal parliamentary democracy. Rather, it was set within a broader array of institutional transformations that aimed at the creation of a socialist republic. This was based on Kautsky's understanding that parliaments could change their meaning and significance depending on the balance of forces between classes and the broader political system within which they were located. Following Marx and Engels defence of universal suffrage, Kautsky considered national elections based on universal suffrage to be the most democratic means of establishing the basis of a new socialist republic in which all citizens would enjoy equal rights.

In the early 1880s Kautsky was sceptical of the possibilities for parliamentary activity: 'Social Democracy harbours no illusion that it can directly achieve its goals through elections, through the parliamentary road.'[84] In these early articles, Kautsky's arguments to 'demolish the bourgeois state' and 'create the state anew' brought him much closer to Lenin's position in 'The State and Revolution'.[85] However, by the Erfurt Programme, his suspicion of participation in elections had been cast aside:

> The proletariat has, therefore, no reason to distrust parliamentary action; on the other hand, it has every reason to exert all its energy to increase the power of

[83] Hal Draper, *The Dictatorship of the Proletariat* (New York: NYU Press, 1987), 54.
[84] Quoted in Salvadori, *Karl Kautsky and the Socialist Revolution 1880–1938*, 22. [85] Ibid.

> parliaments in their relation to other departments of government and to swell to the utmost its own parliamentary representation.[86]

Kautsky's consistent position from this point onwards was that parliamentary activity was an important and necessary task of social democracy and that the struggle both for and within parliamentary institutions was a crucial pillar of socialist strategy.

Parliamentary activity was significant first of all as a means of increasing the power of the working class through gaining greater influence over lawmaking. Even in the relatively weak and ineffective 1890s Reichstag, Kautsky considered it important for the proletariat 'to influence the state authorities, to bend them to its purposes'.[87] Participation in parliament also served an educative function for workers in teaching them the necessary skills for self-government:

> This very participation of the proletariat proves to be the most effective means of shaking up the hitherto indifferent divisions of the proletariat and giving them hope and confidence. It is the most powerful lever that can be utilized to raise the proletariat out of its economic, social and moral degradation.[88]

It was essential for the struggle for the demands of the minimum programme that the working class utilized every means available to steadily grow its power within the capitalist system. Although it should never join coalition governments, the task of the workers' party was to develop the power of its opposition through growing its independent organizations and increasing its parliamentary share until it could obtain a majority.

Finally, parliamentary competition was important for workers to obtain a realistic assessment of their strength, which would bring the conflict further into the open and also increase their confidence:

> The election of a Constituent Assembly is an urgent necessity. Not in order to neutralize conflicts among classes and parties, but rather to permit a more accurate assessment of their strength and thus to lend their struggles a more rational foundation.[89]

Kautsky grounded his strategy of parliamentary activity on an analysis of the role of parliaments in modern states. The power of parliament, Kautsky argued, depended on the particular configuration of forces and balance of power between classes within a given regime: 'The representative system is a political form that

[86] Kautsky, 'The Class Struggle'. [87] Ibid. [88] Ibid.
[89] Karl Kautsky, 'Stockholm', *Die Neue Zeit* 35, no. 2 (1916–17), 507.

can assume, and has assumed, the most diverse content.'[90] For Kautsky, parliaments do not have an inherently bourgeois character, nor were they even an invention of the bourgeoisie. Representative institutions such as parliaments predate the emergence of capitalism and can be traced back into the Middle Ages. The content of a parliament is dependent on the forces that act within it: 'Whenever the proletariat engages in parliamentary activity as a self-conscious class, parliamentarism begins to change its character. It ceases to be a mere tool in the hands of the bourgeoisie.'[91] In *Parliamentarism and Democracy*, Kautsky went further still, arguing that 'a real parliamentary regime can be just as well an instrument for the dictatorship of the proletariat as it is an instrument for the dictatorship of the bourgeoisie'.[92]

In Kautsky's analysis, the role of parliament would be circumscribed by other forces within the socialist republic. First, the regime itself would be drastically decentralized such that significant power and decision-making capacity would devolve to regional and municipal assemblies. This aspect of Kautsky's political programme has been highlighted above. Second, the political parliament would sit alongside a constellation of economic bodies from worker and consumer groups to regional and industry-wide councils, right up to a national economic body. The power of the national parliament would therefore be counterbalanced by these various bodies. This aspect of the socialization of the economy will be treated further below. Third, Kautsky advocated for the institutionalization of pressure on parliament from below through civic organizations. For Kautsky:

> The introduction of a parliament is one aspect of democratization, but it is not sufficient in itself. Important as the dependence of the government on parliament may be, it leads to democratization only when it is accompanied by the growing dependence of parliament on the popular masses.[93]

In this passage, Kautsky referred to the process of democratization as containing two key elements. Equally as important as the establishment of a parliament was the close relationship between democratic institutions and the organized masses. It was the role of socialists to enable the masses to bring their political weight to bear on representative institutions. Kautsky believed that a 'parliament is deprived of strength when it cannot rely on the mass of the people.'[94] Contrary to the frequent assertion that Kautsky advocated some form of 'parliamentary only' tactics, he claimed 'a parliament that does not derive its support from the mass of the people is powerless. On the other hand, the people in a parliamentary state

[90] Karl Kautsky, 'Parliamentarianism and Democracy', in *Karl Kautsky on Democracy and Republicanism*, 132.

[91] Kautsky, 'The Class Struggle'.

[92] Kautsky, 'Parliamentarianism and Democracy', 109.

[93] Kautsky, 'The Bolsheviki Arising', 15 November 1917.

[94] Ibid.

that leaves its fate exclusively in the hands of the parliament is likewise impotent.'[95] All of this Kautsky believed could be found directly in the Marxian tradition:

> Marx acknowledged the necessity for the parliament in modern politics, but just as much the necessity of pressure on the parliament from without. He who demands the supreme power be lodged in the parliament, but at the same time holds back the proletariat from all efforts to influence the parliament through methods corresponding to the nature of the proletariat as a class, he does not seriously desire the democratization of the (German) political system.[96]

This interpretation of the role of parliament led Kautsky to support elections to a National Assembly during the German Revolution, which positioned him against Luxemburg and on the side of the SPD. Kautsky believed that the temporary functionaries of the socialist parties must be replaced by democratically elected representatives to ensure the legitimacy of the new regime. He first put this view forward in his criticisms of the Bolshevik's decision to abolish the Constituent Assembly. Kautsky contrasted two different methods and institutions: on the one hand the Russians could have 'put all political power in the hands of a representative body elected through equal, direct, and secret universal suffrage, as Engels demanded in 1891'. Instead the Bolsheviks believed 'new political institutions should be elected on the basis of an indirect, unequal, class-based, and limited suffrage reserved for certain privileged strata of workers, soldiers and peasants.'[97] Kautsky came to the defence of universal suffrage on the grounds that the permanent institutionalization of power based on any other more limited grounds would lead to civil war and severe economic disruptions.[98]

Workers' Councils and Socialization

The final goal of social transformation for certain radical council theorists was a council republic based on participatory workers' councils as the fundamental political and economic institutions. Most versions of council democracy were conceived of as a pyramidal structure of local and regional councils organized into a federal model with a national council as the executive organ. For Rosa Luxemburg and the Spartacus League, the goal was the '[e]limination of all parliaments and municipal councils, and takeover of their functions by workers' and soldiers' councils'.[99] But with the achievement of a democratic republic, Kautsky believed it was no longer the case that an autonomous system of workers'

[95] Ibid. [96] Ibid. [97] Kautsky, *Demokratie oder Diktatur*, 9. [98] Ibid., 56–7.
[99] Luxemburg, 'What Does the Spartacus League Want?'.

councils would provide a more adequate realization of democracy than these institutions.

Kautsky doubted whether there was any qualitative difference between the two arrangements that gave the council system a distinctive proletarian character: 'you search in vain for evidence that a national assembly by its nature must oppose socialism, or that a soldiers' council inherently must support socialism.'[100] The major difference between the two systems was a matter of who could vote. Kautsky argued that the national assembly would be elected through 'a precisely defined franchise that is equal for the entire population, excluding any doubt over who has the right to vote', whereas the councils would have no way of properly determining which layers of the workforce and related groups would be able to vote. Such a system would not prove superior to universal suffrage for several reasons. First, it would succumb to local and particular interests within specific factories and industries attempting to gain advantage over others. Second, it would not be able to generate the same authority over the population because of its ambiguities and potential exclusions: the councils were only elected by one small section of workers, which would therefore disenfranchise not only the bourgeoisie, but also potentially, certain women, peasants, and the unemployed, among others.[101] Third, it would divide rather than unite the workers because in the elections it would put them in competition with each other rather than using the election campaign as a form of class struggle. Numerically, the capitalist class was extremely small, so Kautsky believed they would benefit from universal rather than particular suffrage: 'To think that the capitalists exercise any power whatsoever in the elections through strength of numbers, or that with universal, equal suffrage they would thereby receive some kind of weapon, is nothing but superstition.'[102]

Kautsky was accused by the left radicals of opposing the workers' councils and supporting the forces of the bourgeoisie. However, in 'National Assembly and Council Assembly', Kautsky claimed that workers' councils and a national assembly are 'both equally necessary'. In the first phase of the revolution, the councils were 'indispensable and highly beneficial' to spreading the revolution and establishing the power of workers over the old ruling class. During the second phase of 'consolidation and construction', Kautsky believed parliamentary institutions should be the basis of a more permanent and legitimate authority, but this 'does not make the workers' councils superfluous'. In Kautsky's view:

> it is no less important that the popular masses energetically participate in this activity, strengthening the power of the representatives in parliament and

[100] Kautsky, 'National Assembly and Council Assembly', 96.
[101] Karl Kautsky, *The Dictatorship of the Proletariat*.
[102] Kautsky, 'National Assembly and Council Assembly', 95.

> spurring on their zeal with constant pressure from without.... Moreover, the workers councils are uniquely competent to safeguard proletariat class interests ...the actual workers' councils would retain important political functions.... Therefore it is not a question of either national assembly or workers councils, but *both.*[103]

Kautsky believed that there should be institutionalized pressure from below in order to hold representatives accountable and struggle for the particular interests of the working class.

The claim for reading Kautsky as a *socialist* republican rests on his extensive plans to socialize the economy. Not only did Kautsky argue that '[t]he German republic should become a democratic republic', he believed 'it should be even more than that: a socialist republic—a commonwealth in which there is no longer any place for the exploitation of man by man.'[104] This involved plans 'to convert the capitalist mode of production into the socialist mode of production'.[105] The essence of this process of socialization was not merely the nationalization of industries, it was the democratic intervention of workers into the economy and 'the democratic organization of economic life'.[106] Kautksy was aware of the dangers of a bureaucratic autocracy forming under state socialism and argued that without sufficient forms of local control and robust democratic organization 'a communist economy' could become 'a basis for despotism'.[107] But similarly, a democratic republic that maintained the rule of the bourgeoisie through a system of private property would also be deficient. Thus for Kautsky, socialization would need 'to extend democracy from the political to the economic system'[108] in order to transform the basis of a democratic republic 'into a social republic, instigating a new era in the history of humanity'.[109]

Kautsky believed there were two important preconditions before full socialization could be undertaken. First, the political foundations of a new decentralized administrative apparatus had to be laid in order for responsible bodies to establish new structures of ownership and management in industry. In many parts of Germany, remnants from the feudal era persisted, which required reform and the creation of a full democratic republic. Second, there had to be a dramatic increase in production. Kautsky feared that processes of socialization would prove disruptive and that the socialists might be blamed for a sharp economic downturn. These preconditions did not preclude the immediate commencement of plans to socialize key industries, but they were important steps that would have to be taken

[103] Karl Kautsky, 'National Assembly and Council Assembly'.
[104] Kautsky, 'Guidelines for a Socialist Action Programme'.
[105] Kautsky, 'Driving the Revolution Forward'.
[106] Kautsky, 'Guidelines for a Socialist Action Programme'.
[107] Kautsky, *Demokratie oder Diktatur.* [108] Ibid., 23.
[109] Kautsky, 'Guidelines for a Socialist Action Programme'.

for the process of socialization to function effectively. In the beginning, Kautsky estimated that 'nothing stands in the way of nationalizing all mines, forests and large estates (roughly, those over 100 acres), as well as all municipal land (excluding the houses built on it).'[110] Then once more preparatory work had been undertaken, it would be preferable that 'whole branches of industry should be nationalised, not individual firms', in order to undertake the transformation efficiently and to avoid negative side effects.

Kautsky and Luxemburg differed on the pace of socialization based on their different conceptions of a gradualist versus an immediate approach. For Kautsky, 'it cannot be carried out in the blink of an eye, but only gradually, following a careful examination of actual relations and preparation of the new order.'[111] He considered a modern economy as large as Germany's to be a complex and interconnected system that would require careful planning before any intervention could take place. Kautsky used a biological analogy in making his case: if the state was like a mechanism, then the economy was more comparable to an organism, which was more complicated and hence could not be transformed as quickly. He insisted that his gradualist approach did not mean that he was any less committed to the end goal of a socialized economy: 'It says nothing against the need to use all the energy we have to work on this transformation.'[112]

Kautsky remained vehemently opposed to the Spartacus League for what he considered their overly hasty approach. He argued that if one were to employ mass strikes to completely disrupt the economy until it collapsed this would destroy the livelihood of workers and turn them against the revolution. He emphasized that Luxemburg had no concrete plans for how socialization would occur aside from offering workers the right of control over their factories. As Nicholas Vrousalis has persuasively demonstrated, Kautsky's conception of socialization sought to avoid two undesirable extremes of what Vrousalis has called 'the socialization dilemma'.[113] On the one hand, Kautsky feared a Bolshevik-styled 'bureaucratic autocracy' in which the state usurped workers' power through the centralization of decision-making over the economy. The danger here consisted of the creation of a new despotism in which state officials became a new privileged class with complete control over political and economic life. On the other hand, the syndicalist alternative of transferring control over workplaces directly to the workers themselves posed another set of potential dangers: 'the workers would raise wages, reduce hours of labour, diminish the volume of production, and increase the prices of their products, without troubling about the community.'[114] Without any counterbalancing power representing the interests of the community as a whole, the risk of particularism and a labour aristocracy would arise if workers were provided with incentives to benefit themselves over the rest of the

[110] Ibid. [111] Kautsky, 'Driving the Revolution Forward'. [112] Ibid.
[113] Vrousalis, 'The Socialisation Dilemma'. [114] Kautsky, 'What is Socialisation?'

community. Kautsky believed it necessary to balance the need to provide greater democracy to workers within the workplace with organizing production for community needs on a national scale.

He emphasized that no single blueprint could cover every complexity of how socialization would be applied to various industries and specific cases: 'The starting-points and forms of socialization will be as infinitely varied as modern social life, and they will succeed and thrive all the better, the less occasion there is for bureaucratic intervention.'[115] The two overriding goals of the process of socialization would be the democratic organization of the production process and the replacement of production for profit with production to satisfy community needs. The first could be provided by the democratization of workplaces to accord workers greater control over their working lives:

> our duty will be to replace bureaucratic autocracy by a type of management which would accord a wide measure of self-government to the workers without losing sight of the consumers' interest or creating a Labour aristocracy of the municipal workers.[116]

Under a socialist form of production, 'instead of the worker confronting a boss who owns and controls the means of production, he confronts society, of which he is also a part.'[117] It would be necessary to radically transform the hierarchical and disciplinarian structure of workplaces 'to displace autocracy with democracy, in the economy as in politics'.[118] Kautsky argued that the need to transform the organization of workplaces 'is valid even more so for the economic machine of capitalism than for the state machine. In both cases, it is necessary to implement the most complete democracy.'[119] However, socialization cannot exist solely in the transfer of workplaces to workers because 'the interests of the workers and consumers clash to a certain extent: the former strive for higher wages and shorter hours; the latter for lower prices.'[120]

Drawing from Austrian Marxist writers such as Otto Bauer, Kautsky proposed the creation of a new form of economic organization that would assist with the management and coordination of a socialist economy. This organization would consist of one-third workers' representatives, one-third organized consumers, and one-third representatives of the state administration in order to adequately balance the interests of different sections of the community:

[115] Kautsky, *The Labour Revolution*. [116] Kautsky, *The Labour Revolution*.
[117] Kautsky, 'Guidelines for a Socialist Action Programme'.
[118] Kautsky, *Sozialdemokratische Bemerkungen zur Ubergangswirtschaft*, 159. [119] Ibid., 160.
[120] Kautsky, 'Guidelines for a Socialist Action Programme'.

> With each branch of production that is transferred from capitalist to State or municipal ownership, a new organization should be created, which would enable the workers and the consumers, as well as science, to exercise the necessary influence upon the adaptation of the processes of production. Such an organization would be quite different from State bureaucracy as we have hitherto understood it.[121]

Crucial to Kautsky's plans was the role of state bureaucrats who would occupy one-third of the positions in the highest body of this organization to represent the interests of the community as a whole above the sectional and particular interests of any one factory, region, or industry:

> If workers and consumers were combined in an association in such wise that neither section could dominate the other, they would have to endeavour to overcome their antagonism by means which would be beneficial to both.... To discover these means is the task of the men of science, whose services would be enlisted as the third party in the organization of economy. Their duty would be to ensure that the most perfect technical appliances and organization were adopted in the undertaking, so that the greatest possible result would be obtained with the smallest expenditure of energy.[122]

Importantly for Kautsky, this new economic organization would not be coterminal with the state. Kautsky was adamant that socialization should not be viewed as synonymous with nationalization and state ownership: 'The State is not the appointed instrument of socialization in all branches of industry.'[123] In fact, in certain cases municipal control over production would be sufficient. In cases where 'branches of production or of communications serve narrow local ends' then '[m]unicipal ownership and management is the proper solution of the problem.'[124] Under a socialized economy the municipality would become an important site of local management and control. Kautsky believed it could 'socialise bread production for itself alone... It can become one of the factors in the socialisation of agriculture'. It also 'falls to the municipality to socialise the production of housing, to build and manage sound and cheap housing for the masses'.[125] Yet it would be the state that was responsible for passing worker protection laws and for working alongside representatives from specific industries and workplaces in order to oversee the implementation of decisions.

[121] Kautsky, 'What is Socialisation?' Report submitted to the second congress of the Workers' Councils of Germany.
[122] Kautsky, *The Labour Revolution.* [123] Ibid.
[124] Kautsky, 'Guidelines for a Socialist Action Programme'. [125] Ibid.

Kautsky advised a slower course when it came to the socialization of agriculture: 'In agriculture we cannot quite proceed as we do in industry. It would not be practical to expropriate farmers' land.'[126] The priority for agriculture would be to utilize more efficient methods through investment in agricultural machinery and the promotion of its use.

He also considered that a certain amount of compensation should be provided to capitalists for their businesses.[127] Kautsky noted that this was an idea first proposed by Marx in an article discussing the agrarian question in England and was not foreign to Marxist thought. Capitalists would be offered money by a socialist state in return for productive and well-maintained enterprises which would then be socialized. Kautksy saw that there were principled and strategic reasons for proposing compensation:

> This is not just a question of justice: confiscation would only hit a few of the capitalists, not the majority of them—and it would not only hit capitalists, but smaller business people, too. There are also economic reasons: at a time when the productive process requires the utmost protection, confiscation would most greatly alarm and disrupt the productive capitalists. Compensation would best occur by issuing government bonds at a moderate rate of interest.[128]

If compensation were provided to business owners, this would help alleviate a common criticism of gradualist approaches to socialization that they would lead to economic chaos because capitalists would have no incentive to keep operating their business during the slow period of socialization.

Internationalism

A final key aspect of Kautsky's programme was a policy of spreading the class struggle to other countries: 'Alongside *democratization* and *socialization*, a proletarian government has yet another task: *internationalization*.'[129] Kautsky called for a dramatic departure from Germany's old strategy of power politics against other nations and argued that its foreign policy should be based on establishing an international league of all nations in which 'the German people can participate as equals amongst equals—with full self-determination and with the enthusiastic recognition of this right for other nations too.'[130] Democratization and socialization at home must also be accompanied by the promotion of these principles abroad. For Kautsky, a German socialist republic should not resort to the use of secretive methods in spreading these principles, but rather engage in acts of

[126] Ibid. [127] Ibid. [128] Ibid. [129] Ibid. [130] Ibid.

international solidarity with other peoples. While he agreed with other proponents of proletarian internationalism that socialist revolution is part of a single global struggle against capitalism, he rejected the methods of class struggle adopted by the Bolsheviks and did not see the Russian Revolution as a genuine socialist revolution.

One controversial aspect of this programme was the decision of Kautsky and the German provisional government to refuse recognition of the Russian Bolshevik government. In a cabinet meeting of the Council of People's Representatives on 18 November 1918 at which Kautsky was also present, he advised delaying any official recognition, stating that 'the soviet government will not last long; in a few weeks it will be finished.'[131] While Luxemburg and Liebknecht argued for supporting the Bolsheviks and believed the German Revolution must join forces with the Russian, Kautsky was critical of the Bolsheviks and believed that recognizing their government would risk war with other nations. In the meeting Kautsky argued that '[w]e want to live with the whole world in peace and friendship, even with the Russian republic. No one can begrudge us such a peaceful position.'[132] As a result, Kautsky's form of international solidarity differed greatly from traditional Marxist international socialism, which involved spreading class struggle in other countries through political agitation and support of communist groups overseas.

In spite of his efforts, Kautsky's programme had little practical impact during the revolution. He called for organizational unity between the SPD and USPD and campaigned against attempts by the Spartacus League to overthrow the provisional government. Over the course of the revolution, Kautsky increasingly shifted his attention towards the revolutionary Left, blaming them rather than the Ebert–Scheidemann government's collaboration with right-wing forces for the growing problems of the revolution. After 1918, Kautsky's primary aim was an ongoing polemic against the Bolshevik regime, which led to heated exchanges with Lenin and Trotsky.[133] He viewed Bolshevism as a threat to the workers' struggle due to the Soviet government's attacks on political freedoms and its use of dictatorial methods. Kautsky's involvement in the Socialization Commission from December 1918 to April 1919 amounted to little more than a few reports, which were never acted upon by the SPD-led government. Despite the unwillingness of the SPD to

[131] 'Meeting Minutes from the Council of People's Representatives, 18 November 1918', in *The German Revolution and the Debate on Soviet Power*, ed. John Riddell (New York: Anchor Foundation, 1986), 69.

[132] Ibid.

[133] Kautsky, *The Dictatorship of the Proletariat*; Karl Kautsky, *Terrorism and Communism: a Contribution to the Natural History of Revolution*, trans. W. H. Kerridge (London: The National Labour Press, 1920 [1919]); Karl Kautsky, *Von der Demokratie zur Staatssklaverei. Eine Auseinandersetzung mit Trotzki* (Berlin: Freiheit, 1921); Vladimir Lenin, 'The Proletarian Revolution And The Renegade Kautsky', *Lenin's Collected Works, Volume 28* (Moscow: Progress Publishers, 1974) 104–12; Leon Trotsky, *Terrorism and Communism* (London: Verso, 2007 [1920]).

begin serious processes of socialization, Kautsky failed to develop an analysis of the conservatism of the SPD and their compromises with the old regime. During his brief appointment as under-secretary of State in the Foreign Office, Kautsky worked on retrieving documents which proved the guilt of the German regime for the war.[134] Following 1920, Kautsky became even more isolated in the USPD and never regained his previous influence within the party.

As can be seen, the institutional arrangements of Kautsky's socialist republicanism differed greatly from Pannekoek's idea of a society based on a system of workers' councils. Kautsky's socialist action programme sought to combine a Marxist analysis of capitalist exploitation with a modern system of representative government that would extend and modify Marx's analysis of the state to the sociological realities of twentieth-century German society. In addition to institutional questions about how best to organize a self-determining society, council theorists also debated the cultural aspects required to live as a free people. Political transformation was seen as one part of a broader emancipatory process requiring widespread changes in cultural norms and shared social understandings. The theorists of the German council movements were among the first and sharpest observers of the bourgeoisie's ideological domination of workers and the need for a change in workers' intellectual frameworks and mindsets. In chapter five, I further examine the writings of Rosa Luxemburg and her conception of the development of 'socialist civic virtues' as one possible response to this urgent problem.

[134] The results were published as Graf Max Montgelas and Walther Schücking, eds., *Outbreak of the World War: **German Documents collected by Karl Kautsky and edited by Max Montgelas and Walther Schücking*** (New York: Oxford University Press, 1924).

5
Socialist Civic Virtues

In 1917, reflecting upon the prospects for the Russian Revolution, Karl Kautsky wrote, '[i]n order to liberate themselves, the workers not only need certain material preconditions at their disposal and to be numerically strong; they also have to become new people, endued with the abilities that are required for the reorganization of state and society.'[1] Writing to his friend Leo Kestenberg during the German Revolution, Gustav Landauer envisaged 'a new humanity and a new spirit' that would be born out of a period of 'fundamental social transformations' to Germany society.[2] For Rosa Luxemburg, '[s]ocialism in life demands a complete spiritual transformation in the masses degraded by centuries of bourgeois rule. Social instincts in place of egotistical ones, mass initiative in place of inertia, idealism which conquers all suffering.'[3] Throughout this revolutionary epoch, council theorists would return to these themes of cultural transformation and spiritual renewal as necessary requirements of a political revolution.

The council movements struggled not only for political and economic changes but also for a broader project of human emancipation couched in terms of ideological transformation and cultural rejuvenation. The idea of the socialization of the economy was inextricably tied to the development of the German peoples' 'spirit' [*Geist*] and culture. Workers were gripped by the strong ideological hold of bourgeois mentalities, which hindered the development of a working-class culture. As a result, theorists such as Anton Pannekoek, Rosa Luxemburg, and Gustav Landauer emphasized the subjective role that a people's class consciousness played in political struggle. While many of these ideas were developed in the radical sections of the Second International before the German Revolution, it was this event which clearly demonstrated the great impediment that ideological backwardness posed to social change. Workers who had been socialized in capitalist societies had developed deep-seated mentalities and patterns of behaviour that were barriers to the reorganization of political life.

Sparked by her experiences of the revolutionary period of 1917–19, Rosa Luxemburg made an important contribution to these debates which has been

[1] Karl Kautsky, 'Prospects of the Russian Revolution', *Worker Weekly*, 14 January 2010.
[2] Landauer, 'Letter to Leo Kestenberg, Krumbach (Swabia), 22 November 1918', 173–4. See also Landauer, *Revolution and Other Writings: A Political Reader.*
[3] Luxemburg, *The Russian Revolution.*

Building Power to Change the World: The Political Thought of the German Council Movements. James Muldoon, Oxford University Press (2020). © James Muldoon. DOI: 10.1093/oso/9780198856627.003.0006

passed over by many of her interpreters.[4] The German Revolution prompted Luxemburg to consider in much greater detail the necessary conditions of revolutionary transformation. While her early work on political economy is marked by a view of socialism as based primarily on the transformation of the economy towards rational and planned production, she later developed a more expansive vision of social and cultural transformation. In later writings such as 'What Does the Spartacus League Want?' and 'The Socialisation of Society', Luxemburg argued for the importance of a widespread change in social norms and patterns of behaviour to ensure the success of revolutionary transformation. Adopting the republican-inspired language of 'socialist civic virtues', she considered that worker-controlled institutions would need to be supported by widely accepted socialist norms that would be common knowledge and followed as a matter of habit. Luxemburg argued that workers should direct themselves away from the egoism, individualism, and competition that predominated in capitalist societies and towards socialist virtues of self-discipline, political judgement, self-activity, and solidarity.

Luxemburg explicitly drew upon a republican political vocabulary of political autonomy, civic virtue and participation in public life. Classic republican thinkers have long argued for the importance of civic virtue in maintaining a republican state against corruption and decay.[5] Republicans understood corruption to mean individuals or factional interests placing their private ends ahead of the common good. Citizens cultivated civic virtue through the development of habits oriented towards the collective aims of the community.[6] This chapter will argue that Luxemburg followed this democratic republican tradition in interpreting civic virtues as a set of dispositions and habitual behaviours directed towards collective goals. However, it will go on to show that she significantly altered the meaning of civic virtue by interpreting it as habitual action in solidarity with other workers in political struggle rather than as action aimed at preserving a state's institutions. Oriented by a desire for transformation rather than preservation, socialist civic virtues were directed at the struggle against capitalist exploitation and for the creation and sustenance of a socialist society. While Luxemburg deployed republican language, it will be argued that it was reconfigured within a revolutionary socialist ideology.

Building on the democratic republican heritage present in Marx and Engels' writings, Luxemburg expressed the contents of socialism as the active

[4] Peter Hudis, 'Rosa Luxemburg's Concept of a Post-capitalist Society', *Critique* 40, no. 3 (2015), 323–35; See also Steve D'Arcy, 'Rosa Luxemburg on "the Socialist Civic Virtues"', *The Public Autonomy Project*, 9 September 2014.

[5] Richard Dagger, *Civic Virtues: Rights, Citizenship, and Republican Liberalism* (Oxford: Oxford University Press, 2007).

[6] Dagger, *Civic Virtues*, 14.

participation of individuals in a post-capitalist, self-determining society.[7] One of the fundamental goals of political struggle was to resist capitalist alienation through workers reasserting their control over social institutions and reclaiming their political agency. Luxemburg envisaged cultural transformation as part of a broader emancipatory process—political, economic, and social—of workers becoming free and self-conscious agents exercising control over the direction of their lives. The ideal of freedom as self-determination and her political strategy of mass action was part of her fundamental commitment to the concept of self-emancipation: 'the emancipation of the working classes must be conquered by the working classes themselves.'[8]

Luxemburg also offered a different take on the question of how civic virtues should be cultivated. Classic republicans considered that civic virtue should be transmitted through state institutions and policies.[9] Adrian Oldfield summarizes the position as follows: 'The moral character which is appropriate for genuine citizenship does not generate itself; it has to be authoritatively inculcated.'[10] State institutions were in charge of delivering a civic education of the traditions and customs of the community to direct citizens toward their civic duties and a defence of the state. In contrast, Luxemburg argued that the only way civic virtue should be developed was through self-education and self-organization. She believed it was primarily through their own political activity and experience of political struggle that workers could acquire the necessary habits and dispositions of self-government important for living in an autonomous and community-directed society.

This chapter proceeds as follows. First, I outline the importance of questions of ideology and culture to radical theorists within the council movements. I show how council theorists' experience of the German Revolution demonstrated the importance of cultural factors in political struggle. I then turn to Karl Kautsky's early theorization of the necessary psychological developments in workers to achieve political transformation. I argue that this was a precursor and model for Luxemburg's own writings. Following this, I turn to Luxemburg's institutional vision for a post-capitalist society during the German Revolution. I then analyse her formulation of socialist civic virtues and outline the main conceptual innovations from a republican theory of civic virtues. I sketch each virtue and conclude by discussing the problems and possible criticisms of her theory.

[7] On Marx's democratic republicanism see Bruno Leipold, *Citizen Marx: Republicanism, Communism and Capitalism*. Princeton: Princeton University Press, (forthcoming).

[8] Karl Marx, 'General Rules of the International Workingmen's Association'.

[9] Pettit, *Republicanism*, 97; Dagger, *Civic Virtues*, 17–31; Sandel, *Democracy's Discontent*, 25–54.

[10] Adrian Oldfield, *Citizenship and Community: Civic Republicanism and the Modern World* (New York: Routledge, 1990), 164.

Cultural Transformation

Radical council theorists were adamant that a fundamental political transformation required a corresponding shift in ideology and culture. Rather than viewing culture as entirely determined by the underlying economic relations of production, these council theorists viewed cultural belief systems as a semi-autonomous domain in a reciprocal relationship with economic factors, which was of equal significance in the struggle for a socialist transformation of society. Revolutionary transformation was not just a question of institutional change at the top of society, but of a fundamental shift in culture that would take place amongst all workers. The problem could not be addressed by simply establishing new political and economic institutions, as the oppressive relations were deeply rooted in the national psyche and could only be overcome through more profound changes of mentality. They envisaged a revolutionary dynamic which would lead to a 'new humanity' and a new ethics of coexistence. The spiritual renewal of German politics was viewed as a necessary requirement for realizing the political goals of the revolution.

The question of cultural transformation has traditionally been granted less significance in Marxist theory. Marx and Engels rarely analysed cultural phenomena in much detail and tended to focus on the economy as a determining factor of historical development. There are instances in Marx's writings, such as the famous preface to *A Contribution to a Critique of Political Economy*, in which he writes as though culture is an outgrowth and product of more fundamental economic structures: 'The mode of production of material life conditions the general process of social, political, and intellectual life. It is not the consciousness of men that determines their existence, but their social existence that determines their consciousness.'[11] Yet Engels cautioned against simplistic interpretations of their theory as a mechanical base/superstructure model in which the economy determines all other aspects of society. He insisted that historical development was a reciprocal and dynamic process between different sources and that economics cannot be considered the sole determining factor.[12] For Marx and Engels, cultural ideas of a particular historical epoch served to justify and legitimize the interests of the ruling class. Ideology helps to promote the dominant ideas of the ruling class and to cover up forms of oppression by framing the status quo as a necessary and universal form of life. While Marx and Engels began a critique of ideology, these ideas were further developed within the Dutch and German sections of the Second International before the First World War.

The importance of subjective factors of class consciousness and spiritual development was already identified in different ways by theorists such as Anton

[11] Marx, *Preface to A Contribution to a Critique of Political Economy.*
[12] Friedrich Engels, 'Letter to J. Bloch', 21 September 1890.

Pannekoek and Rosa Luxemburg. Pannekoek, for example, turned attention towards the question of a people's 'spirit', or more precisely, the role that class consciousness and ideology played in political struggle. A true revolution would have to bring about a change of consciousness and a gradual development in the political ideology of the masses alongside economic changes. He believed that the workers must combat the 'spiritual superiority of the ruling minority' which 'presides over all spiritual development, all science'.[13] For Pannekoek it was this 'spiritual dependence of the proletariat on the bourgeoisie', which represented the 'main cause of the weakness of the proletariat'.[14] The development of a culture that promoted human freedom and emancipation had to be a central pillar of political struggle.

Pannekoek developed these views through a synthesis of the work of Marx with another of his influences, Joseph Dietzgen. Pannekoek believed that the question of human 'spirit' was underdeveloped in Marx's writings. He contested a rigid interpretation of the Marxian position that systems of thought could be directly derived from specific material conditions. Pannekoek believed that a system of ideas was not simply a reflection of the current economic reality but was also transmitted from the past, reflecting a certain historical lag in frameworks of understanding in comparison to current material conditions. For Pannekoek, certain prior modes of thought retained their spiritual force because they were still present in the collective memory of society. In Pannekoek's words, this was 'the perpetuation of collective ideas, systematized in the form of prevailing beliefs and ideologies, and transferred to future generations in books, in literature, in art and in education.'[15] This emphasis on the subjective dimension of political struggle led Pannekoek to a position that the socialist revolution in economic production 'must be accompanied by an equally fundamental spiritual revolution... the new understanding gains ground step by step, waging a relentless battle against the traditional ideas to which the ruling classes are clinging, this struggle is the mental companion of the social class struggle.'[16]

While these ideas were first developed before the war, the events of the German Revolution brought to light the urgency of this fundamental problem. It became apparent to a number of theorists within the council movements that despite the political power that workers had gained, they still lagged in ideological development. Nobody was a keener observer of this problem than Pannekoek, who saw that the problem of ideology lay at the centre of the revolution. The strength of the

[13] Anton Pannekoek, 'Mass Action and Revolution', *Die Neue Zeit* 30 (1912), 609–16.

[14] Ibid.

[15] Anton Pannekoek, 'Society and Mind in Marxian Philosophy', *Science and Society* (Summer 1937).

[16] Anton Pannekoek, 'The Position and Significance of Joseph Dietzgen's Philosophical Works', in Joseph Dietzgen, *The Positive Outcome of Philosophy* (Chicago, 1906), 12–13.

bourgeoisie, in Pannekoek's view, did not emanate solely from their economic or political resources, but from their control of cultural and educational institutions:

> In November 1918, state power slipped from the nerveless grasp of the bourgeoisie in Germany and Austria . . . the masses were in control; and the bourgeoisie was nevertheless able to build this state power up again and once more subjugate the workers. This proves that the bourgeoisie possessed another hidden source of power which had remained intact and which permitted it to re-establish its hegemony when everything seemed shattered. This hidden power is the bourgeoisie's ideological hold over the proletariat. Because the proletarian masses were still completely governed by a bourgeois mentality, they restored the hegemony of the bourgeoisie with their own hands after it had collapsed.[17]

Ultimately, it was council delegates themselves who voted for the abolition of the councils as permanent centres of power, leading certain radical council theorists to complain that they had little understanding of the organizational tasks and historical role of the councils. Karl Korsch considered that 'causes of an ideological kind must be mentioned as having played a role' in the defeat of the German Revolution. He continued:

> in the brief period of time when the real preconditions for laying the foundations for and building a solid proletarian dictatorship existed in Germany, the opportunity was necessarily wasted due to the fact that, among broad swaths of the revolutionary proletariat, even in its own functioning 'Councils', there was an almost total lack of real understanding concerning the organizational bases of a revolutionary Council System and the essential tasks which it must perform.[18]

Rosa Luxemburg wrote of the lack of revolutionary consciousness amongst the workers, arguing that '[t]he masses of workers who are already organized in workers' and soldiers' councils are still miles away from having adopted such an outlook, and only isolated proletarian minorities are clearly conscious of their tasks.'[19] Ernst Däumig also believed in the need for education and cultural development. He considered that 'the German people have to get used to self-management instead of governance' and that 'the new world can only be built by the political, economic, and cultural activities of the entire German people.'[20]

The battle for human emancipation, then, was not restricted to the economic sphere but was also fought on the level of ideology, entailing a control over

[17] Anton Pannekoek, 'World Revolution and Communist Tactics', in *Pannekoek and Gorter's Marxism*, ed. D. A. Smart (London: Pluto Press, 1978), 130.
[18] Korsch, 'Evolution of the Problem of the Political Workers Councils in Germany'.
[19] Luxemburg, 'Our Program and the Political Situation'.
[20] Däumig, 'The National Assembly Means the Councils' Death', 48.

education, schools, the press, and the cultural forces that aimed to stifle the revolution. The German education system was thoroughly pervaded by the state's authoritarian ideology. In 1889, Wilhelm II announced his plans for the schooling system:

> For a long time the thought has occupied me . . . to make the schools at each grade level useful in working against the spread of socialistic and communistic ideas. Of the first importance is that the school, by cultivating fear of God and love of the fatherland, lays a foundation for a healthy view of state and social conditions.[21]

The SPD also operated a network of cultural apparatuses which penetrated the lives of workers from magazines, libraries, workers' sports teams, theatres, publishers, cooperative shops, 'red' singing choirs, beer halls, and nature walking clubs. These associations created a feeling of solidarity among workers and 'developed an alternative culture in which members helped construct the notion of what it meant to be a Social Democrat'.[22]

The conclusions drawn by many of the participants in the German council movements were similar to positions developed by Antonio Gramsci, who briefly participated in council movements in Italy. Even before his writings from 1930 in which he developed his well-known concepts of a 'war of position' and a 'war of manoeuvre', Gramsci had identified how the bourgeoisie used cultural hegemony to maintain their power. In 1920, during the rise of the councils across Europe, Gramsci described how:

> [t]ogether with the problem of gaining political and economic power, the proletariat must also face the problem of winning intellectual power. . . . This revolution also presupposes the formation of a new set of standards, a new psychology, new ways of feeling, thinking and living that must be specific to the working class, that must be created by it, that will become 'dominant' when the working class becomes the dominant class.[23]

Gramsci would further develop these ideas through his notion of hegemony, which described how a ruling group in society would maintain its domination through ideas and cultural forms that induced the consent of other classes to the status quo. While Gramsci's theory of cultural hegemony is well known, Luxemburg's insistence on the importance of socialist civic virtues has received less scrutiny. Luxemburg adds to our understanding of the positive content of a

[21] Quoted in Albert Schmelzer, *The Threefolding Movement, 1919: Rudolf Steiner's Campaign for a Self-Governing, Self-Managing, Self-Educating Society* (Forest Row: Rudolf Steiner Press, 2017), 17.

[22] Pelz, *A People's History of the German Revolution*, 20.

[23] Unsigned, *Avanti!*, 14 June 1920, in *The Gramsci Reader: Selected Writings 1916–1935*, ed. David Forgacs (New York: New York University Press, 2000), 70.

socialist culture and provides a vision of a post-capitalist society. In his early work, Gramsci gestures to the necessity of constructing a new cultural framework, whereas Luxemburg provides a provisional answer to the outlines of a working-class culture.

Karl Kautsky's Psychological Foundations of a Socialist Society

Luxemburg's vision for cultural transformation and the development of a socialist ethos draws heavily from an earlier formulation by Karl Kautsky in *The Social Revolution* (1902), which proved influential over the left wing of the SPD.[24] In this political pamphlet, Kautsky reflected upon the 'moral re-birth of the proletariat' as a significant factor in preparing 'the ethical foundations of the new [socialist] society'.[25] While still privileging economic considerations as the most essential determining factor in socialist development, Kautsky acknowledged the importance of 'psychological preliminary conditions in order to enable it to be realized'.[26] He identified the necessity of overcoming the prevalence of 'egoism and brutality' in bourgeois society and developing the 'psychological foundations' of a socialist society: 'high intelligence, strict discipline and complete organization'.[27] His characterization of a socialist ethos is remarkably similar to the one Luxemburg would articulate during the German Revolution. Given the striking parallel, it is conceivable that Luxemburg developed the basis of her ideas on cultural transformation from this initial sketch.

A first point of comparison is on the notion of proletariat discipline, which Luxemburg also analysed in her polemic against Lenin in 'Organizational Questions of Russian Social Democracy'. Kautsky argued that the initial steps for the development of a new socialist ethic were already present in the capitalist mode of production due to the discipline and organization of workers in large factories. But in a manner that prefigured Luxemburg's position, Kautsky described the 'prison regimentation' enacted in capitalist production as of 'a wholly different character' to the forms of discipline required for a socialist society. Rather than a militaristic and authoritarian discipline of physical compulsion, workers would need to develop a freely chosen and self-willed discipline that would enable them to cooperate in new forms of labour organization. A second parallel is the argument that the nature of labour itself would need to be transformed into a more appealing activity to engender a spirit of industriousness and productivity in workers. He suggested a shortening of the workday along with making the workplace 'more hygienic and friendly'. A final similarity to Luxemburg is that Kautsky insisted that it was through 'the struggle of the

[24] Bronner, *Socialism Unbound*, 45. [25] Kautsky, 'The Social Revolution'. [26] Ibid.
[27] Ibid.

proletarian against this [capitalist] exploitation' that would lead to 'the psychological conditions for socialist production'. Otherwise put, it was through taking part in political struggle that workers would develop the necessary discipline, organization, and skills for self-government.

Kautsky's emphasis in this pamphlet on the necessary cultural preconditions for socialist revolution might give us cause to reconsider the economic determinist interpretation of the Second International due to the importance accorded to cultural factors. For Kautsky, people's behaviour reflected their place in the economic system, but this could be challenged and altered through the spread of scientific truths about the corrupt nature of existing norms.[28] However, for Kautsky, there were limits to the cultural development that could be achieved within a capitalist mode of production. Kautsky argued that 'the creation of a higher type of mankind' could only be the *result* of socialist transformation rather than its precondition. Unlike Pannekoek and Gramsci, who had begun to view cultural factors as of equal significance to economic developments, orthodox members of the Second International still considered the economy as the underlying driving force. Trotsky expressed the basics of this position in the following way:

> The economic conditions are the fundamental factor of history, but we as a communist party, and as a workers' state, can only influence economics with the aid of the working class, and to attain this we must work unceasingly to promote the technical and cultural capacity of the individual element of the working class.[29]

Trotsky held that 'a dialectic dependence exists between the two spheres' and that '[i]n order to reach a higher stage of culture, the working class—and above all its vanguard—must consciously alter its morals. It must work consciously towards this goal.'[30] However, for most Marxists at the beginning of the twentieth century, economic development was still considered the driving force.

Luxemburg's Institutional Vision

The Russian and German revolutions thrust the question of the necessary conditions of socialist transformation on to the agenda with fresh urgency. In 'What does the Spartacus League Want?' published in *Die Rote Fahne* on 16 December 1918, Luxemburg set out the position of the Spartacus League in relation to the now pressing question: how to establish a socialist order of society? For

[28] Karl Kautsky, *Ethik und materialistische Geschichstsauffassung* (Berlin: J. H. W. Dietz 1927), 142.
[29] Leon Trotsky, 'Transformation of Morals'. [30] Ibid.

Luxemburg, '[t]his task requires a complete transformation of the state and a complete overthrow of the economic and social foundations of society.'[31] This question contained an important institutional dimension that Luxemburg addressed by arguing for the need to 'replace the inherited organs of bourgeois class rule—the assemblies, parliaments, and city councils—with its own class organs—with workers' and soldiers' councils'.[32] This would also involve productive assets passing into common ownership and production planned according to community needs.

The text is a political pamphlet and call to arms. As such, it does not aim to set out the complete institutional framework of a post-capitalist society but merely to address urgent questions of revolutionary struggle. Yet in its immediate demands the text nevertheless offers a general idea of the socialist society advocated for by Rosa Luxemburg and the Spartacus League. Like Kautsky, Luxemburg demanded the dissolution of a standing army and the formation of a workers' militia. She argued for the 'abolition of the command authority of officers and noncommissioned officers' and the 'creation of a Red Guard of proletarians as an active part of the militia for the constant protection of the Revolution against counter-revolutionary attacks and subversions'.[33] She also sought to eliminate immediate threats to the achievements of the revolution by disarming the conservative police force, military officers, and all members of the ruling class. All former legal and political sources of authority would be replaced by the workers' and soldiers' councils. This appeared to include all questions of national defence, internal security, and law and order.

Her focus was on the need for the working class 'to get the entire political power of the state into its own hands'.[34] She called for the 'establishment of a united German Socialist Republic', consisting of the institutional structure of workers' and soldiers' councils with a central executive council at its head.[35] Workers' and soldiers' councils would be elected by 'the entire adult working population of both sexes, in the city and the countryside', which was not as expansive as Kautsky's call for universal suffrage but appeared to include the vast majority of the population and was designed only to exclude the former capitalist class from the vote. This institutional framework of a council system relied on a unified government without a separation of powers. Since Karl Marx's essay on the Paris Commune, council systems were generally conceived of as 'working institutions', which combined legislative and executive functions in order to directly create and administer laws.[36] Writing on the separation of powers, Marx stated: 'Here we have the old constitutional folly. The condition of a "free government" is not the

[31] Luxemburg, 'What Does the Spartacus League Want?'. [32] Ibid. [33] Ibid.
[34] Luxemburg, 'The Socialisation of Society'.
[35] Luxemburg, 'What Does the Spartacus League Want?'.
[36] Däumig, 'The National Assembly Means the Councils' Death', 48; Luxemburg, 'What does the Spartacus League Want?'.

division but the unity of power.'[37] Radical council theorists criticized bourgeois parliaments as 'talk shops' of speeches, which masked the undemocratic and unaccountable decisions that were being made in the executive and government bureaucracy. Rather than subject it to reform, Luxemburg believed that the old government bureaucracy should be completely abolished.

Marx also criticized the judiciary in liberal democracies for their 'sham independence' that 'served to mask their abject subservience to all succeeding governments'.[38] Marx proposed that 'like the rest of public servants, magistrates and judges were to be elective, responsible, and revocable.'[39] Luxemburg also believed the courts were 'organs of class justice' whose primary role was to enforce private property claims and uphold the dominance of the bourgeoisie.[40] Although it is not explicitly addressed in this pamphlet, it appears that questions of justice would also be administered by the councils as they were the only source of legitimate authority. Following Marx's criticisms of the doctrine of the separation of powers, council systems have usually been conceived of as unified systems of governance with no separate judiciary.[41] In his essay on the Paris Commune, Marx called for the popular election of judges, although it is unclear the extent to which Luxemburg endorsed this proposal.

Luxemburg envisaged a radically democratic structure of governance with a central council that met at least every three months 'with new elections of delegates each time'.[42] Her proposal for new delegates to the central council (at least) every three months involved more frequent rotations than even the ancient Athenian political system in which members of the Council of 500 served for a year. She was concerned with the possibility that representatives would usurp the power and political agency of workers. For Luxemburg, parliamentary representatives governed in the interests of the bourgeoisie and prevented workers from exercising political and economic power. The question, then, was how a workers' government could institute a form of representation which did not lead to a permanent usurpation of the people's power. Karl Marx's answer in 'The Civil War in France' was for the election of councillors by universal suffrage at short terms, who would also be revocable at any time.[43] Ernst Däumig concurred that the problem of political power could be solved so long as the council delegates 'cannot hold any powers long-term but must be under constant control by the

[37] Karl Marx, 'The Constitution of the French Republic Adopted November 4 1848', *Notes to the People*, London, no. 7 (June 1851). Quoted in Hal Draper, *Karl Marx's Theory of Revolution: Volume 1, The State and Bureaucracy* (London: Monthly Press Review, 1977), 316.

[38] Marx, 'The Civil War in France'. [39] Ibid.

[40] Rosa Luxemburg, 'Auf die Schanzen', *Die Rote Fahne*, no. 30, 15 December 1918.

[41] However, Marxists are not unanimous in their desire for an elimination of a separation of powers. Karl Kautsky is one example of an attempt immediately following the Russian Revolution to advocate for a proper separation of powers.

[42] Luxemburg, 'What Does the Spartacus League Want?'. [43] Marx, 'The Civil War in France'.

voters who can recall councils or council members whenever they have lost their trust'.[44] In a desire to create stronger accountability mechanisms on representatives and to prevent the creation of a new class of elites ruling over society, Luxemburg considered revocable delegates with short terms of office and subject to the possibility of immediate recall as an important feature of a socialist republic.

With workers' and soldiers' councils as the central institutions of political and economic authority, workplaces took on a new sense of political importance as centres of power that would elect representatives to the highest political institutions of the republic. Luxemburg called for workplace democracy to be instituted in all enterprises so that workplaces would become worker-managed through 'enterprise councils', which would function alongside workers' councils.[45] Another institutional feature of Luxemburg's socialist republic that differed markedly from Kautsky's proposal was her support for the establishment of a central strike commission. Kautsky believed that the right to strike would be considered differently in a socialist republic due to the harmful effect it would have on the socialist economy. In contrast, Luxemburg called for the strike movement to be provided with a 'unified leadership' and 'the strongest support by the political power of the workers' and soldiers' councils'.[46]

During the German Revolution, in spite her earlier criticisms of certain aspects of the Bolshevik's programme, Luxemburg supported a system of workers' councils as the institutional basis of a socialist republic. In her final speech for the Communist Party of Germany (KPD) before she was murdered, she argued for the councils as the institutional embodiment of the self-liberation of the working class. She did not consider this to be the act of an organized minority, but the beginning of the self-conscious rule of the majority of workers through these new institutions of a republic. Luxemburg seemed to have misjudged the mood of the masses in her complete dismissal of the national assembly. The KPD had decided to boycott elections to the assembly and Rosa Luxemburg, writing to her friend Clara Zetkin, advised:

> In reality, the rush of events has put the question of [participating] in the national assembly on the back burner and, if things continue in this way, it is highly doubtful whether there will be elections and a national assembly.[47]

This letter, written only eight days before the elections, undoubtedly shows a miscalculation in terms of the political realities of Germany and the likelihood of workers' power being based in a council system. However, there was more to

[44] Däumig, 'The Council Idea and its Realization', 52.
[45] Luxemburg, 'What Does the Spartacus League Want?'. [46] Ibid.
[47] Quoted in Stephen Bronner, ed., *The Letters of Rosa Luxemburg* (New Jersey: Humanities Press, 1993), 300.

Luxemburg's programme than the outlines of an institutional framework for a new political and economic order.

Rosa Luxemburg's Socialist Civic Virtues

Luxemburg understood the most important aspect of the socialist revolution not simply as a change in institutions but as a fundamental shift in the identity and self-understanding of workers:

> The essence of socialist society consists in the fact that the great laboring mass ceases to be a dominated mass, but rather, makes the entire political and economic life its own life and gives that life a conscious, free, and autonomous direction.[48]

She believed that capitalism engendered ignorant, selfish, and mindless individuals whose ethos and culture would have to be transformed. The problem was that the majority of workers under capitalism were required to be little more than 'living machines', rather than developing a capacity to think independently and use their critical faculties.[49] They were encouraged to adopt an individualistic perspective on life rather than identifying with other workers in social struggle. In order to accomplish widespread social transformation, Luxemburg considered that it would be necessary for all workers to actively participate in this change. Without the wholesale transformation of practices and institutions from the factory floor to the government, a revolution would be unlikely to have its intended transformative effect.

In the following crucial passage, Luxemburg described the necessary transformation in disposition and habits required for the realization of a socialist society:

> From dead machines assigned their place in production by capital, the proletarian masses must learn to transform themselves into the free and independent directors of this process. They have to acquire the feeling of responsibility proper to active members of the collectivity which alone possesses ownership of all social wealth. They have to develop industriousness without the capitalist whip, the highest productivity without slavedrivers, discipline without the yoke, order without authority. The highest idealism in the interest of the collectivity, the strictest self-discipline, the truest public spirit of the masses are the moral foundations of socialist society, just as stupidity, egotism, and corruption are

[48] Ibid. [49] Luxemburg, 'The Socialisation of Society'.

> the moral foundations of capitalist society.... All these socialist civic virtues, together with the knowledge and skills necessary to direct socialist enterprises, can be won by the mass of workers only through their own activity, their own experience. [50]

This is perhaps Luxemburg's most succinct attempt to capture the essence of a proletarian culture through which workers would struggle against capitalist exploitation and build the foundations of a socialist society. It is important to note that this conception of culture is not one of pure refusal and resistance but rather puts forward positive virtues that underlined the need for new forms of order, discipline, and self-government. Luxemburg shifted her attention from the disruption and dislocation of mass strikes that would paralyse capitalist society towards a more expansive vision of the positive requirements of a socialist society. She sketched the outlines of a culture that would help workers support institutions of self-government in the absence of economic compulsion and oppressive state apparatuses.

Of what did these socialist civic virtues consist? First, they contained a psychological dimension, which involved the cultivation of a disposition to act in solidarity with others. Second, they consisted of a behavioural aspect: stable and enduring patterns of conduct supported by widely accepted social norms. Philip Pettit has argued that there are three conditions required for a civic norm to be established:

> first, that relevant parties generally display the pattern of behaviour in question; second, that they generally approve of someone's doing so and/or disapprove of someone's not doing so; and third, that this habit of approval makes the behaviour more likely or secure than it would otherwise be.[51]

For Luxemburg's socialist civil virtues to be so established it would entail most members understanding them, seeing them as desirable and viewing them as producing the common good.

Luxemburg followed a radical participatory republican tradition concerned not just with the civic virtue of government officials, but with the virtuous conduct of the broader citizenry. For Luxemburg, without widespread social norms encouraging collective action and self-discipline, the social and political institutions of socialism would not be able to function effectively. Just as republicanism demands strong public-spiritedness and active participation from citizens, socialism requires the active participation of workers in a struggle against capitalist exploitation and oppression. Socialism is not just about the abolition of private property

[50] Luxemburg, 'What Does the Spartacus League Want?'.

[51] Pettit, *Republicanism*, 244.

and the collective ownership of the means of production, it concerns the development of human potential through transforming passive subjects into active citizens of a self-determining community.

The appearance of the republican-inspired language of socialist civic virtues in Luxemburg's writings raises the question of the extent of the influence of republicanism over her political thought. Several commentators have sought to interpret Luxemburg along republican lines.[52] The most prominent and radical of these interpretations is that of Hannah Arendt, who goes so far as to suggest that on account of Luxemburg's republicanism 'it might be doubted that she was a Marxist at all.'[53] For Arendt, Luxemburg 'remained passionately engaged in public life and civil affairs ... outside the immediate interests of the working class, and hence completely beyond the horizon of all Marxists.'[54] Arendt argued that Luxemburg's insistence on a 'republican program' 'separated her most decisively from all others'.[55] Arendt's insistence on Luxemburg's adherence to a non-Marxist republicanism offers a radical new interpretation on a figure that is widely accepted to be a revolutionary socialist. Stephen Eric Bronner has sought to enlist Luxemburg in debates over socialist strategy on the Left and has argued that Luxemburg supported the establishment of a liberal republican state and was never fully committed to the project of workers' councils.[56]

I argue that while republican themes and language can be found in Luxemburg's writings, they are recast within an overriding socialist framework. Writers attempting to reclaim Luxemburg for the republican tradition have overstated their claims in distancing her from Marx and a revolutionary socialist tradition.[57] In her articulation of *socialist* civic virtues, Luxemburg modifies many of the underpinning ideas of the republican tradition.

First, the political subject of 'the people' is replaced by class-specific language of 'workers' and 'the proletariat'. While Luxemburg believed that all oppressed classes would benefit from a social revolution, it was primarily organized workers who would be the main actors in social struggle. This was also not a homogenous and nationally bounded community of property-owning citizens. Instead, Luxemburg's vision was of an internationally organized federation of working-class associations, which would act in solidarity with each other. Civic virtue was not put in the service of a defence of state institutions but in their transformation towards a self-determining society. Workers would play an instrumental role in

[52] See Stephen Eric Bronner, 'Red Dreams and the New Millennium: Notes on the Legacy of Rosa Luxemburg', in Jason Schulman, ed., *Rosa Luxemburg—Her Life and Legacy* (New York: Palgrave Macmillan, 2013); Sidonia Blättler and Irene M. Marti, 'Rosa Luxemburg and Hannah Arendt: Against the Destruction of Political Spheres of Freedom', *Hypatia* 20, no. 2 (2005), 88–101.

[53] Arendt, *Men in Dark Times*, 38. [54] Ibid., 51. [55] Ibid., 52. [56] Ibid., 38.

[57] For a critique of republican readings of Luxemburg see Norman Geras, *The Legacy of Rosa Luxemburg* (London: New Left Books, 1976).

undermining the conditions that allowed a capitalist class to rule through the state and its coercive apparatuses.

Second, Luxemburg rejected the patriotism and militarism of the ancient republican tradition and sought to foster an international spirit of solidarity among workers of all nations.[58] Solidarity should extend beyond the members of territorially bounded political communities and had to be spread to all workers. Luxemburg recognized that nationalism could be used by the ruling classes to promote imperialism and war, which would ultimately harm workers. She recognized that, historically, republican city states practised a politics of exclusion of slave populations, women, and noncitizens and also tended to exercise colonial domination over other peoples. The idea of cultivating a militaristic culture was vehemently rejected by Luxemburg who campaigned as a pacifist when many socialists within the SPD lent their support to the First World War.

Third, the cultivation of socialist civic virtues would not take place in state institutions but through political struggle as part of a broader workers' movement. The self-education and self-organization of the working classes required an institutional framework in which workers could gain a greater consciousness of their position and learn the basic habits of cooperation and solidarity. Luxemburg considered that civic virtues could be best cultivated in the associational life of workers, which was particularly vibrant in early twentieth-century Germany. It was through participation in these institutions, with a particular emphasis on political struggle against the capitalist class, that Luxemburg envisaged the growth of civic virtue.

Finally, Luxemburg replaced the ideal of a democratic republican state with the image of a stateless proletarian democracy organized through workers' councils. By 1917, Luxemburg agreed with Trotsky that a socialist revolution would not have to first achieve a democratic republican state as a preliminary stage, but could undertake an uninterrupted transition to a socialist society. During the German Revolution, Luxemburg consistently supported the formation of workers' councils and was opposed to the maintenance of the old institutions of the German *Kaiserreich*. Contrary to arguments that Luxemburg remained ambiguous on the question of workers' councils, her vision of a socialist society involved the complete replacement of the institutional framework of the state with worker-led institutions such as workers' councils. Ultimately, in Luxemburg's political theory, republican ideals are significantly transformed through their incorporation into a project of revolutionary socialism. She abandoned many of the more conservative and militaristic aspects of republican political theory in favour of a transformative vision of workers' solidarity in social struggle, which placed her at a significant distance from the classic republican tradition.

[58] Iseult Honohan, *Civic Republicanism* (London: Routledge, 2002), 166; Pettit, *Republicanism*, 150–3.

A Socialist Order of Society

At the same time as Luxemburg was writing 'What does the Spartacus League Want?' she was also thinking about the question of the future form of a socialist society in another pamphlet, 'The Socialisation of Society', which expanded on a number of themes related to socialist civic virtues. Through reading these two texts alongside each other, it becomes clear that Luxemburg's ideal of socialist civic virtues was intended to support the institutions of an emerging socialist society. Her conception of socialist civic virtue was not only an ethics of class struggle against the bourgeoisie, but was intended to lay the moral foundations of a sense of social obligation, mutual respect and reciprocity in a new society. This was important for two reasons. First, in order to continue large-scale production, workers would need to be ready to sacrifice their own immediate personal interests and devote themselves to continuing to work for the community. Without the profit motive or the wage labour system, workers would have to find a new source of motivation to continue working in a socialist society. Society would depend not just on well-ordered institutions, but on the dispositions of workers to work towards the common good. Second, Luxemburg feared the consequences of a deformed revolution and believed that the development of civic virtues would be a superior alternative to the use of dictatorial methods for enforcing behaviour. For workers to be truly free in a post-capitalist society, their adherence to social norms should be self-imposed and freely chosen rather than brought about by enforcement from party leaders. If workers did not believe it necessary to devote themselves to the common good, large-scale social transformation would be neither practical nor desirable.

Most Marxists of the Second International considered it unnecessary to speculate on any future form of a socialist society due to their belief in the inevitability of the collapse of capitalism and the unpredictability of future developments in social struggle. Kautsky famously argued that 'it is not our task to invent recipes for the kitchens of the future.'[59] For Kautsky, 'the party could not lay out a definite road for conditions of which we can have only a dim presentiment and which may easily surprise us with much that is wholly unexpected.'[60] Any future revolution would be dependent on a variety of contingent historical circumstances impossible to predict. As Marx never systematically addressed the structure of a future socialist society, it was taken for granted that this was an unnecessary task for later Marxists. The creation of blueprints of future systems was viewed as part of a surpassed utopian idealist tradition.

Yet following the workers' seizure of power in Germany and the appointment of Richard Müller, a revolutionary socialist, as the head of the Executive Council

[59] Kautsky, 'The Social Revolution'. [60] Ibid.

of Workers' and Soldiers' Councils, more concrete plans were necessary for the transition to a socialist society. While Luxemburg did not write explicitly on the institutional question beyond a call for workers' and soldiers' councils to retain political power in the face of the possibility of a national assembly, she did expand upon the dispositions and cultural habits necessary for a self-determining society.

Perhaps the most striking characteristic of Luxemburg's essay is her call for workers to develop new habits of self-discipline in the absence of the domination and control of the bourgeoisie. Workers would need to find an alternative source of motivation to work based on their desire for their community to flourish and be productive. They must want to work 'for the public good and benefit', which required developing new affective attachments and a 'passion and enthusiasm for the general well-being, full of self-sacrifice and sympathy for his fellow human beings'.[61] The development of what Luxemburg elsewhere referred to as a 'new discipline' and a 'self-discipline' would be an important step in workers' casting aside their old habits of 'obedience and servility'.[62] In 'Organizational Questions of Russian Social Democracy', Luxemburg had sought to distinguish between two forms of discipline based not only on who was undertaking the disciplining but also on the mode of discipline that was employed. Luxemburg argued that this new discipline should not entail 'the replacement of the authority of bourgeois rulers with the authority of a socialist central committee'.[63] It was the workers themselves who should provide this discipline through new forms of self-organization. She was critical of Lenin for failing to see the important distinction between the slave-like discipline of the capitalist factory and state versus the maturity and self-organization of workers. Luxemburg criticized Lenin, who 'glorifies the educative influence of the factory, which, he says, accustoms the proletariat to "discipline and organization"'.[64] Luxemburg believed that there was a fundamental difference between these modes of discipline:

> We misuse words and we practice self-deception when we apply the same term—discipline—to such dissimilar notions as: 1. the absence of thought and will in a body with a thousand automatically moving hands and legs, and 2. the spontaneous coordination of the conscious, political acts of a body of men.[65]

Self-discipline is 'freely assumed', whereas the organization under capitalism is little more than 'the regulated docility of an oppressed class'.[66] The self-discipline of a group of workers relied upon complex processes of cooperation and coordination between individuals. It required conscious effort and determination to work together and achieve a common goal. This was vastly different than being

[61] Luxemburg, 'The Socialisation of Society'.
[62] Luxemburg, 'Organizational Questions of the Russian Social Democracy'. [63] Ibid.
[64] Ibid. [65] Ibid. [66] Ibid.

told one's place in a hierarchically ordered structure controlled by an external agent. There was also a necessary psychological aspect of self-motivation in the absence of what Luxemburg frequently referred to as 'the capitalist whip'.

In order to achieve this dramatic reorganization of production, Luxemburg argued that it would require a transformation of the conditions and experience of labouring. First, Luxemburg believed there would need to be a 'general requirement to work' in a socialist society, 'from which small children, the aged and sick are exempted'.[67] Luxemburg also thought that it would require a transformation in the nature of labour. This required changes in how the labour process was organized and how workers would be treated:

> In a socialist society, where everyone works together for their own well being, the *health* of the workforce and its *enthusiasm for work* must be given the greatest consideration at work. Short working hours that do not exceed the normal capability, healthy workrooms, all methods of recuperation and a variety of work must be introduced in order that everyone enjoys doing their part.[68]

Factories could still be organized with technical managers who gave directives based on their expertise, but these managers would be elected delegates held accountable and would also not profit from surplus-value produced by the workers. Workers should still be 'maintaining discipline and order, of not causing difficulties or confusion'.[69] This would be a question of maintaining 'order without authority'. However, it would be necessary to reform the conditions of work to make workplaces more humane and agreeable spaces.

Luxemburg's emphasis in 'The Socialisation of Society' on transforming the activity of labouring mirrors many of the themes of Marx's 1844 Manuscripts, which were discovered and published much later in 1932. In these manuscripts Marx argued that the abolition of private property and the end of alienated labour would usher in a post-capitalist and self-determining society in which free agents would be in conscious control over the production process.

Luxemburg also realized that after the abolition of the profit motive and oppressive forms of organizing human society, new motivations and organizational mechanisms would be needed to ensure productivity:

> In a word: the worker in a socialist economy must show that he can work hard and properly, keep discipline and give his best without the whip of hunger and without the capitalist and his slave-driver behind him. This calls for inner self-discipline, intellectual maturity, moral ardour, a sense of dignity and responsibility, a complete inner rebirth of the proletarian.[70]

[67] Luxemburg, 'The Socialisation of Society'. [68] Ibid. [69] Ibid. [70] Ibid.

In addition to this self-discipline, workers would require another fundamental socialist civic virtue: the capacity for political judgement. Also described by Luxemburg as workers' intellectual and political maturity, sound political judgement would be crucial to assuming full political responsibilities in a self-determining society. Luxemburg considered 'the existence of a large contingent of workers educated in the class struggle' as an 'indispensable condition' for the realization of socialist goals.[71] One important aspect of this judgement was the development of workers' theoretical knowledge. In her analysis of the Russian Revolution, Luxemburg made it clear that she opposed 'the guardianship methods of the German Social-Democracy' and argued that it was:

> only by an insight into all the fearful seriousness, all the complexity of the tasks involved, only as a result of political maturity and independence of spirit, only as a result of a capacity for critical judgement on the part of the masses, whose capacity was systematically killed by the Social-Democracy for decades under various pretexts, only thus can the genuine capacity for historical action be born in the German proletariat.[72]

The proletariat must be educated through political struggle to develop their ability to understand and take part in political events. This required a breakdown of the division between theorists and workers or intellectual and manual labour. For Luxemburg, 'No coarser insult, no baser aspersion, can be thrown against the workers than the remarks: "Theocratic controversies are only for academicians."'[73] Workers should be armed with theoretical insight, since '[t]he entire strength of the modern labour movement rests on theoretic knowledge.'[74]

For Luxemburg, the working class as a whole would be the primary catalyst and agent of a future revolution. Marxism had provided an analysis of the objective laws of capitalism, but the movement of history was dialectically connected to the actions of the working class. It was therefore imperative that workers rather than a revolutionary vanguard be educated and empowered to act, for it was only through their activity that socialism could be realized. Luxemburg called for 'the most intensive political training of the masses and the accumulation of experience' in order to develop their capacity for political judgement.[75] This was also underpinned by Luxemburg's belief that a revolution could not be 'made' or brought about by the actions of party leaders. Mass movements could only be produced through the long-term education and development of the working class based on 'the existing degree of tension between the classes, the degree of intelligence of the

[71] Luxemburg, 'Organizational Questions of the Russian Social Democracy'.
[72] Luxemburg, 'The Russian Revolution'. [73] Luxemburg, 'Reform or Revolution'.
[74] Ibid. [75] Luxemburg, 'The Russian Revolution'.

masses and the degree or ripeness of their spirit of resistance'.[76] Not only were party leaders unable to effectively bring about mass action, they actually posed a danger to it through overly centralized and restrictive forms of organizing. The antidote to rigid centralization for Luxemburg was 'the independent revolutionary action of the proletariat, as a result of which the workers acquire the sense of political responsibility and self-reliance'.[77]

Finally, political judgement had to be developed by the workers themselves through their own action, including experimentation with new methods which may lead to deviations and errors. But it was only in having its own experiences and making its own errors that the proletariat would truly learn the adequate lessons:

> Its tasks and its errors are both gigantic: no prescription, no schema valid for every case, no infallible leader to show it the path to follow. Historical experience is its only school mistress. Its thorny way to self-emancipation is paved not only with immeasurable suffering but also with countless errors. The aim of its journey—its emancipation depends on this—is whether the proletariat can learn from its own errors. Self-criticism, remorseless, cruel, and going to the core of things is the life's breath and light of the proletarian movement.[78]

As Luxemburg noted in her criticisms of Lenin's rigid centralism: 'the mistakes that are made by a truly revolutionary workers' movement are, historically speaking, immeasurably more fruitful and more valuable than the infallibility of the best possible "Central Committee."'[79]

Luxemburg considered self-activity [*Selbsttätigkeit*] to be a third important socialist civic virtue, which she defined as the capacity for the masses to take self-directed political action rather than receiving orders from party leaders. She believed in the necessity for 'workers to develop their own political activity through direct influence on public life, in a party press, and public congresses, etc.'.[80] Her insistence on workers' political initiative was in response to what she considered the bureaucratic tendencies of the SPD. Her polemic against Lenin's democratic centralism can also be read as directed at the leadership of the SPD and their preference for a command and control style of leadership in which workers were figured as passive recipients of orders from a party leadership. Luxemburg called for the cultivation of a 'positive and creative spirit' amongst workers so they would be directly involved in the creation of tactics and strategy. Rather than have a central committee oversee every important decision,

[76] Luxemburg, 'The Junius Pamphlet'.
[77] Luxemburg, 'Organizational Questions of the Russian Social Democracy'.
[78] Luxemburg, 'The Junius Pamphlet'.
[79] Luxemburg, 'Organizational Questions of the Russian Social Democracy'. [80] Ibid.

Luxemburg believed that 'the party sections and federations need the liberty of action which alone will permit them to develop their revolutionary initiative.'[81]

The principle of self-activity was also part of a more general ideal that workers must also 'bring socialism step by step into life' through their own activity.[82] In the final months of her life she insisted: 'Socialism will not and cannot be created by any government, however socialistic. Socialism must be created by the masses, by every proletarian. Only that is socialism, and only thus can socialism be created.'[83] In a self-determining society, it is workers themselves who should be in charge of major decision-making. It is therefore necessary that they develop such habits through their struggle for socialism.

Moving on to the fourth civic virtue, an ongoing concern for Luxemburg was the tendency of individuals within a capitalist society to ignore their membership of a social whole and to focus on their own immediate needs and interests at the expense of the common good. Part of the moral degradation of bourgeois society that had to be overcome was the way it isolated individuals and encouraged them to seek their private gain by whatever means necessary. Luxemburg would often refer to this problem as the 'egoism' or 'individualism' of bourgeois society. The end product of this alienation and individualism was an incapacity to identify with a broader collective group and a tendency to exploit others. In *The Russian Revolution*, Luxemburg phrased this problem in the traditional republican language of corruption, referring to 'how easily all sections of bourgeois society are subject to such degeneration.'[84] Since one of the organizing principles of bourgeois life is 'the exploitation of man by man', a wide range of self-serving and avaricious behaviours would have to be combatted, such as 'commercial profiteering, fictitious deals, adulteration of foodstuffs, cheating, official embezzlement, theft, burglary and robbery'.[85]

The socialist civic virtue that Luxemburg believed would provide an antidote to this problem was solidarity with fellow workers and an identification with the interests of the community. Luxemburg argued that 'the only effective means' against egoistic behaviours are:

> radical measures of a political and social character, the speediest possible transformation of the social guarantees of the life of the masses—the kindling of revolutionary idealism, which can be maintained over any length of time only through the intensively active life of the masses themselves under conditions of unlimited political freedom.[86]

[81] Ibid. [82] Luxemburg, 'What does the Spartacus League Want?'. [83] Ibid.
[84] Luxemburg, 'The Russian Revolution'. [85] Ibid. [86] Ibid.

Luxemburg advocated 'the truest public spirit of the masses' as the moral foundation of a socialist society.[87] She believed that solidarity was best exercised through defending the freedom of others. To act in solidarity with another involved working with them to overcome relationships of exploitation and domination, even if one was not personally affected by such issues. Luxemburg envisioned solidarity as a way of building relationships with others that enhanced their freedom. She believed that it was only possible for an individual to be free when they lived in a society that enabled the free development of all. Such a conception of solidarity could outlast the immediate event of the revolution since it was not based exclusively on a shared position of oppression but on a desire to enhance human flourishing and development. Luxemburg was committed to the development of political community and the maintenance of its capacities for self-determination.

A Misguided Ideal?

Critics of republican civic virtue have worried that it involves an overly demanding ideal of self-sacrifice and public-spiritedness.[88] If citizenship is to be understood as requiring high levels of participation and engagement in politics, this could be seen to make unrealistic demands on modern citizens' time and energy. Critics have asserted that it is more realistic to assume that people will primarily act in ways that further their own interests and devote little time to issues of public concern. Citizens should be considered as self-interested rational actors who will maximize their expected utility by focusing on personal rather than public matters.[89] Luxemburg's socialist civic virtues could be vulnerable to similar criticisms of the impractical demands they place on citizens.

Liberals have criticized advocates of a republican civic humanism for their failure to acknowledge the drastically changed circumstances of modern politics and the decline of a politics of virtue and active citizenship.[90] Richard Dagger has noted that 'the size, diversity, and complexity of the modern state make it difficult for us to see ourselves as members of a body politic that is also a cooperative enterprise.'[91] Even in the eighteenth century, Rousseau was already concerned that modern ways of life were eroding the basic conditions that could sustain a republican political community. The rise of a commercial society led to a growing

[87] Luxemburg, 'What Does the Spartacus League Want?'.

[88] Robert E. Goodin, 'Folie Républicaine', *Annual Review of Political Science* 6 (2003), 55–76; Dagger, *Civic Virtues*, 105.

[89] Joseph Schumpeter, *Capitalism, Socialism, and Democracy*. 3rd ed. (New York: Harper and Row, 1962); Anthony Downs, *An Economic Theory of Democracy* (New York: Harper and Row, 1957).

[90] Jürgen Habermas, 'Three Normative Models of Democracy', *Constellations* 1, no. 1 (1994), 2.

[91] Dagger, *Civic Virtues*, 98.

pursuit of individual independence and the satisfaction of material desires. Benjamin Constant noted:

> The aim of the ancients was the sharing of social power among the citizens of the same fatherland: this is what they called liberty. The aim of the moderns is the enjoyment of security in private pleasures; and they call liberty the guarantees accorded by institutions to these pleasures.[92]

He considered that modern forms of social organization had rendered obsolete an older view of politics as participation in government and the collective exercise of power. Citizens today could not be counted on to actively participate in public affairs or to approach political questions from the perspective of the common good.

Moreover, might the project of cultural transformation be based on a dangerously utopian idea of changing fundamental aspects of our human nature? Council theorists held a transformative vision of overcoming capitalist alienation and often phrased this in terms of the development of a new 'spirit' or human nature. The problem of how current alienated and individualistic citizens could be transformed into the kinds of public-spirited individuals that would be required in a socialist society appeared to rest on idealistic expectations of a fundamental change in human character. Socialist Henry Pachter was sceptical of such promises of transformation:

> Ultraleft utopians have given it an even sharper, or perhaps more ludicrous form. It seems to them that under socialism people will undergo a fundamental change of character; not being alienated, they will have neither different interests nor different opinions, but will gladly cooperate in any reasonable assignment that the government decides upon.[93]

There are certainly times at which Luxemburg appears to be calling for heroic acts that would dramatically break from older ways of practising politics. She argued that individuals must strive for 'the highest idealism in the interest of the collectivity, the strictest self-discipline, the truest public spirit of the masses'; it was only 'through tenacious, tireless struggle by the working mass along its entire front' that socialism could be achieved.[94]

However, Luxemburg might also respond through recourse to a modified understanding of self-interest. Under conditions of capitalist exploitation, it is in the interest of workers to act collectively against this injustice and to organize

[92] Benjamin Constant, 'The Liberty of Ancients Compared with that of Moderns'.

[93] Pachter, *Socialism in History*, 46.

[94] Luxemburg, 'What Does the Spartacus League Want?'.

society in a manner which enables them to benefit from the full fruits of their labour. In what Alexis de Tocqueville described as 'self-interest properly understood', attention to the common good will ultimately benefit individuals as members of the social collective. For Tocqueville, the understanding of one's place in society 'does not lead the will directly to virtue, it establishes habits which unconsciously turn it that way'.[95] While Tocqueville's description of the 'temperate, moderate, careful, and self-controlled citizens' is a long way from Luxemburg's combative and militant workers, they would agree that producing public goods benefits the individual and the collective. Therefore, work directed towards the public good need not entail a great sacrifice of personal interest. Luxemburg would add that with the elimination of class-based exploitation there will be more substantial agreement between personal and public interest in a socialist society. Socialist civic virtues would therefore appear more practical in a society in which the common good is more in accord with workers' personal interests.

However, there is also an undeniable utopian element of Luxemburg's project insofar as she did not accept the terms of contemporary capitalist society. Her political programme called for a radical transformation of all spheres of life and the replacement of existing social conditions with new ones. This was not a nostalgic project of returning to a lost utopia of classic republics, but a forward-looking programme of social transformation aimed at radically changing the way in which human beings lived in modern industrial societies. Yet as a radical project, it is necessarily vulnerable to charges of utopian thinking. She struggled for enormous changes to social relations and to how individuals conceived of their place in society. But she considered such transformations as the only possible way to avoid the increasing barbarism of capitalist society. For her, it was utopian to believe that capitalism could be reformed or that the world could continue under present conditions. While her ideal necessitated large-scale social transformation, this was based on her analysis of the decline of capitalism and the need for a radical alternative. Such an argument would be unlikely to convince critics sceptical of her analysis of capitalism, but it was an integral aspect of her worldview.

A second problem that could be identified with Luxemburg's socialist civic virtues is the issue of paternalism. Luxemburg appears to demand a specific set of dispositions and behaviours from workers as necessary aspects of their social struggle. Could such a prescription be seen as itself a source of coercion and unfreedom? Republican writers have been criticized for the coercive socialization involved in state institutions teaching citizens how to behave virtuously. Quentin Skinner has noted that republican theorists have turned to institutions that could

[95] Alexis de Tocqueville, *Democracy in America*, trans. George Lawrence, ed. J. P. Mayer (Garden City, NY: Doubleday, 1969), 526–7.

'force us out of our habitual patterns of self-interested behavior' and 'into discharging the full range of civic duties'.[96] How would individuals be treated within a socialist society in view of Luxemburg's theory of character transformation? There is much evidence in Luxemburg's writings that she would be against any kind of tutelage model of civic education. She is insistent that social transformation 'cannot be decreed by any bureau, committee, or parliament', but must be 'the work of the working class itself... won by the mass of workers only through their own activity, their own experience'.[97] Luxemburg does not offer us much in the way of a theory of pedagogy, but the notion of a prescribed morality is foreign to other aspects of her political thought. It is likely that Luxemburg was attempting to clarify the psychological conditions of social transformation in order to help guide the workers' movement but did not consider that her specific interpretation of those values should be viewed as a prescriptive doctrine.

Third, Luxemburg's notion of socialist civic virtues differs markedly from traditional republican accounts due to her argument that there will be no coercive state or system of laws in a socialist society. In republican political theory, civic virtues have been thought to support republican laws. As Philip Pettit has stated:

> If the state is to be able to find a place in the hearts of the people, and if the laws of the state are to be truly effective, those laws will have to work in synergy with norms that are established, or that come to be established, in the realm of civil society. The laws must give support to the norms and the norms must give support to the laws.[98]

This follows many precedents in the republican tradition of the mutual reinforcement of political laws and civic virtue. Machiavelli, for example, argued 'just as good morals, if they are to be maintained, have need of the laws, so the laws, if they are to be observed, have need of good morals.'[99] Are Luxemburg's socialist civic virtues simply incoherent or destined to fail without a corresponding system of laws?

Marx's general view was that legal systems would disappear in a socialist society following the withering away of the state.[100] Marx and Engels considered the ideal of the rule of law as part of a bourgeois ideology that obscured the true nature of class domination in the state.[101] As a result, subsequent Marxists wrote little about

[96] Quentin Skinner, 'The Republican Ideal of Political Liberty', in *Machiavelli and Republicanism*, ed. Gisela Bock, Quentin Skinner, and Maurizio Viroli (Cambridge: Cambridge University Press, 1990), 293–309, 304–5.

[97] Luxemburg, 'What Does the Spartacus League Want?'.

[98] Pettit, *Republicanism*, 242.

[99] Niccolò Machiavelli, *The Complete Works and Others*, trans. Allan Gilbert (Durham, NC: Duke University Press, 1965), 241.

[100] Laurence Lustgarten, 'Socialism and the Rule of Law', *Journal of Law and Society* 15, no. 1 (1988), 25–41.

[101] Hugh Collins, *Marxism and Law* (Oxford: Oxford University Press, 1994).

the need for a socialist system of laws as they assumed that a feature of a truly free society would be the absence of a coercive legal system. There are notable exceptions such as Karl Kautsky who considered that 'law and order are preconditions to accomplishing socialism and the socialist revolution.'[102] However, although Luxemburg wrote little on this subject, her view that the legal system was an organ of class justice indicates that she believed that such a system would be abolished in a socialist society.[103] One could argue that the rejection of a specific 'capitalist' legal system does not necessarily entail the abolition of all legal systems, but there is no indication in her writings of how a non-capitalist legal system could be conceived.

It seems that socialist civic virtues might play a different role in Luxemburg's socialist society than in republican political theory. Social norms would be more important in Luxemburg's socialist thought due to the lack of a coercive state apparatus for punishing harmful social behaviour. Socialist civic virtues would be the primary mechanism through which citizens could develop public-spirited dispositions and habits. Here, Luxemburg is again vulnerable to the charge of utopianism from republicans because it could be doubted whether individuals would indeed act in the common good without a combination of coercive laws and socially endorsed norms. For Luxemburg, the development of social norms would occur through citizens' participation in political activity and their direct organizing of economic and social life. The overcoming of capitalist relations of production would eliminate the primary source of political conflict in society and would dramatically reshape the possibilities for human life. Without the need to protect property relations, a legal system would be unnecessary as socialist civic virtues would help form workers' character and direct their conduct towards the common good.

Council theorists argued for the self-organization and self-education of workers in processes of widespread cultural transformation. They believed that any changes in the economic sphere would need to be accompanied by a shift in the dispositions and habits of workers. Luxemburg's conception of socialist civic virtues was an attempt to conceptualize the nature of such a transformation through the republican-inspired language of civic virtue. Rather than directing civic virtue towards the preservation of state institutions, Luxemburg reinterpreted these virtues as the habits of discipline, political judgement, self-activity, and solidarity necessary for social transformation. She did not consider it the job of the socialist party or other state institutions to inculcate workers with a prescribed ideology. Instead, she believed that civic virtues had to be learnt by the workers themselves in political struggle. Such virtues would be important for

[102] Karl Kautsky, 'National Assembly and Council Assembly', 103.
[103] Luxemburg, 'Auf die Schanzen'.

political struggle against capitalist alienation, but they would also form the basis of a new socialist society. In this way, although Luxemburg utilized the republican language of civic virtue, she significantly altered its underlying meaning by reimagining it within a socialist ideology. Luxemburg's politics of civic virtue became a theory of solidarity and social transformation rather than a conservative state-centred ideology.

6

Conclusion

After the Councils

The purpose of this book has been to recover political debates surrounding the experience of council movements in Germany and to reassess their transformative potential. The council movements emerged spontaneously across the country, leading to the resignation of the Kaiser and the establishment of a new parliament and institutional arrangement. The formation of councils following a sailors' mutiny in Kiel on 4 November 1918 took both the authorities and the socialist leaders by surprise. Within a week, the entire authority structure of the governmental apparatus had collapsed and the leaders of the councils had unwittingly taken de facto power of the country. It is worth recalling just how quickly these events transpired. Writing the day after the declaration of the republic, Theodor Wolff, liberal editor of the *Berliner Tageblatt*, wrote:

> The greatest of all revolutions, like a suddenly rising storm, has crushed the Imperial regime with everything that belonged to it, above and below. It can be called the greatest of all revolutions, because never has such a sturdily built, solidly walled Bastille been taken in such a siege. Only a week ago there was a military and civil administrative apparatus that was so branched, so interlinked, so deeply ingrained that it seemed to have secured its rule beyond the changing of times. The grey cars of the officers were speeding through the streets of Berlin, in the squares stood policemen like the pillars of power, a giant military organization seemed to embrace everything, a seemingly invincible bureaucracy sat enthroned in the offices and ministries. Yesterday morning, at least in Berlin, everything was still there. Yesterday afternoon, none of it existed anymore.[1]

Yet in spite of the speed of its collapse, there was no single clear demand for what should replace the authority structure of the old regime. The contested nature of the revolution is starkly demonstrated by the image of the simultaneous proclamation of two different republics on 9 November 1918. Friedrich Ebert had planned on taking the Chancellorship himself following the abdication of the Kaiser. But throughout the morning of 9 November, demonstrators gathered in great

[1] Theodor Wolff, 'Der Erfolg Der Revolution', *Berliner Tageblatt und Handels-Zeitung* 47 (10 November 1918), 576..

Building Power to Change the World: The Political Thought of the German Council Movements. James Muldoon, Oxford University Press (2020). © James Muldoon. DOI: 10.1093/oso/9780198856627.003.0007

numbers outside the Reichstag demanding the complete abolition of the monarchy. Philipp Scheidemann was eating lunch in the Reichstag when he was interrupted with news that Karl Liebknecht, recently released from prison, had refounded the Spartacus League and was about to proclaim Germany a socialist republic. Not willing to allow momentum to gather behind the Spartacists, Scheidemann decided to seize the initiative and rushed to a balcony window to proclaim Germany a republic against the wishes of Friedrich Ebert. Only a few hours later, Karl Liebknecht declared Germany a free *socialist* republic to an assembled crowd of workers outside the Berlin Palace. This scene of two alternative declarations set the stage for the bitter disagreements between the SPD and USPD over the council movements and the future of the German state.

The council movements gave voice to widespread demands for the radical transformation of German society and for the democratization of politics and the economy. Council delegates sought to address the fundamental power imbalance between classes as a question central to ensuring the strength and vitality of a democratic polity. They considered political and economic elites a threat because of their tendency to utilize their wealth and power to dominate political institutions and shape decisions to suit their own class interests. Workers called for new forms of ownership and management over workplaces and a transformation of the military and bureaucratic state apparatuses that had led them to war. A new form of socialism gained ground that emphasized bottom-up grassroots organizing and mass participation in political institutions. Against the traditional hierarchies of the SPD, the councils opened participatory spaces for workers to directly engage with political issues and elect mandated and recallable delegates to sit on higher councils. Both the centrists and radicals of the USPD envisaged a participatory socialist society in which citizens would play an active role in determining the character and direction of social institutions. The council movements passed resolutions for the socialization of German industry and to transfer the ownership and management of industrial enterprises into public control. There were widespread discussions about the most effective pathways to socialization, which remained a popular policy amongst workers even though the SPD failed to institute such reforms.

The council movements were able to hold political power, however imperfectly and temporarily, because they represented the organized power of the workers' movement that directly challenged the hierarchical authority structures of the German Empire. Over the preceding decades, theorists within the workers' movement had debated effective strategies for the development of workers' power and how this could be deployed to support a transformative political programme in the interests of the majority of workers. Their central insight was that only through an established power base would workers be able to successfully implement their plans and achieve thoroughgoing social reforms. They rejected a liberal focus on the moral persuasion of elites and piecemeal reforms which did not threaten the balance of power in existing institutions. The council movements empowered workers through a new institutional model that provided mechanisms for delegates to be held accountable and for power to remain at the base of the structure.

The final goal of social transformation for many radical council theorists was a council republic based on participatory workers' councils as the underlying political and economic institutional structure of a new society. Most versions of a council system were conceived of as a pyramidal structure of local and regional councils organized into a federal model with a national council as the executive organ.[2] For Rosa Luxemburg and Karl Liebknecht of the Spartacus League and Richard Müller and Ernst Däumig of the Revolutionary Shop Stewards, for example, the goal was the '[e]limination of all parliaments and municipal councils, and takeover of their functions by workers' and soldiers' councils'.[3] Over the course of 1919, the Revolutionary Shop Stewards developed extensive plans for how a council system would be organized in the journal, *Der Arbeiter-Rat* [The Workers' Council].[4] For Ernst Däumig, the councils heralded a new era in which the institutions of bourgeois democracy, with its ballots, parliaments, and system of private property, would give way to an emerging proletariat democracy, embodied in the institutions of a national network of workers' and soldiers' councils. Däumig believed this institutional form would have ongoing significance because 'the council system is, and has to be, the organizational structure of modern revolutions.'[5] But in the early 1920s the emphasis of certain council theorists began to shift from understanding the councils as the basis of an institutional framework for a post-capitalist society towards a method of revolutionary struggle, which facilitated the mass action of the working class. While Richard Müller and Ernst Däumig of the Revolutionary Shop Stewards were more inclined towards viewing specific council institutional schemas as superior to liberal institutions, council communism began to be developed as a method of struggle based on the principle of the self-emancipation of the working class in opposition to traditional political parties and trade unions.

A distinction can be drawn between those who directly participated in the German council movements which arose in November 1918 and the later development of council communist political thought. The term 'council communism' began to be used in 1921 after the council movement had already largely been defeated in Germany. As we have seen, the first delegates elected to councils did not see themselves as council communists or as representing a distinctive and unified doctrine. Political ideologies and strategies varied across local councils

[2] For an overview of different theories of council democracy see James Muldoon, 'Council Democracy: Towards a Democratic Socialist Politics', 1–29.

[3] Luxemburg, 'What Does the Spartacus League Want?'.

[4] Hoffrogge, *Working-Class Politics in the German Revolution*, 109–20.

[5] Däumig, 'The National Assembly Means the Councils' Death', 42.

with participants disagreeing on the proposed structure and purpose of workers' councils. The origins of the council communist ideology first developed in the German and Dutch sections of the Communist International amongst socialist who were searching for more participatory models of socialism and more immediate and direct methods of class struggle. When the councils arose across Europe, theorists such as Herman Gorter and Henriette Roland-Holst in the Netherlands and Otto Rühle, Karl Korsch, Karl Schröder, Franz Pfemfert, Karl Plättner, Gustav Landauer, Erich Mühsam, and Paul Mattick in Germany began to see in them an organizational form for the self-emancipation of the working class.

The experience of the German council movements was decisive for the development of council communist political thought because it tested the conditions for a socialist revolution in the West. The first split between Lenin's Bolsheviks and the council communists was over the universal applicability of the Bolshevik's strategy and whether it could be applied outside of Russia. The failure of the German Revolution demonstrated to council communists that bourgeois ideology was far more advanced in the West and that new strategies would need to be developed to overcome the resilience of bourgeois mentalities over workers. From 1919, council communists began to turn away from traditional trade unions and workers' parties since they considered participation in these institutions to reinforce bourgeois attitudes amongst workers. Council communists were critical of the usurpation of political agency by party and trade union leadership and believed their influence was stifling the self-organization of the working class. The outlines of council communism emerged slowly following the German Revolution and into the 1920s. Criticisms of the Bolshevik model and the Russian Revolution emerged through debates within the Communist International between Lenin and what he called the 'left-wing communists'. Council communism reflected on the experience of workers' councils, but was not developed at the time the councils first arose.

Building Workers' Power Today

Even for those sceptical of the possibilities of the specific institutional proposal of a council system, there is much that is useful and interesting in the political struggle of the council movements that speaks to contemporary concerns. Over a century now separates us from the council movements. Socio-economic conditions and forms of political organizing are now vastly altered, which leads to necessary caution in drawing lessons for political action in the present. Yet, many of the problems addressed by the council movements are similar to those faced by democratic collectives today. Powerful economic interests have attempted to subvert public goods for their own private gain. Corporations are increasingly less able to be constrained by democratic action and are growing in power to rival nation states as political actors. Economic inequalities continue to rise as democratic systems appear unable to intervene. New forms of authoritarianism are on the rise across the globe that have eroded some of the hard-fought social and political rights of the previous century. The task democratic collectives now face is how to counter powerful undemocratic forces and structures that have overtaken the agency of ordinary citizens. While it must be recognized that the council movements were struggling against monarchical and authoritarian regimes rather than liberal democracies, it is also important to note that many of the goals they strived for are yet to be obtained.

First, the council movements inspire reflection upon how democratic principles can be extended from the liberal state to broader spheres of society. They demanded that the principles of self-government, citizen control, and effective participation be introduced into a wide range of democracy-resistant institutions and practices such as the workplace, schools, economic regulatory bodies, cultural institutions, the army, and the civil service. In the absence of more wide-reaching transformations of social institutions, the formal political equality of liberal democracy leaves relations of domination intact in the private sphere. One of the most important and innovative aspects of the council movements' programme was their attempt to impose democratic relations on previously closed and hierarchical institutions. The council movements challenged entrenched structures of private power by intervening in what had hitherto been considered non-political domains. They claimed a right to exercise democratic control over institutions in which no such right had existed. Unsurprisingly, the first targets of the council delegates were the immediate sources of their daily oppression: the factory and the barracks. Extensive reforms were proposed that would have overturned and reconfigured these institutions. They offered a far-reaching critique of the limitations of proposed plans for a liberal democracy and put forward a vision of a participatory society in which major political and economic institutions would be placed under democratic control.

Rosa Luxemburg conceptualized this aspect of social transformation based on her analysis of the limitations and inadequacies of 'bourgeois democracy'. For Luxemburg, the 'fate of democracy was bound up with the socialist movement'.[6] For it was only in the further democratization of society and the economy that democratic citizens could exercise control over key economic institutions that had been monopolized by capitalists. The crux of the matter was the relationship between political equality and social and economic privileges. Liberal democracies guaranteed citizens equal political rights in the public sphere (rights such as citizenship, suffrage, freedom of speech and association), while enforcing systems

[6] Luxemburg 'Reform or Revolution'.

of property rights and social hierarchies that maintained vast inequalities in the private sphere. Luxemburg wrote:

> we have always revealed the hard kernel of social inequality and lack of freedom hidden under the sweet shell of formal equality and freedom ... not in order to reject the latter but to spur the working class into not being satisfied with the shell, but rather, by conquering political power, to create a socialist democracy to replace bourgeois democracy—not to eliminate democracy altogether.[7]

The major difference from the Bolsheviks was that Luxemburg did not believe that democracy itself should be dismissed as meaningless. Rather, the underlying democratic principles of citizen control and accountability should be practised more widely and applied to a broader set of social institutions. Existing democratic rights should be expanded and introduced into the material bases of social life. For Luxemburg, institutions which supported private relationships of domination should be transformed into accountable and citizen-controlled structures.

This interventionist approach is particularly effective because it undermines the elite's preferred strategy for the containment of emancipatory movements: cede ground in the public sphere, while protecting private regimes of power in the factory, army, and family. When faced with the rise of the council movements in Germany, all shades of reactionaries and conservatives began supporting democracy and elections to liberal parliamentary institutions. The bourgeoisie viewed parliamentary elections and the suppression of the council movements as the best method to maintain their social and economic dominance and restore their position of privilege within a new democratic regime. By restricting struggle to electoral politics, it was hoped that the domain of contestation could be shifted away from more wide-ranging demands of socialization and institutional transformation. However, democracy, to the council movements, entailed a broader programme of the democratization of society and the economy. By challenging the elite's private institutions of power, the council movements sought to overcome this strategy of containment. Inspired by these interventionist strategies of the council movements, a transformative democratic strategy today should include the democratization of society and the economy.

In particular, returning to the council delegates' programme provides impetus to refocus democratic theory on the undemocratic nature of workplaces, which have traditionally been of only marginal interest to democratic theory. The dominant approach within deliberative democracy and participatory governance has been to focus on increasing and deepening levels of participation and citizen empowerment in existing democratic institutions from the local level up to

[7] Luxemburg, *The Russian Revolution*.

national representative institutions.[8] Deliberative theorists have sought to extend democratic principles to a wide variety of institutions including 'experiments with citizen juries and panels, advisory councils, stakeholder meetings, lay members of professional review boards, representations at public hearings, public submissions, citizen surveys, deliberative polling, deliberative forums, and focus groups'.[9] More recently, the turn to deliberative systems has extended the focus of the deliberative ideal beyond individual institutions to examine the interaction of a number of processes and sites of contestation in a broader system. This expanded scope enables an analysis of how empowered democratic institutions relate to other possibly non-deliberative institutions in society.[10] However, even in the most recent literature, economic institutions are usually not explicitly addressed as a desirable site for increased deliberation and citizen control. It is easy to see how one could conclude that the workplace, and economic institutions more generally, have been a 'forgotten topic in democratic theory'.[11]

Questions of the democratization of the economy go back to early socialists and Marxists, with an ongoing interest in 'industrial democracy' throughout the early twentieth century from revolutionary socialists. One can count John Stuart Mill, John Dewey, and Pierre-Joseph Proudhon among early proponents for such an ideal.[12] The councils of the early twentieth century represent one prominent tradition of workers who sought to institute direct decision-making procedures over workplaces and the economy. In Anglo-American political theory, participatory and economic democracy arose on the back of the student movements in the 1960s and 1970s, influencing a generation of theorists who would propose various forms of greater participation in economic life.[13] The Port Huron statement of the Students for a Democratic Society is the most well-known document that calls for a participatory democracy, which Jane Mansbridge parses as a

[8] Joshua Cohen and Joel Rogers, *Associations and Democracy* (New York: Verso, 1995); Archon Fung and Olin E. Wright, *Deepening Democracy: Institutional Innovations in Empowered Participatory Governance* (London: Verso, 2003).

[9] Nadia Urbinati and Mark E. Warren, 'The Concept of Representation in Contemporary Democratic Theory', *Annual Review of Political Science* 11 (2008), 387–412, 405.

[10] John Parkinson and Jane Mansbridge, eds., *Deliberative Systems: Deliberative Democracy at the Large Scale* (Cambridge: Cambridge University Press, 2012).

[11] David Ellerman, 'The Workplace: A Forgotten Topic in Democratic Theory?' *Kettering Review* 27, no. 2 (2009), 51–7.

[12] Pierre-Joseph Proudhon, *What is Property? Or, an Inquiry into the Principle of Right and of Government* (New York: Humboldt Publishing Company, 1980); Sidney and Beatrice Webb, *Industrial Democracy* (London, New York, Bombay: Longmans, Green & Co, 1897); Herbert Croly, *Progressive Democracy* (Memphis, TN: General Books, 2010 [1914]), chap. 18; John Dewey, *Political Writings*, ed. Ian Shapiro (Indianapolis, IN: Hackett, 1993), 121–4; John Stuart Mill, *Principles of Political Economy with Some of Their Applications to Social Philosophy*, 9th edition, ed. W. J. Ashley (New York: Longmans, Green, 1915 [1848]), 752.

[13] Robert Dahl, *A Preface to Economic Democracy* (Berkeley: University of California Press, 1985); Carole Pateman, *Participation and Democratic Theory* (Cambridge: Cambridge University Press, 1970); Benjamin Barber, *Strong Democracy: Participatory Politics for a New Age* (Berkeley and Los Angeles: University of California Press, 1984).

combination of equality, direct participation, and consensus decision-making.[14] As Robert Dahl has noted, 'if democracy is justified in governing the state, then it is also justified in governing economic enterprises. What is more, if it cannot be justified in governing economic enterprises, we do not quite see how it can be justified in governing the state.'[15] The council movements direct attention back to this neglected perspective on democratic politics.

Furthermore, the radical council movements did not view democracy in the sociologically anonymous terms of liberal discourse. Instead, they considered that class antagonisms would proliferate without more thoroughgoing social and economic reforms. Democracy, to the radical socialists, entailed a programme of empowering workers against the ruling class. The way in which the language of democracy was employed in Russia in 1917 exhibited a strong influence of a socialist conception of class and antipathy towards the elite. Historian Boris Kolonitskii, has argued that during the February revolution in Russia '"democratic" was often used as the opposite not of dictatorship or autocracy, but of the upper and even middle classes, toward whom it was antagonistic.'[16] Democracy had quite specific connotations during this period and was used as a term of self-identification by all of the socialist groups and often served as a synonym for the 'democratic strata' or 'democratic classes'. The term 'democratic camp' [*demokraticheskii lager*] designated the forces of the working masses and the socialist intelligentsia who supported the councils. While there was much division between the various socialist groups in Russia, they all agreed on the term 'revolutionary democracy' as that which distinguished them from the conservatives and the bourgeoisie.[17] From the Provisional Government, Alexander Kerensky was able to offer 'a bow to all democracy: to workers, soldiers, and peasants'.[18] Another example is the authors of the *Guide to Political Terms and Politicians*, published in Russia by a moderate liberal publishing house in 1917, who defined democracy as 'all classes in a country who live by their own labor: workers, peasants, servants, intelligentsia'.[19] It was liberals such as the Kadets and other propertied elements of society that were excluded through the use of this term. Liberalism was an unpopular political ideology at the time and was considered the language of the elite.[20]

[14] Jane Mansbridge, *Beyond Adversary Democracy* (Chicago: University of Chicago Press, 1980).

[15] Dahl, *A Preface to Economic Democracy*, 134–5.

[16] Boris Kolonitskii, '"Democracy" in the Political Consciousness of the February Revolution', in *Revolutionary Russia: New Approaches*, ed. Rex A. Wade (New York and London: Routledge, 2004), 75.

[17] Anweiler, *The Soviets*, 76.

[18] Alexander Kerensky, *Russia and History's Turning Point* (New York: Duell, Sloan & Pearce, 1965), 411.

[19] Quoted in Kolonitskii, '"Democracy" in the Political Consciousness of the February Revolution', 82.

[20] Anweiler, *The Soviets*, 129–30; See also Mandel, *The Petrograd Workers and the fall of the Old Regime*, 18–19.

In Germany, there was also a struggle over the meaning and interpretation of the concept of democracy. The leadership of the SPD, who were supporters of a call for a national assembly and the dismantling of the councils, preferred to frame the question as 'democracy or dictatorship', painting the councils as a dangerous flirtation with a Bolshevist dictatorship. However, although there was a general consensus that the new republic would be a democratic regime, the true question concerned what form that democracy would take. 'Today it is not a question of democracy or dictatorship', argued Rosa Luxemburg, '[t]he question that history has placed on the agenda is: bourgeois democracy or socialist democracy?'[21] Although the SPD leadership were satisfied with the establishment of a democratic republic, many council delegates saw the importance of struggling for a socialist republic which would enshrine workers' control over economic institutions as an essential aspect of the new regime.

An analysis of the council movements can make a distinct and important contribution to current debates over the meaning and significance of democracy. Democracy is commonly understood as a form of rule based on a principle of political equality in which power is vested in the people and exercised by them either directly or indirectly. In most conceptions, democratic government should be responsive to the people's expressed preferences and is usually actualized through a majoritarian decision-making procedure.[22] The radical council delegates' understanding of democracy challenged the sufficiency of the liberal conception of political equality as universal suffrage and equality under the law. It presented a more substantive idea of equality as influence and control over decision-making, not simply as an abstract right, but in terms of actual power to determine outcomes. Rather than consider political equality according to the proceduralist criteria of one-person/one-vote, council delegates conceived of political equality as the equal capacity to participate effectively. They believed that political equality should embody what Robert Dahl has named effective participation. Dahl argued that 'citizens ought to have an adequate opportunity, and an equal opportunity, for expressing their preferences as to the final outcome.'[23] They argued that given the enormous differences in the effective capacities of different citizens to act politically, greater attention was required to mechanisms that would aim to achieve a more substantive equality of influence and control over decision-making. Council delegates were acutely aware of how wealthy actors could utilize their economic resources to dominate political institutions and processes. By attending to the underlying socio-economic conditions

[21] Luxemburg, 'The National Assembly'.

[22] Robert Dahl, *Democracy and Its Critics* (New Haven, CT: Yale University Press, 1989), 109–11; Charles Beitz, *Political Equality: An Essay in Democratic Theory* (Princeton, NJ: Princeton University Press, 1989), 17. For a critical disambiguation of these three concepts see Ben Saunders, 'Democracy, Political Equality, and Majority Rule', *Ethics* 121, no. 1 (2010), 148–77.

[23] Dahl, *Democracy and Its Critics*, 109.

of political practices, the council movements sought to counteract the negative consequences of the elite domination of politics.

A Self-Determining Society

The struggles of the council movements serve as a prescient reminder that liberal democracy does not exhaust the possibilities of democratic government. The overall vision of council theorists was for the radical reorganization of social relations towards a self-determining society. This involved deepening democracy in existing institutions and extending democratic principles to institutions where they had been excluded. The development of practices of discipline and solidarity was important for the cultivation of active citizens taking part in worker-controlled political and economic institutions. The vision of a self-determining society in which all citizens participate in self-government poses a challenge to the growing domination of commercial interests and the privatization of public goods. The power and the fragility of this vision comes from the desire for an awakening of new appetites for political freedom understood as collective self-determination. But this was not a nostalgic turn to models of ancient Athens or agrarian republican societies. Council theorists envisaged a thoroughly modern and industrialized society jointly owned and managed by workers. They considered a new political ethos of public-spiritedness and solidarity to be essential to this social transformation. Returning to this vision not only reminds us of an important and often forgotten chapter in the history of political thought, but invites reflection on what democracy can and should mean today.

Bibliography

Acton, Edward. *Rethinking the Russian Revolution*. London: Bloomsbury Academic, 1990.

Allgemeiner Kongreß der Arbeiter- und Soldatenräte Deutschlands vom 16. bis 21. Dezember 1918 im Abgeordnetenhause zu Berlin. Stenographische Berichte [Congress Report] (Berlin, 1919).

Anweiler, Oskar. 'Die Räte in der ungarischen Revolution', *Osteuropa* 8 (1958): 393–400.

Anweiler, Oskar. *The Soviets: The Russian Workers, Peasants, and Soldiers Councils, 1905–1921*. New York: Pantheon Books, 1974.

Arendt, Hannah. *Between Past and Future*. New York: Viking Press, 1961.

Arendt, Hannah. *Crises of the Republic*. New York, NY: Harcourt Brace Jovanovich, 1972.

Arendt, Hannah. *The Human Condition*. Chicago: The University of Chicago Press, 1998.

Arendt, Hannah. *The Jewish Writings*. New York: Schocken Books, 2007.

Arendt, Hannah. *Men in Dark Times*. New York: Harcourt Brace and Company, 1968.

Arendt, Hannah. *On Revolution*. New York: Penguin, 2006.

Arendt, Hannah. 'Totalitarian Imperialism: Reflections on the Hungarian Revolution', *The Journal of Politics* 20.1 (1958): 5–43.

Aristotle. *Politics*, ed. Ernest Barker, revised by Richard Stalley. Oxford: Oxford University Press, 1995.

Arnold, Volker. *Rätebewegung und Rätetheorien in der Novemberrevolution*. Hamburg: Junius Verlag, 1985.

Avrich, Paul. *Kronstadt 1921*. Princeton: Princeton University Press, 1970.

Avrich, Paul. *The Russian Anarchists*. Princeton: Princeton University Press, 2015.

Baden, Prince Max von. *Erinnerungen und Dokumente*, ed. Golo Mann. Stuttgart: Ernst Klett, 1968.

Barber, Benjamin. *Strong Democracy: Participatory Politics for a New Age*. Berkeley and Los Angeles: University of California Press, 1984.

Bayat, Assef. *Work, Politics and Power: An International Perspective on Workers' Control and Self-management*. New York: Monthly Review Press, 1991.

Beckett, Ian. *The Great War*. London: Pearson/Longman, 2007.

Beitz, Charles. *Political Equality: An Essay in Democratic Theory*. Princeton, NJ: Princeton University Press, 1989.

Berkman, Alexander. 'The Russian Tragedy', in *The Life of an Anarchist: The Alexander Berkman Reader*, ed. Gene Fellner. New York: Seven Stories Press, 1992.

Berlin, Isaiah. 'Two Concepts of Liberty', in *Four Essays on Liberty*. Oxford: Oxford University Press, 1969.

Blackledge, Paul. 'Karl Kautsky and Marxist Historiography', *Science & Society* 70.3 (2006): 337–59.

Blättler, Sidonia and Irene M. Marti. 'Rosa Luxemburg and Hannah Arendt: Against the Destruction of Political Spheres of Freedom', *Hypatia* 20.2 (2005): 88–101.

Bluhm, Felix, *'Die Massen sind aber nicht zu halten gewesen.' Zur Streik- und Sozialisierungsbewegung im Ruhrgebiet 1918/19*. Berlin: edition assemblage, 2014.

Bock, Hans Manfred. 'Anarchosyndicalism in the German Labour Movement: a Rediscovered Minority Tradition', in *Revolutionary Syndicalism: An International Perspective*, ed. Marcel van der Linden and Wayne Thorpe. Aldershot, England: Scholar Press, 1990, 59–80.

Bock, Hans Manfred. *Syndikalismus und Linkskommunismus von 1918 bis 1923*. Meisenheim am Glan: Verlag Anton Hain, 1969.

Boyd, John. 'The Origins of Order Number 1', *Soviet Studies* 19.3 (1967): 359–72.

Breaugh, Martin. *The Plebeian Experience: A Discontinuous History of Political Freedom*. Columbia: Columbia University Press, 2013.

Breen, Keith. 'Freedom, republicanism, and workplace democracy', *Critical Review of International Social and Political Philosophy* 18 (2015): 470–85.

Bricianer, Serge. *Pannekoek and the Workers' Councils*. Saint Louis: Telos Press, 1983.

Brinton, Maurice. *The Bolsheviks and Workers' Control, 1917–1921*. London: Solidarity, 1970.

Bronner, Stephen Eric. ed. *The Letters of Rosa Luxemburg*. New Jersey: Humanities Press, 1993.

Bronner, Stephen Eric. 'Red Dreams and the New Millennium: Notes on the Legacy of Rosa Luxemburg', in *Rosa Luxemburg—Her Life and Legacy*, ed. Jason Schulman. New York: Palgrave Macmillan, 2013.

Bronner, Stephen Eric. *Socialism Unbound: Principles, Practices, and Prospects*. 2nd ed. New York: Columbia University Press, 2011.

Browder, Robert and Alexander Kerensky. eds. *The Russian Provisional Government: Documents Vol. 1*. Stanford: Stanford University Press, 1961.

Bukharin, Nicholas and Yevgeni Preobrazhensky. *The ABC of Communism*. Harmondsworth: Penguin, 1969.

Callinicos, Alex. *Social Theory: A Historical Introduction*. London: Polity Press, 1999.

Canovan, Margaret. 'Trust the People! Populism and the Two Faces of Democracy', *Political Studies* 47 (1999): 2–16.

Carter, Ian. *A Measure of Freedom*. Oxford: Oxford University Press, 1999.

Castoriadis, Castoriadis. *Political and Social Writings Volume 2 1955–1960: From the Workers' Struggle Against Bureacracy to Revolution in the Age of Modern Capitalism*. Minneapolis: University of Minnesota Press, 1988.

Central Committee of the Russian Social-Democratic Labour Party. *The Bolsheviks and the October Revolution: Minutes of the Central Committee of the Russian Social Democratic Labour Party (Bolsheviks) August 1917–February 1918*. London: Pluto Press, 1974.

Christman, John. 'Freedom in Times of Struggle: Positive Liberty Again', *Analyse & Kritik* 1/2 (2015): 171–88.

Coffee, Alan. 'Two Spheres of Domination: Republican theory, social norms and the insufficiency of negative freedom', *Contemporary Political Theory* 14 (2015): 45–62.

Cohen, Joshua and Joel Rogers. *Associations and Democracy*. New York: Verso, 1995.

Collins, Hugh. *Marxism and Law*. Oxford: Oxford University Press, 1994.

Comack, Martin. *Wild Socialism: Workers Councils in Revolutionary Berlin, 1918–1921*. Lanham: University Press of America, 2012.

de Condorcet, M. *Sketch for a Historical Picture of the Progress of the Human Mind*. Westport: Hyperion Press, 1955.

Constant, Benjamin. 'The Liberty of Ancients Compared with that of Moderns', accessible at http://oll.libertyfund.org/titles/constant-the-liberty-of-ancients-compared-with-that-of-moderns-1819.

Croly, Herbert, *Progressive Democracy*. Memphis, TN: General Books, 2010 [1914].

D'Arcy, Steve. 'Rosa Luxemburg on "the Socialist Civic Virtues"', *The Public Autonomy Project*, 9 September 2014, accessible at https://publicautonomy.org/2014/09/09/rosa-luxemburg-on-the-socialist-civic-virtues/.

Dagger, Richard. *Civic Virtues: Rights, Citizenship, and Republican Liberalism*. Oxford: Oxford University Press, 2007.

Dahl, Robert A. 'The concept of power', *Behavioral Science* 2 (1957): 201–15.

Dahl, Robert A. *Democracy and Its Critics*. New Haven, CT: Yale University Press, 1989.

Dahl, Robert A. *A Preface to Economic Democracy*. Berkeley: University of California Press, 1985.

Däumig, Ernst. 'The Council Idea and its Realization', in *All Power to the Councils! A Documentary History of the German Revolution of 1918–1919*, ed. Gabriel Kuhn. Oakland: PM Press, 2012.

Däumig, Ernst. 'The National Assembly Means the Councils' Death', in *All Power to the Councils! A Documentary History of the German Revolution of 1918–1919*, ed. Gabriel Kuhn. Oakland: PM Press, 2012.

Dauvé, Gilles. *Eclipse and Re-Emergence of the Communist Movement*. London: PM Press, 2015.

Davis, Angela. *Freedom is a Constant Struggle: Ferguson, Palestine and the Foundations of a Movement*. Chicago: Haymarket Books, 2016.

Dewey, John. *Political Writings*, ed. Ian Shapiro. Indianapolis, IN: Hackett, 1993.

Dikovich, Albert. 'Heroismus und Sorge um das Selbst. 1919 im Lichte der frühen politisch-ethischen Schriften György Lukács', in *Die Ungarische Räterepublik 1919 in Lebensgeschichten und Literatur*, ed. Albert Dikovich and Edward Saunder. Vienna 2017.

Downs, Anthony. *An Economic Theory of Democracy*. New York: Harper and Row, 1957.

Draper, Hal. *The Dictatorship of the Proletariat*. New York: NYU Press, 1987.

Draper, Hal. *Karl Marx's Theory of Revolution: Volume 1, The State and Bureaucracy*. London: Monthly Press Review, 1977.

Dubigeon, Yohan. *La démocratie des conseils: Aux origins modernes de l'autogouvernement*. Paris: Klincksiek, 2017.

Ebert, Friedrich. *Schriften, Aufzeichnungen, Reden, Vol. 2*. Dresden: Carl Reissner Verlag, 1926.

Ellerman, David. 'The Workplace: A Forgotten Topic in Democratic Theory?' *Kettering Review* 27.2 (2009): 51–7.

Elster, John. *Making Sense of Marx*. Cambridge: Cambridge University Press, 1985.

Engels, Friedrich. 'Letter to J. Bloch', 21 September 1890, accessible at https://www.marxists.org/archive/marx/works/1890/letters/90_09_21.htm.

Erdmann, Karl Dietrich. 'Die Geschichte der Weimarer Republik als Problem der Wissenschaft', *Vierteljahrshefte für Zeitgeschichte* 3 (1955): 1–19.

European Commission for Democracy through Law, 'Report on the Imperative Mandate and Similar Practices'. Venice, 2009.

Foerster, Friedrich. *Weltpolitik und Weltgewissen*. München, 1919.

Forgacs, David. ed. *The Gramsci Reader: Selected Writings 1916–1935*. New York: New York University Press, 2000.

Fowkes, Ben. ed. *The German Left and the Weimar Republic: A Selection of Documents*. Ledien: Brill, 2014.

Frankel, Emil. 'The Status of "Socialization" in Germany', *Journal of Political Economy* 32.1 (1924): 68–85.

Fung, Archon and Olin E. Wright, *Deepening Democracy: Institutional Innovations in Empowered Participatory Governance*. London: Verso, 2003.

Gaido, Daniel and Richard B. Day. eds. *Witnesses to Permanent Revolution: The Documentary Record*. Leiden: Brill, 2009.

Geary, Dick. *Karl Kautsky*. Manchester: Manchester University Press, 1982.

Geary, Dick. 'Radicalism and the Worker: Metalworkers and Revolution 1912–23', in *Society and Politics in Wilhelmine Germany*, ed. Richard J. Evans. London: Croom Helm, 1979.

Geras, Norman. *The Legacy of Rosa Luxemburg*. London: New Left Books, 1976.

Gerber, John. *Anton Pannekoek and the Socialism of Workers' Self Emancipation, 1873–1960*. Dordrecht: Kluwer Academic Publishers, 1989.

Getzler, Israel. *Kronstadt 1917–1921: The Fate of a Soviet Democracy*. Cambridge: Cambridge University Press, 1983.

Gilcher-Holtey, Ingrid. *Das Mandat des Intellektuellen. Karl Kautsky und die Sozialdemokratie*. Berlin: Siedler, 1986.

Gluckstein, Donny. *The Western Soviets: Workers' Councils versus Parliament, 1915–20*. London: Bookmarks, 1985.

Gluckstein, Donny. 'Workers' Councils in Europe: A Century of Experience', in *Ours to Master and to Own: Workers' Control from the Commune to the Present*, ed. Immanuel Ness and Dario Azzellini. Chicago: Haymarket Books, 2011.

Golder, Frank. ed. *Documents of Russian History, 1914–1917*. New York: The Century Co., 1927.

Goodin, Robert E. 'Folie Républicaine', *Annual Review of Political Science* 6.1 (2003): 55–76.

Gorter, Herman. 'Open Letter to Comrade Lenin', accessible at https://www.marxists.org/archive/gorter/1920/open-letter/index.htm.

Gourevitch, Alex. *From Slavery to the Co-operative Commonwealth*. Cambridge: Cambridge University Press, 2014.

Gourevitch, Alex. 'Labour and Republican Liberty', *Constellations* 18.3 (2011): 431–54.

Gourevitch, Alex. 'Labour Republicanism and the Transformation of Work', *Political Theory* 41.4 (2013): 591–617.

Grebing, Helga. 'Konservative Republik oder soziale Demokratie? Zur Bewertung der Novemberrevolution in der neueren deutschen Historiographie', in *Vom Kaiserreich zur Republik*, ed. Eberhard Kolb. Köln: Kiepenheuer and Witsch, 1972.

Groh, Dieter. *Negative Integration und revolutionärer Attentismus. Die deutsche Sozialdemokratie am Vorabend des Ersten Weltkrieges*. Berlin: Propyläen, 1973.

Groos, Otto. *Der Krieg in der Nordsee*. Berlin: E. S. Mittler, 1922.

Grunberger, Richard. *Red Rising in Bavaria*. London: Arthur Barker, 1973.

Guerin, Daniel. ed. *No Gods, No Masters: An Anthology of Anarchism. Vol. 1*. Edinburgh: AK Press, 1998.

Habermas, Jürgen. 'Three Normative Models of Democracy', *Constellations* 1.1 (1994): 2–10.

Haffner, Sebastian. *Die deutsche Revolution 1918/19*. Berlin: Kindler, 2002.

Hansen, Mogens. *The Athenian Democracy in the Age of Demosthenes: Structure, Principles, and Ideology*. Norman: University of Oklahoma Press, 1991.

Haugaard, Mark. 'Power: a "family resemblance" concept', *European Journal of Cultural Studies* 13.4 (2010): 1–20.

Hautmann, Hans. *Die Geschichte der Rätebewegung in Österreich 1918–1924*. Vienna: Europaverlag, 1995.

Heimann, Eduard. 'Die Sozialisierung', *Archiv für Sozialwissenschaft und Sozialpolitik* 45.3 (1919): 527–90.

Hobbes, Thomas. *Leviathan*. Cambridge: Cambridge University Press, 2003.

Hoffrogge, Ralf. 'From Unionism to Workers' Councils: The Revolutionary Shop Stewards in Germany, 1914–1918', in *Ours to Master Ours to Own, Workers' Councils: Workers'*

Control from the Commune to the Present, ed. Immanuel Ness and Dario Azzellini. Chicago: Haymarket Books, 2011.

Hoffrogge, Ralf. *Working-Class Politics in the German Revolution: Richard Müller, the Revolutionary Shop Stewards and the Origins of the Council Movement.* Chicago: Haymarket Books, 2015.

Holden, Alice M. 'The Imperative Mandate in the Spanish Cortes of the Middle Ages', *American Political Science Review* 24.4 (1930): 886–912.

Holzheuer, Walter. *Karl Kautskys Werk als Weltanschauung*. Munchex C. H. Beck, 1972.

Honohan, Iseult. *Civic Republicanism*. London: Routledge, 2002.

Hudis, Peter. 'Rosa Luxemburg's Concept of a Post-capitalist Society', *Critique* 40.3 (2015): 323–35.

Institut für Marxismus-Leninismus. *Dokumente und Materialien zur Geschichte der Deutschen Arbeiterbewegung, Band 2 November 1917–Dezember 1918*. Berlin: Dietz Verlag, 1957.

Jones, Mark. *Founding Weimar*. Cambridge: Cambridge University Press, 2016.

Kalyvas, Andreas, *Democracy and the Politics of the Extraordinary*. Cambridge: Cambridge University Press, 2009.

Kautsky, Karl. '"A Destroyer of Vulgar Marxism": Review of Karl Korsch's "Marxism and Philosophy" by Karl Kautsky', *Platypus Review* 43 (2012), accessible at https://platypus1917.org/2012/01/30/destroyer-of-vulgar-marxism/.

Kautsky, Karl. 'The Bolshevki Rising', accessible at https://www.marxists.org/archive/kautsky/1918/03/bolsheviki.htm.

Kautsky, Karl. 'The Class Struggle', accessible at https://www.marxists.org/archive/kautsky/1892/erfurt/.

Kautsky, Karl. *Das Erfurter Programm*. Stuttgart: J. H.W. Dietz Nachf, 1920.

Kautsky, Karl. *Demokratie oder Diktatur*, accessible at https://www.marxists.org/deutsch/archiv/kautsky/1918/demo/index.htm.

Kautsky, Karl. *Demokratie oder Diktatur*. Berlin: Paul Cassirer, 1920.

Kautsky, Karl. 'The Dictatorship of the Proletariat', accessible at https://www.marxists.org/archive/kautsky/1918/dictprole/index.htm.

Kautsky, Karl. 'Die Aktion der Masse', https://www.marxists.org/deutsch/archiv/kautsky/1911/xx/masse.htm.

Kautsky, Karl. 'Die neue Taktik', accessible at https://www.marxists.org/deutsch/archiv/kautsky/1912/xx/taktik.htm.

Kautsky, Karl. *Die proletarische Revolution und ihr Programm*. Stuttgart: J. H.W. Dietz Nachf, 1922.

Kautsky, Karl. 'Driving the Revolution Forward', accessible at https://www.marxists.org/archive/kautsky/1918/12/forward.html.

Karl Kautsky, 'Eine Neue Strategie', accessible at https://www.marxists.org/deutsch/archiv/kautsky/1910/xx/strategie.htm.

Kautsky, Karl. *Ethik und materialistische Geschichstauffassung*. Berlin: J. H. W. Dietz, 1927.

Kautsky, Karl. 'Guidelines for a Socialist Action Programme', accessible at https://www.marxists.org/archive/kautsky/1919/01/guidelines.html.

Kautsky, John H. *Karl Kautsky: Marxism, Revolution and Democracy*. New Jersey: Transaction, 1994.

Kautsky, Karl. 'The Labour Revolution', accessible at https://www.marxists.org/archive/kautsky/1924/labour/index.htm.

Kautsky, Karl. 'National Assembly and Council Assembly', in *The German Revolution and the Debate on Soviet Power*, ed. in John Riddell. New York: Anchor Foundation, 1986.

Kautsky, Karl. 'Prospects of the Russian Revolution', *Weekly Worker* (14 January 2010), accessible at https://weeklyworker.co.uk/worker/800/supplement-prospects-of-the-russian-revolution/.

Kautsky, Karl. *The Road to Power*, accessible at https://www.marxists.org/archive/kautsky/1909/power/index.htm.

Kautsky, Karl. 'The Social Revolution', accessible at https://www.marxists.org/archive/kautsky/1902/socrev/.

Kautsky, Karl. 'Speech on "the Socialisation of Economic Life" at the Second Congress of Councils in April 1919', in *The German Left and the Weimar Republic: A Selection of Documents*, ed. Ben Fowkes. Ledien: Brill, 2014.

Kautsky, Karl. 'Stockholm', *Die Neue Zeit* 35, no. 2 (1916–17).

Kautsky, Karl. *Terrorism and Communism: A Contribution to the Natural History of Revolution*, trans. W. H. Kerridge. London: The National Labour Press, 1920 [1919].

Kautsky, Karl. *Von der Demokratie zur Staatssklaverei. Eine Auseinandersetzung mit Trotzki*. Berlin: Freiheit, 1921.

Kautsky, Karl. 'Wahlen und Attentate', *Der Sozialdemokrat* 23 (5 June 1881).

Kautsky, Karl. 'Was Nun?', accessible at https://www.marxists.org/deutsch/archiv/kautsky/1910/xx/wasnun.htm.

Kautsky, Karl. 'Was will die deutsche sozialistische Republik?', accessible at https://reader.digitale-sammlungen.de/de/fs1/object/display/bsb11125769_00005.html.

Kerensky, Alexander. *Russia and History's Turning Point*. New York: Duell, Sloan & Pearce, 1965.

Kets, Gaard and James Muldoon. eds. *The German Revolution and Political Theory*. London: Macmillan, 2019.

Keyt, David. 'Aristotelian Freedom', in *The Oxford Handbook of Freedom*. eds. David Schmidtz and Carmen Pavel. Oxford: Oxford University Press, 2016.

King, Martin Luther, Jr. '"The Death of Evil upon the Seashore," speech delivered at the Cathedral of St. John the Divine', New York City, 17 May 1956, accessible at https://kinginstitute.stanford.edu/king-papers/documents/death-evil-upon-seashore-sermon-delivered-service-prayer-and-thanksgiving.

King, Martin Luther, Jr. 'Letter from a Birmingham Jail', August 1963, accessible at https://web.cn.edu/kwheeler/documents/Letter_Birmingham_Jail.pdf.

Kluge, Ulrich. *Die deutsche Revolution 1918–1919*. Frankfurt am Main: Suhrkamp, 1985.

Kluge, Ulrich. *Soldatenräte und Revolution. Studien zur Militärpolitik in Deutschland 1918/19*. Göttingen: Vandenhoeck and Ruprecht, 1975.

Kolb, Eberhalb. *Die Arbeiterräte in der deutschen Innenpolitik, 1918–1919*. Berlin: Droste, 1962.

Kolb, Eberhard. ed. *Quellen zur Geschichte der Rätebewegung in Deutschland 1918/1919, Band I: Der Zentralrat der deutschen sozialistischen Republik 19.12.1918–8.4.1919, Vom Ersten Zum Zweiten Rätekongress*. Leiden: E. J. Brill, 1968.

Korsch, Karl. 'Evolution of the Problem of the Political Workers Councils in Germany', accessible at https://www.marxists.org/archive/korsch/1921/councils.htm.

Korsch, Karl. *Karl Marx*. Leiden: Brill, 1930.

Korsch, Karl. *Marxism and Philosophy and Other Essays*. London: Monthly Review Press, 1970.

Korsch, Karl. 'The Passing of Marxian Orthodoxy: Bernstein-Kautsky-Luxemburg-Lenin', *International Council Correspondence* 3.11&12 (1937): 7–11.

Korsch, Karl. *Revolutionary Theory*, ed. Douglas Kellner. Austin: University of Texas Press, 2013.

Korsch, Karl. 'What is Socialization? A Program of Practical Socialism', *New German Critique* 6 (1975): 60–81.

Kuhn, Gabriel. ed. *All Power to the Councils! A Documentary History of the German Revolution of 1918–1919.* Oakland: PM Press, 2012.

Laborde, Christine. *Critical Republicanism: The Hijab Controversy and Political Philosophy.* Oxford: Oxford University Press, 2008.

Laclau, Ernesto and Chantal Mouffe, *Hegemony and Socialist Strategy: Towards a Radical Democratic Politics.* London: Verso, 1985.

Landauer, Gustav. 'Letter to Leo Kestenberg, Krumbach (Swabia), 22 November 1918', in *All Power to the Councils! A Documentary History of the German Revolution of 1918–1919.* ed. Gabriel Kuhn. Oakland, CA: PM Press, 2012.

Landauer, Gustav. *Revolution and Other Writings: A Political Reader*, ed. Gabriel Kuhn. Oakland: PM Press, 2010.

Landauer, Gustav. 'The United Republics of Germany and Their Constitution', in *All Power to the Councils! A Documentary History of the German Revolution of 1918–1919.* ed. Gabriel Kuhn. Oakland, CA: PM Press, 2012.

Lange, Dietmar, *Massenstreik und Schießbefehl: Generalstreik und Märzkämpfe in Berlin 1919.* Berlin: edition assemblage, 2012.

Leipold, Bruno. 'Marx's Social Republic: Radical Republicanism and the Political Institutions of Socialism,' in *Radical Republicanism: Recovering the Tradition's Popular Heritage*, eds. Bruno Leipold, Karma Nabulsi and Stuart White. Oxford: Oxford University Press, 2020.

Leipold, Bruno. *Citizen Marx: Republicanism, Communism and Capitalism.* Princeton: Princeton University Press, (forthcoming).

Lenin, V. I. '"Left-Wing" Communism: An Infantile Disorder', in *Collected Works, Volume 31.* Moscow: Progress Publishers, 1965.

Lenin, Vladimir I. 'The Proletarian Revolution And The Renegade Kautsky', in *Lenin's Collected Works, Volume 28.* Moscow: Progress Publishers, 1974.

Lenin, Vladimir I. 'The Political Situation', accessible at https://www.marxists.org/archive/lenin/works/1917/jul/10b.htm.

Lenin, Vladimir I. 'The State and Revolution', accessible at https://www.marxists.org/archive/lenin/works/1917/staterev/.

Lenin, Vladimir I. 'What is to be Done?', accessible at https://www.marxists.org/archive/lenin/works/1901/witbd/.

Lewis, Ben. *Karl Kautsky on Democracy and Republicanism.* Leiden: Brill, 2019.

Lewis, Ben. 'Kautsky: From Erfurt to Charlottenburg', *Weekly Worker*, 10 November 2011, accessible at https://weeklyworker.co.uk/worker/889/kautsky-from-erfurt-to-charlottenburg/.

Lih, Lars T. 'The book that didn't bark', *Weekly Worker* 863, 27 April 2011, accessible at https://weeklyworker.co.uk/worker/863/the-book-that-didnt-bark/.

Lih, Lars T. 'Lenin and Kautsky: The final Chapter', *International Socialist Review* 58 (May–June 2008).

Lih, Lars T. *Lenin Rediscovered: 'What Is to Be Done?' in Context.* Leiden: Brill Academic Publishers, 2005.

Lindemann, Albert S. *The Red Years: European Socialism Versus Bolshevism, 1919–1921.* Berkeley: University of California Press, 1974.

Lovett, Frank. *A General Theory of Domination and Justice.* Oxford: Oxford University Press, 2010.

Lüders, Sven and Johannes Müller-Salo, 'Which Liberalism, Which Republicanism, Constructing Traditions of Political Thought with Philip Pettit', in *Philip Pettit: Five Themes from his Work*, ed. Simon Derpmann and David P. Schweikard. London: Springer, 2016.

Lukács, Georg. *Lenin: A Study on the Unity of his Thought*. Cambridge: MIT Press, 1971.

Lukes, Steven. *Power: A Radical View*. 2nd ed. Basingstoke: Palgrave Macmillan, 2005.

Lustgarten, Laurence. 'Socialism and the Rule of Law', *Journal of Law and Society* 15.1 (1988): 25–41.

Lutz, Ralph Haswell. *The German Revolution, 1918–1919*. Stanford: Stanford University Publications, 1922.

Luxemburg, Rosa. 'An anti-clerical policy of Socialism', accessible at https://www.marxists.org/archive/luxemburg/1903/01/01.htm.

Luxemburg, Rosa. 'Auf die Schanzen', *Die Rote Fahne* 30 (15 December 1918).

Luxemburg, Rosa. 'Introduction to Political Economy', in *The Complete Works of Rosa Luxemburg, Volume I: Economic Writings 1*, ed. Peter Hudis. London: Verso, 2013.

Luxemburg, Rosa. 'Zeit der Aussaat', in *Gesammelte Werke Vol 2*, ed. G. Radczun et al. Berlin: Dietz, 1981 [1910].

Luxemburg, Rosa. 'The Junius Pamphlet', accessible at https://www.marxists.org/archive/luxemburg/1915/junius/.

Luxemburg, Rosa. 'The National Assembly', accessible at https://www.marxists.org/archive/luxemburg/1918/11/20.htm.

Luxemburg, Rosa. 'The Next Step', accessible at https://www.marxists.org/archive/luxemburg/1910/03/15.htm.

Luxemburg, Rosa. 'Organizational Questions of the Russian Social Democracy', accessible at https://www.marxists.org/archive/luxemburg/1904/questions-rsd/index.htm.

Luxemburg, Rosa. 'Our Program and the Political Situation', accessible at https://www.marxists.org/archive/luxemburg/1918/12/31.htm.

Luxemburg, Rosa. 'Reform or Revolution', accessible at https://www.marxists.org/archive/luxemburg/1900/reform-revolution/.

Luxemburg, Rosa, *The Russian Revolution*. London: Workers Age, 1940 [1918].

Luxemburg, Rosa. 'The Russian Revolution', in *The Rosa Luxemburg Reader*, ed. Peter Hudis and Kevin Anderson. London: Monthly Review Press, 2004.

Luxemburg, Rosa. 'The Socialisation of Society', accessible at https://www.marxists.org/archive/luxemburg/1918/12/20.htm.

Luxemburg, Rosa. 'Theory and Practice', accessible at https://www.marxists.org/archive/luxemburg/1910/theory-practice/.

Luxemburg, Rosa. 'What Does the Spartacus League Want?', accessible at https://www.marxists.org/archive/luxemburg/1918/12/14.htm.

MacCallum, G. 'Negative and Positive Freedom', *The Philosophical Review* 76.3 (1976): 312–34.

Machiavelli, Niccolò. *The Complete Works and Others*, trans. Allan Gilbert. Durham, NC: Duke University Press, 1965.

Machiavelli, Niccolò. *The Discourses on Livy*. Chicago. The University of Chicago Press, 1996.

MacIntyre, Alistair. *After Virtue: A Study in Moral Theory*. London: Duckworth, 1981.

Macnair, Mike. *Revolutionary Strategy: Marxism and the Challenge of Left Unity*. London: November Publications, 2008.

Mandel, Ernest. 'The Debate on Workers' Control', *International Socialist Review* 30.3 (May–June 1969).

Mandel, David. 'The Factory Committee Movement in the Russian Revolution', in *Ours to Master and to Own: Workers' Control from the Commune to the Present*, ed. Immanuel Ness and Dario Azzellini. Chicago: Haymarket Books, 2011.

Mandel, David. *The Petrograd Workers and the fall of the Old Regime: From the February Revolution to the July Days, 1917*. London: The Macmillan Press, 1983.

Mandel, Ernest. 'Workers' Control and Workers' Councils', *International* 2.1 (1973): 1–17.

Mandela, Nelson. *The Long Road to Freedom: The Autobiography of Nelson Mandela*. Boston: Little Brown & Co, 1994.

Mansbridge, Jane. *Beyond Adversary Democracy*. Chicago: University of Chicago Press, 1980.

Marx, Karl. 'Address of the Central Committee to the Communist League', accessible at https://www.marxists.org/archive/marx/works/1847/communist-league/1850-ad1.htm.

Marx, Karl. 'The Civil War in France', accessible at https://www.marxists.org/archive/marx/works/1871/civil-war-france/ch05.htm.

Marx, Karl. 'Critique of Gotha Programme', accessible at https://www.marxists.org/archive/marx/works/1875/gotha/.

Marx, Karl. 'General Rules of the International Workingmen's Association', accessible at http://www.marxists.org/history/international/iwma/documents/1864/rules.htm.

Marx, Karl. 'On Freedom of the Press', *Rheinische Zeitung* 139, Supplement (19 May 1842). Available in K. Marx and F. Engels, *Collected Works Vol. 1*, London: Lawrence and Wishart, 1976.

Marx, Karl. *Preface to A Contribution to a Critique of Political Economy*, accessible at https://www.marxists.org/archive/marx/works/1859/critique-pol-economy/preface.htm.

Marx, Karl. *Selected Writings*. Oxford: Oxford University Press, 2000.

Marx, Karl. 'Wage Labour and Capital', in *Collected Works, Vol. 9*, Moscow: International Publishers, 1977.

Marx, Karl and Friedrich Engels, *Collected Works*. London: Lawrence and Wishart, 1975–2001.

Materna, Ingo. *Der Vollzugsrat der Berliner Arbeiter- und Soldatenräte 1918/19*. Berlin: Dietz Verlag, 1978.

Matthias, Erich. 'Kautsky und der Kautskyanismus', in *Marxismusstudien*, ed. Iring Fetscher. Tubingen: Mohr, 1957.

Matthias, Erich. 'Zur Geschichte der Weimar Republik. Ein Literaturbericht', *Die neue Gesellschaft* 3 (1956): 312–20.

Mattick, Paul. *Anti-Bolshevik Communism*. Wales: The Merlin Press, 2007.

Maximoff, Gregori Petrovich. ed. *The Political Philosophy of Bakunin: Scientific Anarchism*. Glencoe, Il: The Free Press, 1953.

McCauley, Martin. *The Russian Revolution and the Soviet State 1917–1921: Documents*. London: Macmillan Press, 1975.

McCormick, John. *Machiavellian Democracy*. Cambridge: Cambridge University Press, 2011.

Medearis, John. 'Lost or Obscured? How V. I. Lenin, Joseph Schumpeter, and Hannah Arendt Misunderstood the Council Movement', *Polity* 36.3 (2004): 447–76.

Medearis, John. *Why Democracy is Oppositional*. Cambridge, MA: Harvard University Press, 2015.

Mill, John S. 'Considerations on Representative Government', in *The Collected Works of John Stuart Mill* (Toronto: The University of Toronto Press, 1977).

Mill, John S. *Principles of Political Economy with Some of Their Applications to Social Philosophy*, 9th edition, ed. W. J. Ashley. New York: Longmans Green, 1915 [1848].

Mitchell, Allan. *Revolution in Bayern 1918/1919. Die Eisner-Regierung und die Räterepublik*. München: Beck, 1967.

Mommsen, Wolfgang J. 'Die Deutsche Revolution 1918/19', *Geschichte und Gesellschaft* 4.3 (1978): 362–91.

Monteglas, Graf Max and Walther Schucking. eds. *Outbreak of the World War: German Documents*. New York: Oxford University Press, 1924.

Muldoon, James. 'A Socialist Republican Theory of Freedom and Government', *European Journal of Political Theory* (forthcoming).

Muldoon, James. ed. *Council Democracy: Towards a Democratic Socialist Politics*. London: Routledge, 2018.

Muldoon, James. 'The Lost Treasure of Arendt's Council System', *Critical Horizons* 12.3 (2011): 396–417.

Muldoon, James. 'The Origins of Hannah Arendt's Council Democracy', *History of Political Thought* 12.3 (2011): 396–417.

Müller, Dirk H. *Gewerkschaftliche Versammlungsdemokratie und Arbeiterdeliegerte vor 1918*. Berlin: Colloquium, 1985.

Müller, Richard. 'Democracy or Dictatorship', in *All Power to the Councils!*, ed. Gabriel Kuhn. Oakland: PM Press, 2012.

Müller, Richard. 'Report by the Executive Council of the Workers' and Soldiers' Councils of Great Berlin', in *All Power to the Councils!*, ed. Gabriel Kuhn. Oakland: PM Press, 2012.

Müller, Richard. 'Speech to congress on 16 December 1918, Zentralrat der sozialistischen Republik Deutschlands', in *Allgemeiner Kongreß der Arbeiter- und Soldatenräte Deutschlands vom 16. bis 21. Dezember 1918 im Abgeordnetenhause zu Berlin. Stenographische Berichte* [Congress Report] Berlin, 1919.

Müller, Richard. *Vom Kaiserreich zur Republik*. Vienna: Malik, 1924–1925.

Negri, Antonio. *Insurgencies: Constituent Power and the Modern State*. Minneapolis: University of Minnesota Press. 1999.

Negri, Antonio. *Subversive Spinoza*. Manchester: Manchester University Press, 2008.

Ness, Immanuel and Dario Azzellini. eds. *Ours to Master and to Own: Workers' Control from the Commune to the Present*. Chicago: Haymarket Books, 2011.

Niess, Wolfgang. *Die Revolution Von 1918/19 in Der Deutschen Geschichtsschreibung. Deutungen Von Der Weimarer Republik Bis Ins 21. Jahrhundert*. Berlin, Boston: Gruyter, 2013.

Norval, Aletta. 'Writing a Name in the Sky: Rancière, Cavell, and the Possibility of Egalitarian Inscription,' *American Political Science Review* 106.4 (2012): 810–26.

Ober, Josiah. *Mass and Elite in Democratic Athens: Rhetoric, Ideology, and the Power of the People*. Princeton NJ: Princeton University Press, 1989.

Oertzen, Peter van. *Betriebsräte in der Novemberrevolution. Eine politikwissenschaftliche Untersuchung über Ideengahalt und Struktur der betrieblichen und wirtschaftlichen Arbeiterräte in der deutschen Revolution 1918*. Berlin: Dietz, 1963.

Oldfield, Adrian. *Citizenship and Community: Civic Republicanism and the Modern World*. New York: Routledge, 1990.

O'Shea, Tom. 'Socialist Republicanism', *Political Theory* (forthcoming).

Pachter, Henry. *Socialism in History: Political Essays*. New York: Columbia University Press, 1984.

Anonymous Pamphlet, 'To the Populace of the Fortress and Town of Kronstadt, Comrades and Citizens!', *Kronstadt Izvestia* 1 (3 March 1921).

Pannekoek, Anton. 'Class Struggle and Nation', accessible at https://www.marxists.org/archive/pannekoe/1912/nation.htm.

Pannekoek, Anton. 'De sociaaldemokracie en de oorlog', *De Nieuwe Tijd* (1915): 69–84, 137–51, 146.

Pannekoek, Anton. 'Die Massenstreikdebatte', *Zeitungskorrespondenz*, 18 June 1910.

Pannekoek, Anton. *Die taktischen Differenzen der Arbeiterbewegung*. Hamburg: Erdmann Dubber, 1909.

Pannekoek, Anton. 'The Failure of the Working Class', accessible at https://www.marxists.org/archive/pannekoe/1946/failure-working-class.htm.

Pannekoek, Anton. 'Friedrich Adler', *Die Nieuwe Tijd* (1916): 640–7, 647.

Pannekoek, Anton. 'General Remarks on the Question of Organisation', accessible at https://www.marxists.org/archive/pannekoe/1938/general-remarks.htm.

Pannekoek, Anton. 'Imperialism and the Tasks of the Proletariat', *Kommunist* 1/2 (Geneva: 1915).

Pannekoek, Anton. 'Marxist Theory and Revolutionary Tactics', accessible at https://www.marxists.org/archive/pannekoe/1912/tactics.htm.

Pannekoek, Anton. 'Mass Action and Revolution', *Die Neue Zeit* 30 (1912).

Pannekoek, Anton. 'Nach vierzig Jahren', *Bremer Bürger-Zeitung* (18 March 1911).

Pannekoek, Anton. 'Party and Working Class', accessible at https://www.marxists.org/archive/pannekoe/1936/party-class.htm.

Pannekoek, Anton. 'The Position and Significance of Joseph Dietzgen's Philosophical Works', in Joseph Dietzgen, *The Positive Outcome of Philosophy*. Chicago: Charles H. Kerr & Company, 1906.

Pannekoek, Anton. 'Socialism and Religion', accessible at https://www.marxists.org/archive/pannekoe/1907/socialism-religion.htm.

Pannekoek, Anton. 'Society and Mind in Marxian Philosophy', *Science and Society* (Summer 1937).

Pannekoek, Anton. 'Theses on the Fight of the Working Class Against Capitalism', *Southern Advocate for Workers' Councils* (1947).

Pannekoek, Anton. 'Was ist Sozialismus?' *Lichtstrahlen* 11 (1915): 220–3.

Pannekoek, Anton. *Workers' Councils*, accessible at https://www.marxists.org/archive/pannekoe/1947/workers-councils.htm.

Pannekoek, Anton. 'Workers' Councils', *International Council Correspondence* 2.5 (1936): 20–7.

Pannekoek, Anton. 'World Revolution and Communist Tactics', accessible at https://www.marxists.org/archive/pannekoe/tactics/index.htm.

Pansardi, Pamela. 'Power to and power over: two distinct concepts of power?', *Journal of Political Power* 5.1 (2012): 73–89.

Parkinson, John and Jane Mansbridge. eds. *Deliberative Systems: Deliberative Democracy at the Large Scale*. Cambridge: Cambridge University Press, 2012.

Parsons, Talcott. 'On the concept of power', *Proceedings of the American Philosophical Society* 107 (1963): 232–62.

Pateman, Carole. *Participation and Democratic Theory*. Cambridge: Cambridge University Press, 1970.

Pelz, William A. *A People's History of the German Revolution*. London: Pluto Press, 2018.

Perry, Matt. *Marxism and History*. London: Palgrave Macmillan, 2002.

Pettit, Philip. 'Freedom in the Market', *Politics, Philosophy & Economics* 5 (2006): 131–49.

Pettit, Philip. 'Joining the dots', in *Common Minds: Themes from the Philosophy of Philip Pettit*, ed. M. Smith, G. Brennan, R. Goodin, and F. Jackson. Oxford: Oxford University Press, 2007.

Pettit, Philip. *On the People's Terms: A Republican Theory and Model of Democracy.* Cambridge: Cambridge University Press, 2012.

Pettit, Philip. *Republicanism: A Theory of Freedom and government.* Cambridge: Cambridge University Press, 1997.

Pipes, Richard. *A Concise History of the Russian Revolution.* New York: Knopf, 1995.

Pitkin, Hanna. 'Are Freedom and Liberty Twins?', *Political Theory* 16 (1988): 523–52.

Pitkin, Hanna. *The Concept of Representation.* Berkeley: University of California Press, 1987.

Pocock, J. G. A. *The Republican Moment. Florentine Political Theory and the Atlantic Republican Tradition.* Princeton, NJ: Princeton University Press, 1975.

Proudhon, Pierre-Joseph. *Oeuvres Complètes, Vol. 17.* Paris: A. Lacroix, 1868.

Proudhon, Pierre-Joseph. *The Principle of Federation.* Toronto: The University of Toronto Press, 1979.

Proudhon, Pierre-Joseph. *What is Property? Or, an Inquiry into the Principle of Right and of Government.* New York: Humboldt Publishing Company, 1980.

Rabinowitch, Alexander. *The Bolsheviks in Power: The First Year of Soviet Rule in Petrograd.* Bloomington and Indianapolis: Indiana University Press, 2007.

Rabinowitch, Alexander. 'The Bolsheviks Come to Power', in *The Russian Revolution: The Essential Readings*, ed. Martin A. Miller. Oxford: Blackwell Publishers, 2001.

Radkey, Oliver H. *Russia Goes to the Polls: The Election of the Russian Constituent Assembly of 1917.* Ithaca: Cornell University Press, 1989.

Rahman, K. Sabeel. *Democracy against Domination.* Oxford: Oxford University Press, 2016.

Rahman, K. Sabeel. 'Democracy against domination: Contesting economic power in progressive and neorepublican political theory', *Contemporary Political Theory* 16 (2017): 41–64.

Rawls, John. *Political Liberalism.* New York: Columbia University Press, 1993.

Riddell, John. ed. *The German Revolution and the Debate on Soviet Power.* New York: Anchor Foundation, 1986.

Ritter, Gerhard A. and Susanne Miller. eds. *Die Deutsche Revolution 1918–1919: Dokumente.* Hamburg: Hoffman und Campe Verlages, 1981.

Rosenberg, Arthur. *A History of Bolshevism: From Marx to the First Five-Year Plan.* Oxford: Oxford University Press, 1934.

Roß, Sabine. *Biographisches Handbuch der Reichsrätekongresse 1918/1919.* Düsseldorf, Drosste Verlag, 2000.

Rühle, Otto, et al. *Non-Leninist Marxism: Writings on the Worker's Councils.* London: Red and Black Publishers, 2007.

Rürup, Reinhard. *Probleme Der Revolution in Deutschland 1918/19.* Wiesbaden: Steiner, 1968.

Salvadori, Massimo. *Karl Kautsky and the Socialist Revolution 1880–1938.* London: Verso, 1990.

Sandel, Michael. *Democracy's Discontent. America in Search of a Public Philosophy.* Cambridge, MA: Harvard University Press, 1996.

Saunders, Ben. 'Democracy, Political Equality, and Majority Rule', *Ethics* 121.1 (2010): 148–77.

Schecter, Darrow. *Radical Theories: Paths Beyond Marxism and Social Democracy.* Manchester: Manchester University Press, 1994.

Schmelzer, Albert. *The Threefolding Movement, 1919: Rudolf Steiner's Campaign for a Self-Governing, Self-Managing, Self-Educating Society.* Forest Row: Rudolf Steiner Press, 2017.

Schumpeter, Joseph. *Capitalism, Socialism, and Democracy*. 3rd ed. New York: Harper and Row, 1962.

Seeling, Otto, *Der Rätegedanke und seine Verwirkung in Sowjetrussland*. Berlin: Pyramidenverl, 1925.

Service, Robert. *A History of Modern Russia from Nicholas II to Vladimir Putin*. Cambridge, MA: Harvard University Press, 2005.

Sirianni, Carmen. *Workers Control and Socialist Democracy: The Soviet Experience*. London: Verso, 1982.

Skinner, Quentin. *Liberty before Liberalism*. Cambridge: Cambridge University Press, 1996.

Skinner, Quentin. 'The Republican Ideal of Political Liberty', in *Machiavelli and Republicanism*, ed. Quentin Skinner, Maurizio Viroli, and Gisela Bock. Cambridge: Cambridge University Press, 1990.

Smith, Stephen, 'Factory Committees', in *Critical Companion to the Russian Revolution, 1914–1921*, ed. Edward Acton, Vladimir Cherniaev, and William Rosenberg. London: Bloomsbury Academic, 2001.

Smith, Stephen A., *The Russian Revolution: A Very Short Introduction*. Oxford: Oxford University Press, 2002.

Steenson, Gary P. *Karl Kautsky, 1854–1938: Marxism in the classical years*. Pittsburgh: University of Pittsburgh Press, 1991.

Steinberg, Mark D. ed., *Voices of Revolution*. New Haven: Yale University Press, 2001.

Stern, Boris. *Works Council Movement in Germany*. Washington: Government Printing Office, 1925.

Students for a Democratic Society. *The Port Huron Statement*. Chicago: Charles H. Kerr Publishing Co., 1990.

Thompson, E. P. *The Making of the English Working Class*. London, Victor Gollancz, 1963.

Thompson, Michael J. 'Reconstructing republican freedom: A critique of the neo-republican concept of freedom as non-domination', *Philosophy & Social Criticism* 39 (2013): 277–98.

Thompson, Michael J. 'The two faces of domination in republican political theory', *European Journal of Political Theory* 17.1 (2018): 44–64.

Thorpe, Wayne. 'Keeping the Faith: The German Syndicalists in the First World War', *Central European History* 33.2 (2000): 195–216.

Tocqueville, Alexis de. *Democracy in America*, trans. George Lawrence, ed. J. P. Mayer. Garden City, NY: Doubleday, 1969.

Tomba, Massimiliano. 'Who's Afraid of the Imperative Mandate?', *Critical Times* 1.1 (2018): 1–12.

Tormin, Walter. *Zwischen Rätediktatur und Sozialer Demokratie: Die Geschichte Der Rätebewegung in Der Deutschen Revolution 1918/19*. Düsseldorf: Droste Verlag, 1954.

Townshend, Jules. 'Reassessing Kautsky's Marxism', *Political Studies* 37.4 (1989): 659–64.

Trotsky, Leon. *History of the 1905 Revolution*. Harmondsworth: Penguin Books, 1972.

Trotsky, Leon. *The History of the Russian Revolution, Vol. 1*. London: Victor Gollancz Ltd, 1932.

Trotsky, Leon. *Terrorism and Communism*. London: Verso, 2007 [1920].

Trotsky, Leon. 'Transformation of Morals', accessible at https://www.marxists.org/archive/trotsky/1923/10/morals.htm.

Urbinati, Nadia. 'Competing for Liberty: The Roman Critique of Democracy', *American Political Science Review* 106.3 (2012): 607–21.

Urbinati, Nadia and Mark E. Warren. 'The Concept of Representation in Contemporary Democratic Theory', *Annual Review of Political Science* 11 (2008): 387–412.

Varlet, Jean. 'Proposal for a Special and Imperative Mandate', in *Social and Political Thought of the French Revolution: An Anthology of Original Texts*, ed. Marc A. Goldstein. New York: Peter Lang, 2001.

Vogel, Angela, *Der deutsche Anarcho-Syndikalismus*. Berlin: Karin Kramer, 1977.

Volker, Arnold. *Rätebewegung und Rätetheorien in der Novemberrevolution*. 2nd ed. Hamburg: Junius Verlag, 1985.

Vrousalis, Nicholas. 'The Socialisation Dilemma', in *Council Democracy: Towards a Democratic Socialist Politics*, ed. James Muldoon. London: Routledge, 2018.

Wade, Rex A. ed. *Revolutionary Russia: New Approaches*. New York and London: Routledge, 2004.

Webb, Sydney and Beatrice Webb. *Industrial Democracy*. London, New York, Bombay: Longmans, Green & Co, 1897.

Weber, Max. *Economy and Society: An Outline of an Interpretative Sociology, Vol. 1*. Berkeley and Los Angeles: University of California Press, 1978.

Wehler, Hans-Ulrich. *Das Deutsche Kaiserreich 1871 bis 1918*. Göttingen: Vandenhoeck u. Ruprecht, 1988.

Weinhauer, Klaus. Anthony McElligott and Kirsten Heinsohn. eds. *Germany 1916–23: A Revolution in Context*. Bielefeld: Transcript, 2015.

Weipert, Axel. *Die Zweite Revolution. Rätebewegung in Berlin 1919/1920*. Berlin: be.bra, 2015.

Winkler, Heinrich August. *Von der Revolution zur Stabilisierung. Arbeiter und Arbeiterbewegung in der Weimar Republik 1918 bis 1924*. Berlin/Bonn: Verlag J. H. W. Dietz, 1984.

Wolff, Theodor. 'Der Erfolg Der Revolution', *Berliner Tageblatt und Handels- Zeitung* 47 (10 November 1918): 576.

Woodcock, George. *Pierre-Joseph Proudhon: His Life and Work*. New York: Schocken Books, 1972.

Zimmerman, Joseph F. *The Recall: Tribunal of the People*. New York: SUNY Press, 2013.

Zinoviev, Grigory. 'Die Sozialdemokratie als Werkzeug der Reaktion', *Die Kommunistische Internationale* 2 (1919).

Index

For the benefit of digital users, table entries that span two pages (e.g., 52–53) may, on occasion, appear on only one of those pages.

A Contribution to a Critique of Political Economy (Marx) 134
Action Committee 41
agriculture 128
All-Russian Congress of Soviets 26, 33–4, 36
American Industrial Workers of the World (IWW) 39
anarchism 22–3, 25–6
anarcho-syndicalism 22–3
Anweiler, Oskar 20–1
Arato, Andrew 8
Arbeiterpolitik (Workers' Politics) 39
Arendt, Hannah 9–11, 64–5, 79, 145
Aristotle 56, 56n.19, 69
Athenian political system 56, 141–2, 168
Austro-Hungarian Empire 10–11
authoritarianism 24–5, 49, 162–3

Bakunin, Mikhail 24–6
Bauer, Gustav 46–7
Bauer, Otto 126
Berkman, Alexander 35
Berlin
  general strike (1919) 18–19
  strike (1916) 39
  strikes in 48–9
Berlin, Isaiah 54, 54n.10
Bismarck, Otto von 77
black freedom movement 71–2
Blackledge, Paul 105
Bolshevik Central Committee 34, 36
Bolsheviks
  and anarchism 25–6
  application of strategy 162
  and bureaucratic autocracy 125–6
  centralizing power 36–7
  and councils 17–18, 42–3
  council system concept 112, 167
  decision to abolish Constituent Assembly 122
  and democracy 110, 164
  disenfranchising the soviets 37
  and failed revolt in July 34
  and failing Provisional Government 34
  introduction 8–10
  and Kautsky 111, 129–30
  and Lenin's slogan 33
  methods of class struggle 128–9
  and October Revolution 35
  power in name of soviets 36–8
  and Rosa Luxemburg 142
bourgeoisie
  confronting in a political struggle 76
  crippling the power of 95
  and democracy 110
  ethics of class struggle against 147
  first source of power for 82
  and ideological hold over proletariat 83
  introduction 7–8
  nature of power of 79–80
  and the proletariat 134–5
  spiritual dependence of the proletariat 134–5
  and the state 96–7
  and suppression of council movements 164
  weakening the power of 92
  and the working class 89, 131
Bremen 22
Bronner, Stephen Eric 145
bureaucratic militaristic 115–16

Canovan, Margaret 72
capitalism
  and agriculture 128
  annihilation of 80–1
  class struggle against 57
  and compensation 128
  and competition 131–2
  control over cultural and ideological apparatuses 61
  deleterious effects of 23
  exploitation of the proletariat 144
  global 52
  and laborers 83
  and Marxism 26, 147, 150–1
  and modes of production 124
  oppression of workers under 81–2
  and parliament 120

capitalism (*cont.*)
power to be eroded through direct assaults 76
regimentation enacted in production 138–9
Rosa Luxemburg's view 143, 155
socialization of 45–6
and the state 90–1
vanquishing of 62
and workers 131–3, 145–6
Carter, Ian 53–4
Castoriadis, Cornelius 69–70
Catholic party 1–2
Cheka (secret police) 37
Chkheidzev, Nikolay 30
Cicero 56
civic virtue 132, 153
civil and political rights 110–11
Civil Society and Political Theory (Cohen/Arato) 8
'Civil War in France, The' (Marx) 141–2
class consciousness 15, 84
Class Struggle, The (Kautsky) 105
Cohen, Jean 8
Cohen, Max 47–8
collective self-determination 70–2
Communism
council 10, 17, 161–2
and despotism 124
and free activity 57
and the Kronstadt uprising 37–8
Communist International 10
Communist Manifesto (Marx) 26
Communist Party of Germany (KPD) 142
compensation 128
competition 15, 52, 58, 74, 108, 123, 131–2
Condorcet, Marquis de 69
Constant, Benjamin 153–4
corruption 132, 143–4, 152
council Communism 10, 17, 161–2
council movements
aim of 80–1
call for an end to the war 44–5
competing ideologies within 98
conclusions 159–68
definition 19–23
disagreements between the SPD and USPD 160
distinctively proletarian 123
in Germany 22–3
history of 16–19
holding political power 160–1
introduction 1–14
need for ideological development of workers 135–6
participants in German 137
precursors 23–9
revolutionary organs 38
struggle for creation of self-determining society 52
struggle for political and economic changes 131
theorists of 130, 134
and works councils 49–50
Council of People's Commissars 36
Council of People's Deputies 41–2, 41n.118, 44
Council of People's Representatives 118, 129
council republics 20–2, 49
council systems
abolition of as permanent centres of power 136
Bolshevik concept 112
conceived as working institutions 140–1
or constituent assemblies 100
and Ernst Däumig 47–8
federal 27–8
and Karl Kautsky 114–15
and national elections 42
and the Paris Commune 4–5
or parliamentary republic 99
precursors 23–5
and social democracy 100
vocal advocates for 99–100
cultural hegemony theory (Gramsci) 137–8
cultural transformation 134–8

Dagger, Richard 153–4
Dahl, Robert 79, 165–7
Däumig, Ernst
and council systems 47–8, 161
freedom as collective self-determination 52–3, 63
need for education and cultural development 136
problem of political power 141–2
Davis, Angela 71–2
Day, Richard B. 106
democracy
justified in governing the state 165–6
and Karl Kautsky 101, 107–10, 128–9
key elements of 121–2
participation 13–14
politics and the economy 160
and the proletariat 109, 146
redemptive face of 72
representative 8
society and the economy 164–6
and violence 111–12
and workplaces 126
democratic camp 166

democratic republicanism 106
Demokratie oder Diktatur (Kautsky) 109
Der Arbeiter-Rat (journal) 99–100, 161
despotism 30–1, 98, 124–6
de Tocqueville, Alexis 154–5
Dewey, John 165–6
Dictatorship of the Proletariat, The (Kautsky) 109–10
Die Neue Zeit 100
Dietzgen, Joseph 52–3, 57–8, 135
direct control 62–4
Discourses on Livy, The (Machiavelli) 56
Draper, Hal 119
'Driving the Revolution Forward' (Kautsky) 113–14, 117–18
Dubigeon, Yohan 18–19
Duma Committee 30–1

Ebert, Friedrich 3–4, 42–5, 99, 112–13, 159–60
Ebert-Scheidemann government 118, 129–30
Eighteenth Brumaire, The (Marx) 115–16
eleutheria (liberty) 56
Engels, Friedrich 70–1, 103, 111–12, 119, 134
Erdmann, Karl Dietrich 17
Erfurt Programme 102, 107–8, 119
Executive Committee 30–2, 118
Executive Council 24–5, 40–1, 43–4, 140–1
Executive Council of Worker's and Soldiers Councils 4, 76–7, 147–8

factories 6, 19–20, 23, 30–1, 35, 39–43, 50, 123, 149
First World War
  chaos and unrest 1
  short-term crises during 29–30
  support for by SPD 146
  union opposition to 40
Förster, Frederick 7, 77–8
Free Association of German Trade Unions 22–3
freedom
  as collective self-determination 52–7, 62–3, 66
  as non-domination 54–5
  and political action 64–9
  as self-determination 133
freedom of speech 110
Freiheit (newspaper) 53
Freikorps 1–2, 48
French Revolution (1848) 106

Gaido, Daniel 106
Geary, Dick 104–5
Gerber, John 58–9
German Revolution
  failure of 162
  importance of cultural factors 133
  and Karl Kautsky 101, 112, 119
  and a National Assembly 122
  need of an accompanying spiritual revolution 135
  question of power in 73–4
  and Rosa Luxemburg 131–2, 142, 146
  socialist groups during 99
  and workers' control over production 83
  and the working class 38–9
German workers' movement 81–2
Germany
  at a crossroads 1–8, 3n.8, 4n.11
  better organized than Russia 74–5
  council movements in 16–17, 16n.2, 22–3, 160–2, 164
  councils betrayed 38–51, 40n.112, 49n.161
  and democracy in 113, 167
  education system of 136–7
  future direction of 10–11, 13–15
  and Karl Kautsky 114–18
  Marxist council delegates in 26
  monarchy toppled 19
  political mass strikes in 18–19
  political thought of *Wilhelmine* 77–8
  and politics 63, 66, 128–9
  refused recognition of Russian Bolshevik government 129
  regime guilty of war 129–30
  and remnants from the feudal era 124–5
  revolution in 98
  socialism in 8–9, 58–9
  and the SPD 86, 104–5
  struggle for universal suffrage in 76
  workers' seizure of power in 147–8
global capitalism 52
Gluckstein, Donny 20–1
Gorter, Herman 82–3
Gramsci, Antonio 137–9
Grebing, Helga 100
Groener, Wilhelm 44
Guchkov, Aleksander 30–1
'Guidelines for a Socialist Action Programme' (Kautsky) 106–7, 110, 113
Guide to Political Terms and Politicians 166

Haase, Hugo 42
Hamburg Points 45
Hegel, Georg Wilhelm 57–8
Hegemony and Socialist Strategy (Mouffe/Laclau) 8
Hilferding, Rudolf 42, 45–7
Hobbes, Thomas 54, 54n.10
Hoffrogge, Ralf 18–19, 22–3

Hungarian Revolution (1956) 9–10
Hungary 22

Independent Social Democratic Party of Germany (USPD)
daily newspaper of 53
disagreements with SPD 160
divided in German Revolution 73–4
and Ebert-Scheidemann government 118
and Karl Kautsky 13, 113, 129–30
and Karl Liebknecht 40
left-wing faction in 42, 42n.122
rise in popularity 49
and socialization 100
individualism 15, 71, 131–2, 152
Instituut voor Sociale Geschiedenis, Amsterdam 103
international socialism 16
International Women's Day 29–30

Jacobin faction 117–18
Jefferson, Thomas 23–4
Junker caste 118

Kant, Immanuel 57–8
Kapp–Lüttwitz Putsch 49
Kautsky, Karl
establishment of a central strike commission 142
and internationalism 128–30
introduction 2, 13–15
'kitchens of the future' remark 147
law and order 156–7
and mass actions 94–5
and organization 73–5, 84–8
and parliamentary elections 95–6
political democracy and civil rights 107–12
political programme of 89–90, 94, 100–2, 100n.9
and power 75–6, 81–2
and the proletariat 76–7, 83
as a renegade 103–30
role of the councils 73–4
socialist society psychological foundations 138–9
and the state 96, 98, 112–19
strategy of attrition 90–4
and the USPD 42
vision for a post-capitalist society 98
workers' councils 122–8
workers and political transformation 133
Kerensky, Alexander 30, 166
Kiel sailor's mutiny 40–1
King, Martin Luther Jr 70–1
Kluge, Ulrich 17–18
Kolb, Eberhard 17–18
Kolonitskii, Boris 166
Korsch, Karl
causes of an ideological kind 136
freedom as collective self-determination 52–3
and intellectual freedom 60
and Karl Kautsky 104–5
and socialization 45–6
universal development of free individuals 69
Kronstadt uprising (1921) 12–13, 37–8

Laclau, Ernesto 8
Landauer, Gustav 15, 53, 131
Lange, Dietmar 18–19
Lasson, Adolf 77
Lenin, Vladimir
and application of Bolshevik strategy 162
attack on council communist tendencies 17
criticisms of radical theorists 10
and destruction of state institutions 34
and Karl Kautsky 103, 105–6, 111, 117, 119, 129–30
and the Kronstadt rebellion 37–8
and the Paris Commune 101
and Rosa Luxemburg 138–9, 148
and worker self-organization 36–7
Lewis, Ben 106, 113, 116–17
liberty
in Athens 56
negative 54–5, 62
as non-domination 56
and political freedom 70
positive 54–5, 62
Liebknecht, Karl 40, 48, 129, 159–61
Lih, Lars T. 105, 116–17
Lukes, Steven 79, 83
Luxemburg, Rosa
advocate of mobilization 73
argued for support of Bolsheviks 129
and class consciousness 131–2, 134–5
contents of socialism 132–3
and council systems 161
criticisms of Lenin 138–9, 151
and cultural transformation 138
democracy and the socialist movement 163–4, 167
freedom as collective self-determination 52–3
future form of a socialist society 147–53
importance of socialist civic virtues 137–8
institutional vision of 139–43
introduction 2, 13–15
and Karl Kautsky 73–4, 105, 119
mobilization theory of 92–4

murdered by the *Freikorps* 48
notion of proletariat discipline 138–9
and the pace of socialization 125
and parliamentary elections 95, 122
political capacity of the masses 94–5
political power 66–7, 78, 89, 91–2
a post-capitalist society 133
and the ruling class 79–80, 111
and the Russian Revolution 90
and socialist civic virtues 6–7, 143–7, 153–8
and the state 96
vision for a post-capitalist society 98
and the workers 60–1, 75–6, 88–9, 122–3, 136

MacCallum, Gerald C. Jr. 59
Machiavelli, Niccolò 56, 156
Macnair, Mike 106, 112
Mandela, Nelson 71
Mansbridge, Jane 165–6
Marxism
and Bakunin's political struggle 25–6
and capitalism 130, 147, 150–1
and cultural transformation 134
democratization of the economy 165–6
and freedom 57–8
German workers steeped in 38–9
and international socialism 129
introduction 8, 10
and Karl Kautsky 103–6, 112
and parliament 121–2
and political strategy 98
and revolutionary struggle 57
and Rosa Luxemburg 145
Marx, Karl
and agriculture 128
alienation of capitalist economic relations 57
canonical status of 24–5
criticism of judiciary in liberal democracies 141, 141n.40
and cultural phenomena 134
and his 1844 Manuscripts 149
and human spirit 135
legal systems disappearing in a socialist society 156–7
and majority rule of the proletariat 111–12
materialist world view of 58–9
and the Paris Commune 20–1, 34, 101, 115–17, 140–1
and prospects of revolutionary action 26–7
and the state 80–1, 130
structure of future socialist society 147
unequal social relationships 60–1
and universal suffrage 119
and the working classes 65
writings of 57–8
Matthias, Erich 104–5
Menshevik Party 36
Mensheviks 20, 26, 33
Military Revolutionary Committee of the Petrograd Soviet 34
Mill, John Stuart 165–6
Milyukov, Pavel Nikolayevich 30–1
mobilization 14, 73, 92–5, 102, 109
Mommsen, Wolfgang 17–18
Mouffe, Chantal 8
Müller, Richard
and council systems 161
Executive Council appointment 147–8
freedom as collective self-determination 52–3
and a national assembly 47–8
questions of power 76–7
revolutionary shop steward 18–19, 40–1
workers' and soldiers' councils 43–4
and works councils 49–50

National Congress of Workers' and Soldiers' Councils 40, 42, 44–5, 73–4
nationalism 146
nationalization 124, 127
natural evolution 105
Nazism 1–2, 38–9
Negri, Antonio 79
Nicholas II, Tsar 29–31

Observation Committee 32
Oertzen, Peter von 17–18, 100
Oldfield, Adrian 133
On Revolution (Arendt) 9–10
organization 14, 85–94
'Organizational Questions of Russian Social Democracy' 138–9, 148

Pachter, Henry 154
Pannekoek, Anton
advocate of mobilization 73
and capitalism 80–1
and class struggle 66–7, 89, 131, 134–6
and cultural development 139
ideas on freedom 57–9, 62–6, 70
introduction 2, 6–7, 10, 13–15
and Kautsky 73–4, 86–7
and mobilization theory 92–4
and one-track perfectionism 55
and political action 67–70, 94–6
and revolutionary action 57
and the Russian Revolution 90
and the state 96–7

Pannekoek, Anton (*cont.*)
  vision of self-determining society 50–3
  and the workers 75–7, 81–2
  and workers's councils 130
Pansardi, Pamela 79, 79n.13
Paris Commune (1871) 20–1, 101, 106, 115–18
Parliamentarism and Democracy (Kautsky) 121
paternalism 155–6
pedagogy 155–6
Pelz, William A. 18–19
Petrograd 29–30
Petrograd Workers and Soldiers Soviet 30–2, 32n.77
Pettit, Philip 54–5, 55n.13, 156
Pipes, Richard 35
Plato 56
politics
  action 67–9
  agency of the masses 94–6
  democracy 107
  judgement 150–1
  nature of power 79
  struggle 89–94
  theory 70
Politics (Aristotle) 56
Port Huron statement of Students for Democratic Society 165–6
private property 24–5, 70–1, 110, 119, 124, 141, 144–5, 149, 161
'proletarian philosophy' (Dietzgen) 52–3
proletariat
  and the bourgeoisie 134–5
  and capitalist exploitation 144
  and democracy 109, 146
  dictatorship of 102
  discipline of 138–9
  and internationalism 128–9
  morality of 84, 138–9
  and participation in parliament 120
  and political power 112
  Red Guard of 140
  and Rosa Luxemburg 88–9, 150–1
  and socialism 152
Proudhon, Pierre-Joseph 24–6, 165–6
Provisional Government 30, 32–4, 36, 166
Prussia 117–18

Rabinowitch, Alexander 38
Red Ruhr Army 49
republicanism 106, 130, 144–6, 153–4, 156–7
Revolutionary Committee 48
Revolutionary Shop Stewards 4–5, 39–41, 40n.111, 42, 99–100, 119, 161
revolutionary syndicalism 22–3
Right Socialist Revolutionaries 36
Road to Power, The (Kautsky) 103–5, 108, 111
Roß, Sabine 26
Rochau, August Ludwig von 77
Rosenberg, Arthur 100
Rousseau, Jean Jacques 57, 153–4
Royal Palace, Berlin 3–4
Ruhr uprising (1920) 49
Rürup, Reinhard 17–18
Russia
  and the Bolsheviks 17–18, 129, 162
  and class affiliation consciousness 34
  council movements in 16
  and councils 24–5, 29–38, 47–8
  and Germany 74–5
  introduction 1–2, 10–13
  language of democracy in 166
  monarchy toppled 19
  revolution in 98
Russian Revolution (1905) 34, 90, 106, 108–9, 117, 128–9
Russian Revolution (1917)
  analysis by Rosa Luxemburg 150
  collapse of the Tsar's government 29–30
  and council movements 16–18
  introduction 8–9
  and Karl Kautsky 101
  orchestrated by Lenin 35
  and power in the soviets 35
Russian Revolution, The (Luxemburg) 152

sailor mutiny 2–3
St Petersburg Soviet of Workers Deputies 20
Salvadori, Massimo 105, 105n.28
Scheer, Reinhardt 2–3
Scheidemann, Philipp 40, 46–7, 99, 112–13, 159–60
Second International 8, 103–4, 131, 134, 139, 147
self-activity 151–2
self-determination 81, 168
separation of powers doctrine 141
Sirianni, Carmen 31–2
Skinner, Quentin 11, 155–6
Smith, Stephen A. 34
social democracy 22–3, 58–9, 88–9, 100, 119–20, 138–9, 148, 150
Social Democratic Party of Germany (SPD) 4, 17, 40–1, 43–4
  and the 1912 parliamentary elections 90
  action during the revolution 49
  banning of 86
  call for a general strike 49
  'democracy or dictatorship' 167
  disagreements 73–4, 160

and Karl Kautsky 100–2, 104–5, 112–14, 118, 129–30
the masses a passive force 88–9
and a National Assembly 122
network of cultural apparatuses 137
and popularity of council movement 42–3, 48
radical tactics and revolutionary action 75
and Rosa Luxemburg 146, 151–2
and socialization of industry 46–7
and the state 98
thriving in the 1880s 87
'Socialisation of Society, The' (Luxemburg) 131–2, 147, 149
socialism
and Anton Pannekoek 58–9, 65
contents of 132–3
created by the masses 152
and democracy 107–10, 165–6
and international solidarity 101
introduction 8, 19–20
new form of 160
and the Paris Commune 116
practical measures towards 98
and the proletariat 152
requires participation of workers 144–5
and Rosa Luxemburg 93
state 124
and universal development of free individuals 69
socialist republicanism 106, 130
Socialist Revolutionary party 26, 26n.48, 33
socialization 45–7
of agriculture 128
call for immediate action 99–100
and compensation 128
deferred indefinitely 99
of the economy 121, 131
and Karl Kautsky 124–6, 128–9
politics of 102
and the state 127
Socialization Committee 45–7, 46n.145, 129–30
Social Revolution, The (Kautsky) 138
'Sources of the History of the Council Movement in Germany (1918–19)' 17–18
soviets
development of power 35–6
disenfranchised by Bolsheviks 37–8
flourishing across Russia 29–32
organs of revolutionary power 34
radicalization of the revolution 44
support from workers in 35
Soviet Union
and the councils 17
a distortion of original aspirations 23
revolutionary committees 20–1, 20n.25, 26
Spartacus League 3–5, 40, 40n.113
advocates for a council system 99–100, 161
attempt to overthrow provisional government 129–30
and Karl Kautsky 112–14, 125–6
socialist society advocated by 140
and workers' councils 122–3
Spinoza, Baruch 79
spirit (*Geist*) 15
state bureaucrats 126–7
State and Revolution, The (Lenin) 119
state, the 96–8, 112
Steenson, Gary 103
strikes, in Germany (April 1917) 39–40
Students for a Democratic Society of the New Left 15

Tactical Differences in the Workers' Movement (Pannekoek) 81–2
Tormin, Walter 17
Treitschke, Heinrich von 77
Trotsky, Leon 29–30, 33, 37–8, 129–30, 139, 146
'Two Concepts of Liberty', (Berlin) 54

Union of Soviet Socialist Republics (USSR) 38
unitary organization (*Einheitsorganization*) 39
universal suffrage 88, 102, 119, 122, 140–1
utopianism 157

Vrousalis, Nicholas 125–6

'Was will die deutsche sozialistische Republik' (Kautsky) 111–12
Weber, Max 79, 81, 81n.21
Weimar Constitution (1919) 12–13
Weimar Republic 1–2, 17–18, 38–9, 49–50
Weipert, Axel 18–19
'What Does the Spartacus League Want?' (Luxemburg) 131–2, 139–40, 146
Wilhelm, Kaiser 3, 40–1, 44, 99, 136–7, 159–60
Winkler, Heinrich August 17–18
Winter Palace 34
Wolffheim, Fritz 39
Wolff, Theodor 159
women's suffrage 1
workers' associations 24–5
workers' councils 39, 146
and the Berlin general strike 18–19
and Mikhail Bakunin 25
official recognition demand 48–9
opposed by Karl Kautsky 123–4
and Richard Müller 40–1

workers' councils (*cont.*)
  and Rosa Luxemburg 146–8
  valued for open institutional structure 69–70
Workers' Councils (Pannekoek) 53
'Workers' Way to Freedom, The'
    (Pannekoek) 53
working classes
  agents of a future revolution 150–1
  and the Bolsheviks 35
  development of consciousness 86
  emancipation of 26, 81
  forces of 90–1
  and the German Revolution 38–9
  introduction 7
  and Karl Marx 65
  organization of 84–5
  outlines of a culture 137–8
  overthrow of old regime 33
  parliamentary action as part of struggle 108
  particular interests of 124
  and political power of the state 140–1
  political unity 102
  and power 74
  in Russia 74–5
  and SPD-USPD coalition 113
  struggles of 66
Works Council Central Committee 49–50

Zetkin, Clara 142
Zinoviev, Grigory 106, 113